Reminiscences
of
A Christian Family

Reminiscences

of

A Christian Family

In The Mid-20th Century South

Silas Dobbs McCaslin

WestBow
PRESS
A DIVISION OF THOMAS NELSON
& ZONDERVAN

WestBow Press books may be ordered through booksellers or by contacting:

WestBow Press
A Division of Thomas Nelson & Zondervan
1663 Liberty Drive
Bloomington, IN 47403
www.westbowpress.com
1 (866) 928-1240

Because of the dynamic nature of the Internet, any web addresses or links contained in this book may have changed since publication and may no longer be valid. The views expressed in this work are solely those of the author and do not necessarily reflect the views of the publisher, and the publisher hereby disclaims any responsibility for them.

Any people depicted in stock imagery provided by Thinkstock are models, and such images are being used for illustrative purposes only.
Certain stock imagery © Thinkstock.

ISBN: 978-1-4908-6874-5 (sc)
ISBN: 978-1-4908-6875-2 (hc)
ISBN: 978-1-4908-6873-8 (e)

Library of Congress Control Number: 2015901841

Printed in the United States of America.

WestBow Press rev. date: 02/10/2015

Silas Dobbs McCaslin is a pediatric dentist in his forty-fifth year of private practice in Savannah, Georgia. His publications are: A STUDY OF ANORGANIC BONE AS A PULP CAPPING AGENT IN HUMAN PERMANENT TEETH, Master of Science in Dentistry thesis, Emory University School of Dentistry, 1968; "A Better Mousetrap. A Program Written for the Computer for the Automation of the Dental Office Appointment Book." THE JOURNAL OF THE GEORGIA DENTAL ASSOCIATION," February, 1987; THE ALSTON JONES McCASLIN FAMILY, published privately, 1988; "Making Child Patient Cooperation a Choice," JOURNAL OF THE AMERICAN ACADEMY OF PEDIATRIC DENTISTRY, January/February 2000, Volume 22, Number 1; "Risk Management For Pediatric Dental Patients: The Philosophy Of One Practice," THE JOURNAL OF THE SOUTHEASTERN SOCIETY OF PEDIATRIC DENTISTRY, Vol. 7, No. 3-2001; THE ANCESTRY OF C. S. LEWIS, www.silasdobbsmccaslin. com, 2006; "Thoughts on the Virtue of Work," by IPC Press, 2011; and LETTERS TO AND FROM A CHRISTIAN MOTHER AND MORE, WestBow Press, 2011.

Dedicated to my family,
especially my two granddaughters,
Ella and Adelaide Murns

TABLE OF CONTENTS

My maternal grandmother was Mary (Mamie) Adams Dobbs. What follows, extracted from a letter from my mother to her cousins after a recent Adams family gathering in Mississippi, dated August 1, 1979 (exactly one year to the day before her death), is a statement concerning Christian heritage with which spirit we fully comply:

> ...I hope all of you first cousins of mine will instill into your children a deep pride and reverence for the splendid heritage we have. There are many people in the United States today who cannot claim ancestral lines in America back five and six and seven generations, as we can. I don't mean to sound snobbish. I give the Lord the praise for my having been born who and where I was! And for His having chosen me to find and accept the Glorious Gospel of His Grace in Jesus Christ our Redeemer.
>
> So my pride in our ancestors is actually gratitude and praise to God, for allowing me to be born of the parents I had. And having the background of such fine lines as those I have discovered. And I think – as things get worse all over the world and even in our own country – that our children are going to recognize and appreciate more and more the worth of such an heritage. But they can't unless they know of it. And that is our duty – to teach them love of family and country and our Great God and Savior Jesus Christ. (Titus 2:13)....

Mary Margaret Dobbs (McCaslin) Ward

FOREWORD

Si McCaslin describes what it was like to grow up in a small Southern town in the 1940s and early 1950s: RC Colas and Moon Pies, Lincoln Logs and Tinker Toys, Red Ryder BB guns, barefoot summers, tree houses and club houses, young boys and their pocket knives, Mumblety-peg, shooting marbles, spinning tops, riding bikes in packs, paper routes, unsupervised hours of outdoor play, unlocked doors, Saturday afternoon "picture shows" (with the standard double-feature), and plenty of mischief; Sunday church and Wednesday prayer meeting, intact families and strict Sunday Sabbaths. He strategically places family developments in the context of broader developments in the world: the New Deal, the outbreak of World War II, Pearl Harbor, the Allied Victories, the Korean War. He recounts the arrival of the refrigerator, washing machine, central air conditioning, television, and the administrations of Presidents Roosevelt, Truman, and Eisenhower. He takes us through the tragic death of his father at the young age of forty-five and the irrepressible determination of his widowed mother.

Above all, Si describes lesson after lesson learned at the knee of that Christian mother, often reinforced with a switch, and always with Scripture and prayer. Devotion to God was cultivated, integrity insisted upon, and commitments honored. These were simpler times, and comparatively, innocent times. Si's wistful narratives of growing up with big brother Jay will bring a smile to your face, as well as a touch of sadness for the loss of the positive side of an imperfect civilization that is lost forever.

Terry L. Johnson

PREFACE

My mother, Mary Margaret Dobbs, was born in Amory, Mississippi, December 11, 1913. Amory was a small town located seventy-five miles northeast of Ackerman, Mississippi.

DOBBS FAMILY HISTORY, published 1971, by Mary Margaret Dobbs McCaslin Ward, was the inaugural and definitive work for the Choctaw County Dobbs. The work finds Mother's great, great grandfather, The Reverend Silas Dobbs, in Anderson County, South Carolina, where he was born to Fortune Dobbs in 1794. Silas came to Noxubee County, Mississippi in 1834 as a circuit Baptist minister. His son, Lieutenant Silas Mercer Dobbs, fought and died in the Civil War following the Battle of Franklin, Tennessee. Silas Mercer's son, Silas Barnabas, Mother's grandfather, was born, reared, and died in Ackerman. Silas Barnabas' son, Estel Bridges Dobbs, married Mary (Mamie) Eunice Adams in 1907 after completing college. They always resided in Ackerman, except while in Amory when Mother was born. The Dobbs family long had been Baptists.

THE ALSTON JONES McCASLIN FAMILY, by Alston Jones McCaslin V and Silas Dobbs McCaslin, published in 1988, traces the McCaslin line back to 1740 North Carolina. This McCaslin line was Presbyterian in their faith.

LETTERS TO AND FROM A CHRISTIAN MOTHER AND MORE, by Silas Dobbs McCaslin, was published in 2011 by WestBow Press. Somewhat autobiographical, it is interwoven principally with the correspondence to and from Mary Margaret from the third decade of the 20th century up to and shortly beyond her death in 1980.

A chance inquiry by my pastor, Dr. Terry L. Johnson, led to my writing *LETTERS TO AND FROM A CHRISTIAN MOTHER AND MORE* for which he wrote the FOREWORD: "I was surprised, even excited, when I encountered a small sample – three letters – of Dr. Silas McCaslin's mother's letters to him, from the middle of the twentieth century. Their literary quality was outstanding. More importantly, they were filled with sound, shrewd, bold, Biblical counsel for her boys, particularly in the years between the beginning of college and the birth of Si and Suzanne's first child, Carey. I wanted to read more and became convinced that others, particularly parents, could benefit from hearing the strong counsel of a Christian mother to her beloved sons."

As I had recently read some stories of Southern, small town family relationships of the early to middle 20th century, the thought was evoked of writing my own early memoirs. I found myself asking: "Why not do the same sort of book, but including more details of the works of God in our family?" These family experiences have not been told. The late Paul Harvey always closed his syndicated radio news program with the segment: "The rest of the story."

I am compelled to elaborate on the three family publications named earlier, which have become the resource of family tradition, both biographical and genealogical. Repeating all of the events would be redundant. Yet, in what is to follow, I wish to tell "the rest of the story."

Experiences of my grandparents and parents blend into the early experiences of my childhood as I was growing up in Mississippi. My personal memories are gleaned from the period of the mid to late 1940s until college in the fall of 1958. Many of my memories emanate from the instruction and admonition of a Christian mother, proffered to her by my maternal and paternal grandparents. That instruction, conveyed to Jay and me later, blended with our own recollections. Hence her memories evolved into my memories. It would be difficult to completely separate the two. The overarching purpose of this book is my desire to convey to the public my experiences in a small town in the mid-20th century South.

Several close friends have aided me in the production of this book. Dr. Terry Lee Johnson, Senior Pastor, Independent Presbyterian Church, graciously agreed to read an early draft and to write the FOREWORD. Paige Cothren, pastor, Christian counselor, speaker, and a native Mississippian, kindly honored my request to review the manuscript. Paige authored twenty-nine books in three decades. Patrick B. McLean consented to produce the pictures for the cover and the back. My niece, Jennifer Dobbs McCaslin Lobel, provided support with technical questions regarding the conversion of the manuscript to Microsoft Word. From all of them came many suggestions. I offer my gratitude to my sister-in-law, Pamela Stanley McCaslin, who refers to herself as "the old English teacher," having taught in and later heading up the Specific Learning Program at Savannah Country Day School for over twenty years. Pam proof-read the last copy prior to my final draft. Finally, to my dear wife, Suzanne Campbell McCaslin, I offer my sincere thanks for her advice. She, also, carefully proof-read an earlier copy of the manuscript. Moreover, Suzanne was patient and positive toward my efforts throughout the entire process.

INTRODUCTION

Found in this work is a collection of events – stories – that define who we are. The stories are centered in Eupora, Mississippi, and nearby towns.

A Memphis, Tennessee, newspaper ran a feature article in 1957 stating essentially that Eupora was a city of beautiful homes, Cadillacs, and churches. In fact, in the early 1950s it was said that Eupora had more Cadillacs per capita than any other town in the state of Mississippi. Along with the text in the newspaper article were pictures of the town and photographs including former Mayor and State Senator, Judge Everette Eudy, and "Town Officials" Marshall Ernest Coleman and Mayor T. F. Taylor, Jr. These men were among the close friends of my parents, and their lives were enmeshed. T. F. was a multi-millionaire by forty years of age. He became Daddy's close friend in the early 1930s when Daddy was a banker. Ten years later he was Daddy's employer and soon after, his business partner. T. F. Taylor, Jr., his wife, Lavinia, or their daughter, Foy, are mentioned over one-hundred and fifty times in this book, which affirms the deep friendship.

My brother, Jay, was sixteen months my senior. Our father died accidentally in July 1953 at the age of forty-five. Having never worked during her nineteen years of marriage, Mother wished first to complete her BA degree in psychology and then to earn the Master's Degree in speech therapy at Mississippi Southern College in Hattiesburg. A lesser alternative was to remain in her home town of Eupora, teaching speech in the high school, with the security of being surrounded by dear friends. Yet, in a huge step of faith, at forty-one years of age, Mother packed up all of our belongings, the moving van arrived, and she left Eupora with her two young teenage boys, and moved to Hattiesburg, Mississippi. There she resumed the college education interrupted in 1932 at Blue Mountain College by the Great Depression. Two years later, we packed again, arranging for a moving van, and this time left our home state of Mississippi for Gainesville, Georgia. At age fifteen, we all were again starting over. The moves were best for our mother, and we loved her and supported her in her decisions. In God's providence, the move to Gainesville resulted three years later in Mother's second marriage. Eugene Long Ward was a recent widower and a physician. His daughter and son were approximally the age of Jay and me. Mother and Gene were married in May 1959. At her death in 1980, they had been married for twenty-one years, longer than either had been married to a first spouse.

The work that is to follow traces the lives of our family from the early 20th century Mississippi up through our high school years. The events following our college years and beyond are but briefly covered. *LETTERS TO AND FROM A CHRISTIAN MOTHER AND MORE*, spans much the same period, but from an entirely different perspective. Here we offer childhood experiences couched in both the grace and the goodness of God. Lest we forget. The experiences of my parents and grandparents are near alien to the young people of the 21st century.

Chapter One

FROM RICHES TO RUIN

Robert E. Lee's distant cousin, Elizabeth Lee, married Joshua Logan Younger. Robert was the son of Henry (Light Horse Harry) Lee. Elizabeth Lee was the daughter of the great Virginia statesman, Richard Henry Lee. Both Robert E. Lee and Elizabeth Lee descended from Richard Lee (b. 1647). Joshua Logan Younger was the great grandfather of Thomas Cole Younger. The outlaw Jesse James and his brothers were relatives of the Younger brothers of Missouri, the relationship being of record.[1]

Joshua Logan Younger was the first cousin of Susannah Younger McCaslin, the wife of John McCaslin. Alston Jones McCaslin was born in 1810 in Tennessee. He was the grandson of John and Susannah Younger McCaslin. Therefore, our great grandfather, Alston Jones McCaslin II, was the fifth cousin of Thomas Coleman (Cole) Younger, the most celebrated of the outlaw Younger brothers. Moreover, as stated above, we have a distant collateral kinship to Robert E. Lee, the commanding general of the Confederacy. From that point on, our family had few other collateral relationships to renowned Americans, be they generals or outlaws, although Arthur Dobbs, Colonial Governor of North Carolina, was a kinsman, as mentioned later, and former Mississippi governor, James Plemon Coleman, distant kin, was a life-long friend of Mother's. More importantly, what our family *did* have was an extraordinary Christian legacy, as proven in twenty-eight hundred pages of family genealogy that I assembled over some twenty-five years.

---

[1]   *Outlaw Youngers*, by Marley Brant, Madison Books, (1992), p. 10, supplies the documentation of the kinship between the Younger and James families.

Alston Jones McCaslin and his father, James McCaslin, pioneered about 1833 to Marshall County, in north Mississippi. Alston died about 1840. Alston Jones McCaslin II, born in 1827 in Tennessee, migrated sixty miles south to Graysport in Yalobusha County. He is found in that county in the 1850, 1860, and 1870 census records. Alston McCaslin II died accidentally at age forty-nine in 1876 while assisting in the loading of cotton bales on a barge on the Yalobusha River in Graysport, Mississippi. (In 1953, his grandson, my father, Alston Jones McCaslin IV, died accidentally in a body of water in Humphreys County, Tennessee, at forty-five years of age).

Alston Jones McCaslin III, my grandfather, was born in the old McCaslin home in the village of Graysport, Mississippi, November 28, 1863. (Today, Graysport is beneath the massive Grenada Lake). He was thirteen years of age when his father died. Although Alston McCaslin II had wealth, as verified in the census records, his widow had no other source of income. Alston McCaslin III received such early education as the town of Graysport could provide. As a young man, he entered business, first in Graysport and later in the adjacent small town of Coffeeville. Although he had to forego higher education, Grandfather McCaslin put two younger sisters through college while he built a successful enterprise selling farm equipment in Coffeeville.

Alston Jones McCaslin III, at thirty-seven years of age, married Mary Bell Lester on April 26, 1901. Born in 1871, Mary Bell was the daughter of Captain George Lester, of the prominent Lester family of Coffeeville. Mary Bell died in childbirth, she and the baby, March 16, 1902. Mary Bell and the newborn were buried in Coffeeville.

In 1904, having established a lucrative business in Coffeeville, Grandfather McCaslin took up residence in Grenada, Grenada County, Mississippi, twenty miles removed from Coffeeville, where he began acquiring real estate, buying a mercantile business, building and operating a bakery, purchasing the Railroad café, and establishing the Eclipse Drug Store, which at that time had the most ornate soda fountain in Mississippi, from Memphis to New Orleans, bar none.

It is estimated that sometime after his marriage in March 1905 to Miss Maude Henry Windham (b. 1886) he began construction of a home in Grenada for his bride. Grandfather McCaslin was twenty-three years her senior (and for her entire life she referred to him as Mr. McCaslin).

The new residence was located at 515 Main Street, in the second block from the Grenada city square. The house was two stories in height and had a parlor, dining room, six bedrooms, and a broad foyer from which the staircase rose to a landing where it divided to the right and to the left. A wide porch extended across the entire front. Mr. McCaslin must have built the house in the anticipation of a large family.[2]

Henry Ford awarded Grandfather McCaslin a Ford dealership in Coffeeville in 1909, ostensibly in view of his experience and success in the farm equipment business. In the words of Daddy's baby sister, Aunt Louise McCaslin Vance: "At that time, my daddy was so intrigued with this newfangled invention that he really investigated it, and as a result, he got the dealership for Ford in Coffeeville." Ford Motor Company had been established only since June 16, 1903.

Soon thereafter, Grandfather established four additional Ford dealerships in north Mississippi towns, the first of which was in 1912 in Grenada. The other three were in Clarksdale, Cleveland, and Calhoun City. During the next few years, Grandfather McCaslin continued to prosper in every business venture. While Henry Ford built his first car in 1903, it was not until 1908 that the first Model "T" was sold. In 1909, Ford built about ten thousand Model "T's," and the demand was so high that Ford would not sell more cars to dealers until they had completely depleted their stock. Production increased each year, and by 1916 Ford had built about five hundred thousand cars. They reached one million in 1922. On reaching that goal, Ford gave a fifty dollar rebate to everyone who bought a new Ford during that year. The timing of Grandfather McCaslin was almost perfect. He picked up the four additional dealerships just as the production was climbing and while the demand for cars was very high. He had about twenty very good years, from 1910 until 1930. He paid more income tax than anyone else in the entire state of Mississippi in 1913, the first year that income tax was collected since having been abandoned after the Civil War. Grandmother McCaslin reaffirmed this fact about income tax on several occasions.

Henry Ford called the Model "T" "A car for the great multitude." Grandmother McCaslin stated that, prior to 1920, Henry Ford personally asked Grandfather McCaslin to divest himself of four of the dealerships to give others the opportunity to own an automobile business. Grandfather McCaslin retained ownership of the Grenada Ford Company, selling those

---

[2]   *THE HISTORY OF GRENADA*, p. 46, provides a view of the McCaslin home at 515 Main Street. It was the first house on the left in a picture bearing the following legend: "Main Street North, one of Grenada's principal thoroughfares."

in Coffeeville, Clarksdale, Cleveland, and Calhoun City. Grandfather McCaslin was literally riding the crest of prosperity. He owned a large 1915 touring car in which he took the entire family on trips to Memphis, to Indianapolis for the races, as well as to the Gulf Coast for vacations.

The new Fords were shipped to dealerships by train, but they could be acquired more quickly if picked up by the dealer. On at least one occasion, Grandfather and a driver took the boys, all whom were teenagers (and Daddy was the oldest), to Detroit. Everyone drove a new Ford home over dirt roads. Louise once stated that Henry, the youngest, fell asleep while driving and his car slipped off of the road into the ditch. Once it was pushed out onto the road, they continued on to Grenada in their caravan.

Daddy was born in May 1908. In 1926, Daddy, Alston Jones McCaslin IV, met William Adams Dobbs, who was about eight months younger, born 1909. They both were in their freshman year at Mississippi College, Clinton. They quickly became friends, and William traveled with Daddy to visit in Grenada on several occasions. In the winter of their freshman year, William invited Daddy to accompany him on a trip to visit with his family in Ackerman. While there, he first saw Mother when she had just turned fourteen years of age. As she was much too young for a college freshman, he apparently decided to wait for her to grow up.

The economy slowly had begun to destabilize in the early 1920s. Speculation in the stock market resulted in countless people's buying stocks with borrowed money. Many used the stock as collateral for buying more stocks. The woes of Wall Street continued to exacerbate until brokers' loans from mid-1928 to September of 1929 went from five million to eight hundred and fifty million. The stock market boom that had occurred was based upon borrowed money and false optimism.

October 29, 1929, was known as "Black Tuesday," but it was also called the "Wall Street Crash." A record more than sixteen million shares of stock were sold, compared with four to eight million shares per day earlier in the year. The stock market crashed, throwing the country into what would be named the Great Depression (which lasted until 1939). By March 1930, there were thirteen million unemployed, and almost every bank was closed.

The Great Depression wrought both physical and psychological havoc on the entire nation. Most people feared the loss of their job, and in spite of the efforts of the government, unemployment ran rampant. Anxiety by many brought on feelings of failure, often leading to depression and, for many, suicide. Thousands of people went hungry, and children's health suffered from poor diet and lack of adequate medical care. Food lines were common across the country. Land owners planted "relief gardens" for food and for barter. Multiple families crowded into small houses, causing deplorable living conditions. The divorce rate decreased, because few couples could afford to live in separate households. Others postponed wedding plans.

By January 1930, four months into the Depression, Grandfather McCaslin already had been terribly saddled with grievous financial losses. Mary, the oldest of his children, had finished at Brenau College, Gainesville, Georgia (to which city, by the sovereignty of God, Mother, Jay, and I moved in 1954). Mary remained at Brenau College for a time, teaching elocution. The rest of Grandfather McCaslin's assets, bank stock, real estate holdings, and business enterprises were in peril.

In 1931, repercussions from Europe had aggravated the crisis in America. President Hoover had opponents in Congress who he believed were sabotaging his government programs for their own political gain. They were unfairly characterizing him as a cruel and callous president.[3]

Daddy earlier had transferred to the University of Mississippi to begin his sophomore year. Now twenty-two years of age, during his senior year at Ole Miss in 1931, he must have been greatly stressed in the face of the state of affairs of the nation. His father, once a wealthy man, had witnessed his assets slip through his fingers during these first two years of the Great Depression. Daddy was the oldest of four boys, and his older sister, Mary, was the oldest of the three sisters. At the end of December 1931, Daddy left Ole Miss to return home to work in his father's business, Grenada Ford Company.

Daddy's brother, Billy, was at Southwest College in Memphis (which today is Rhodes College, affiliated with the Presbyterian Church). Grandfather McCaslin drove to Memphis and called on Billy to reason with him about the value of a college education. He explained to Billy that Daddy had come home to work, but encouraged Billy to remain in school. Billy insisted on leaving school, too, and after a lengthy discussion, Grandfather relented. Having a friend at the Ford plant in Memphis, Grandfather asked this friend if Billy could work for him. Billy began work immediately (and he was an executive with Ford until his retirement about forty years later).

---

[3] Hoover became the target of blame for the Depression and was badly defeated in 1932.

One by one, each of the five remaining McCaslin siblings graduated from Grenada High School.

My mother, daughter of Mamie and Estel Dobbs, was reared in Ackerman, Mississippi. She was very bright academically, finished high school in three years, and then attended Blue Mountain College in Blue Mountain, Mississippi. Her mother earlier had graduated with honors from Blue Mountain College.

Parenthetic: James Plemon Coleman was a life-long friend of Mother's. Although one year her junior, they went all through their school years together in Ackerman. After college and obtaining his degree from The George Washington University School of Law, he served on the staff of Aaron Lane Ford, a U.S. Congressman from Mississippi. In Washington, he made a name for himself by challenging and defeating another young Southern congressional staffer, Lyndon Baines Johnson, for Speaker of the Little Congress, a body that Johnson had dominated before Coleman's challenge. Ironically Plemon Coleman and Lyndon Johnson became friends for a lifetime.

Plemon returned to Mississippi. In 1940, he was elected District Attorney, an office he left in 1946 when he became State Circuit Court Judge. That led to a season as a justice on the Mississippi Supreme Court, from which he stepped down when made Mississippi Attorney General in 1950. He was elected Governor of Mississippi in 1956, and during that tenure, he became friends of Senator John Fitzgerald Kennedy. At the end of his term in 1960, Coleman was elected to a seat in the Mississippi House of Representatives, serving until 1964. He was the only politician in the state of Mississippi to serve in an elected capacity in all three branches of the state's government.

He ran for governor in 1963 against Paul B. Johnson, Jr., whose father was a former governor. (Paul Johnson was governor from 1965 to 1968. His brother's family was close friends of Mother's. The summer of 1965, Mother and I were visiting cousins and friends, and we had dinner with them in Jackson. My dear Mother, the matchmaker, insisted that I meet the Johnson daughter, who visited her grandparents in Decatur, Georgia, in August. I took her to see "Sound of Music" as it premiered in Atlanta. That was our only date. I met my future wife the next month).

President Kennedy attempted to lure Plemon Coleman into politics with the posts of U.S. Secretary of the Army and U.S. Ambassador to Australia. However, he preferred to remain in his native state. Following the assassination of John F. Kennedy, President Johnson appointed Coleman to the United States Court of Appeals, Fifth Circuit, where he served from 1965 to 1981, at which time he reached senior status. He returned to Ackerman, where he practiced law.

In one of the many letters that Plemon wrote to Mother during his stellar career (all of which letters she saved), he reminisced of their close and sustained friendship throughout their lives. Mother paid him a visit at his law office on one of her trips back to Mississippi. They assisted each other, through correspondence, in family genealogy and in Choctaw County history. Five years later I had the privilege of both corresponding with him and conversing by telephone; and we exchanged inscribed books on genealogy that each had authored. He cordially invited me to come for a visit with him at any time.

J.P. Coleman was stricken by a severe stroke in December 1990. He died in September 1991, just a few days before Jay and I visited the Mosses in Ackerman.

Although implicated in many earlier criminal activities, in 1931, the formidable Al Capone was imprisoned for income tax evasion. The Empire State Building was completed, and the U. S. officially acquired a national anthem.

At twenty-five years of age, Charles Lindbergh, the son of a U.S. Congressman, had obtained his wings in the Air Service Reserve Corps, first in his class in March 1925. With the Army needing no additional pilots at that time, he was a flight instructor and barnstormer for a while. Then, as a U.S. Air Mail pilot, he was ushered into international fame by flying nonstop from New York to Paris, France, May 20-21, 1927. Having set a record of thirty-six hundred miles in the single-seat *Spirit of St. Louis*, he was recognized later by receiving the Medal of Honor. He was one of three civilian explorers so recognized.

Aldous Leonard Huxley, English novelist, essayist, critic, and poet, published various books of verse and novels preceding the appearance of *Brave New World* (1932). In this exceptional work, he wrote a bitterly satiric account of an uncivilized society controlled by technology; a culture in which both art and religion had been annulled and human beings reproduced by artificial fertilization. Huxley was distressed with what he regarded as the moral and spiritual bankruptcy of the modern world. In hindsight, his book was prophetic.

On March 1st, the "Crime of the Century" occurred with the kidnapping of the twenty-month-old baby boy of Colonel Charles Lindbergh. As the search continued nationally, evidence was painstakingly uncovered. Over two months later, May 12, 1932, the remains of the baby were found by the FBI in a wooded area, very close to the Lindbergh home. It later was determined that the baby had been dropped accidentally by the kidnapper from a ladder propped against the two-story Lindbergh house and died from massive skull fractures. The tragedy was quite personal to the McCaslin family. Charles Lindbergh and Jesse Windham were friends. Jesse was the brother of my grandmother, Maude McCaslin, and he was a pilot in the Army Air Force. On one visit when Lindbergh had flown into Grenada for a visit with Jesse, he appeared at their back door. He joined the family for dinner.

By early 1932, Daddy was employed by Grenada Bank, where his father had long served on the board of directors. There were numerous branches, among which were Eupora and Charleston, Mississippi. Grandfather McCaslin had stock in the bank and continued to serve on the Board of Directors. By June 1932, Daddy was working in the Eupora Bank when he became a close friend of T. F. Taylor, Jr., who was the son of a wealthy Eupora businessman.

THE HISTORY OF WEBSTER COUNTY, MISSISSIPPI, by Webster County History Association, 1985, is a notable work that provides factual accounts on a great variety of subjects. A biography of the T. F. Taylor family is found on pp. 469-470, in which the families of T. F. Taylor Sr. and T. F. Taylor, Jr. are discussed.

> Parenthetic: The Taylors were very successful businessmen. T. F. Taylor, Jr. earlier had attended five colleges: the University of Mississippi, the University of Texas, the University of Virginia, Harvard University, and the University of Alabama. It was said that T. F. remarked: "I stayed at Harvard only two weeks...I found out Harvard didn't have a thing to offer to a Mississippi fellow going into the sawmill business." T. F. Taylor, Jr. met Lavinia Gertrude Foy while he was attending the University of Alabama. She was from Eufaula, Alabama,

and the same age as Mother. After they married, they settled in Eupora. Their only child, Mary Foy, was born in 1937. T. F. Taylor, Sr. died in 1942. In 1955, Foy enrolled at Ole Miss, where she met Jennings Paige Cothren from Natchez, who was born in 1935. They married in 1957. Lavinia and T. F. Taylor, Jr. moved to Ft. Lauderdale, Florida, on his retirement at age 47. Following their Christian conversion, Paige, with Foy at his side at many Christian counseling seminars, stated: "Foy came to Ole Miss looking for a big football hero and I came looking for a rich Mississippi Delta coed. We found each other." T. F. Taylor, Jr. died in 1968, and Lavinia died in 1982.

Mother's brother, Uncle Willie, after one year at Mississippi College, had been accepted at the U.S. Naval Academy, Annapolis. He graduated in May 1932. In those times, a graduate of West Point or Annapolis had no obligation or requirement of active duty service. Again, the early 1930s were not war years. Mother stated many times, "Brother was determined to get into the business world and make his fortune...and one job led to another, each one a disappointment."

Franklin D. Roosevelt had been Governor of New York since 1928. He was elected president in November 1932, in a resounding defeat of Herbert Hoover.

Daddy first wrote to Mother at Blue Mountain College on November 7, 1932. She was eighteen years of age, soon to turn nineteen. This, the earliest extant letter from Daddy to Mother, was written on Bank of Eupora letterhead stationery. He continued to write Mother, and they talked frequently by telephone.[4] Daddy accompanied Uncle Willie to Blue Mountain College on at least one occasion for a visit. Mother had completed her first semester of her junior year (1932-33).[5] By early February, 1933, at the semester break, she returned to Ackerman. Perhaps there had been discussions with her parents concerning the hardships that everyone was

---

[4]   All of these letters that Daddy wrote to Mother she kept, and are among the earliest of her letters provided among over one hundred of record in *LETTERS TO AND FROM A CHRISTIAN MOTHER AND MORE.*

[5]   In 2000, we obtained a copy of Mother's transcript from Blue Mountain College. Although pre-registered for the second semester of 1932-33, she did not return. We will see later that Mother completed the remaining year and a half of her college courses at Mississippi Southern College in three quarters, graduating with honors in May 1955.

experiencing in the Great Depression. Mother may have insisted on staying at home for a season. She had a year and a half left in college, but it can be assumed that there were notable expenses associated with Blue Mountain College. Moreover, judging from two bits of correspondence, Daddy's January 10th post card and his January 15th "missive," it may have been a desire on Mother's part to be closer to Daddy. He lived in Eupora, only eighteen miles from Ackerman.

Indeed, she remained at home. Mother began teaching elocution at Weir and Ackerman schools. In those days, credentials were not required for teaching. A young man from Louisville, the son of a Methodist minister, was courting her.[6]

Another of Daddy's closest friends, Pete Fortner, became President of The Eupora Bank in 1933. *THE HISTORY OF WEBSTER COUNTY, MISSISSIPPI* supplies a profile of The Eupora Bank and Pete Fortner, as well as other people of interest to our family.

In President Roosevelt's first "hundred days" in 1933, he recommended sweeping proposals and Congress enacted them all. The government programs were designed to bring recovery to business and agriculture, relief to the unemployed, and help to those in danger of losing farms and homes. There followed complex governmental reform, an example of which was the establishment of the Tennessee Valley Authority (TVA).

Daddy began regularly writing "love letters" to Mother (of the twenty-nine extant letters in little more than one year, twenty-eight were prior to mid-February 1934, when they married. None of Mother's letters to Daddy survived). Most of his letters were addressed to her in Ackerman, and all of the letters were written on the Grenada Bank letterhead stationery. The first eleven of these letters were all postmarked Eupora, beginning February 12, 1933, and continuing through July 30. Later correspondence followed Mother wherever she was visiting.

Mary McCaslin returned to Grenada after teaching for a while at Brenau College. A company came to Grenada – the Wayne P. Sewell, Co. – which organization put on musical productions. The Sewell Company provided the scripts and the costumes but utilized local people for the productions. Mary became involved in the musical productions in Grenada, and some of the rehearsals were held in the McCaslin home. Mary soon

---

6   Sara Margaret Adams Moss, Mother's first cousin – they were much like sisters – told
     us in a conversation, during a visit in Savannah in 1998, that in spite of this courtship,
     "Mac kept coming around."

was hired by Sewell, and she traveled around, doing the same work in other small towns. She worked her way to Texas, where she met Alton Johnson, whom she later married.

Representative of the romance that had blossomed, and tantamount to their desire to marry, are three of the last of the letters of this courtship. Daddy expressed his distress in not seeing Mother:

> January 11, 1934
> Dear Margaret,
>
> That you might know when I spend miserable evenings you will know that when you call, inviting me over, and I'm unable to come, who is so unfortunate to be around me that evening will be with "Old man gloomy gus" himself. I saw the dark side of so many angles last night that Ben Burney surprised me out of the blues later, and I've been happy since. Whether I'm just "gripped" out or had a change of heart, I'm thankful, nevertheless.
>
> Bill Sugg told me Tuesday that he with another couple had stopped at your house Sunday evening about 8:30 to get us, but that we looked so comfortable, they drove on. They came back to Eupora and cooked a bird supper themselves, which they regret we did not attend.
>
> I hope to be able to call you early enough soon to make a date to take us to a show, or a chance to be with you.
>
> Most affectionately yours,
> Alston

Nine days later, Daddy advised of anticipated plans of a visit that had been dashed:

> January 20 1934
> Dear Margaret,
>
> T. F., in letting me know he was going to Tuscaloosa tomorrow, said that I might ride by Ackerman with him and then back to Eupora on his return trip late Sunday evening. He will probably leave so early though, and come back so late, it would be an imposition on you, should I ask for such a protracted visit without a car of my own or other means of moving us about.

Thank you for holding a date open so long, but I see no way of visiting you as I'd wish.

Hope your play was a big success.
Alston

In early February, the trip to Mardi Gras was upon them. Daddy inquired, "How are our plans progressing:"

Tuesday morning the 6th
Dear Margaret,

I thought we were coming over last night until after six, then realized Henry and I would be working, which we did until about ten o'clock.

How are our plans progressing? Your brother has not written me.

Bill reminded me this morning that we were going to "She Done Him Wrong" Friday. T. F. wants to go to Louisville tonight. You have your play though.

I expect to hear from Dad at noon about a car.

Affectionately yours,
Alston

On February 8, 1934, Daddy made final plans for the trip to New Orleans in the company of his close friends T. F. Taylor, his fiancé, Lavinia Foy, and Pete and Virginia Fortner. The trip clearly had met with the approval of Mother's parents – they must have adored Daddy, to let their nineteen-year-old daughter make the trip.[7]

Daddy drove to Ackerman on Sunday, February 11, to get Mother, returning to Eupora, where they joined the Taylors and Fortners. They then traveled in two cars to New Orleans for the Mardi Gras Parade. The festivities in New Orleans ended on Fat Tuesday, February 13th. On the drive home, on Ash Wednesday, Valentine's Day, February 14, 1934, Daddy and Mother were married by the Justice of the Peace in Bogalusa, Washington Parish, Louisiana. A county or parish JP often married couples

---

[7]   Sara Margaret Moss told us in 1998 of the sequence of events of this trip. She had a vivid memory of it all.

who did not choose to have a church wedding. Presuming that Mother left Blue Mountain College a year earlier and came home because of the intensification of the Great Depression, that same dearth of funds for the cost of a church wedding probably had a strong bearing on their plans to marry. Ostensibly they discussed the financial hardships of the economy and agreed not to impose the expense of a wedding on Mother's parents. At that time, Daddy's salary from the bank was ninety dollars per month (about sixteen-hundred in 2015 dollars).

Daddy's youngest sister, fifteen-year-old Louise, occasionally told the story of Grandmother McCaslin's receiving word of the marriage. In the McCaslin home in Grenada, the wooden telephone hung from the wall in the broad entrance foyer, adjacent to the elegant flight of stairs leading to the second floor. A bench seat was situated along the wall beneath the telephone, in which the younger children would stand to talk into the telephone. Grandmother McCaslin answered the telephone as Louise sat on the bench listening. Daddy probably presented a carefully crafted explanation of their marriage in Bogalusa. Apparently Grandmother McCaslin was astounded; she had to sit down. But then, Grandmother regained her composure and expressed her sheer joy of the marriage. Mother and Daddy probably visited the family in Grenada soon after their return home with Eupora's being only sixty miles away.

Their romance had led so quickly to marriage in such a short period of time. It had been little more than a year since Daddy first brought Mother to Grenada to introduce her to his parents. Again, according to Aunt Louise, while all of the family was seated at the dinner table, Daddy had been so nervous that he spooned gravy into his iced tea, mindlessly thinking the gravy boat to contain sugar. The mistake resulted in notable embarrassment to Daddy but issued laughter from the rest of the family.

About one month later, Grandfather McCaslin wrote Daddy with the following sad news:

Grenada March 21st, 1934
(29th Wedding Anniversary)

My Dear Son,

I know you will be surprised at the enclosure, however it is for your protection, and all I can possibly do under the existing condition that confronts my interests here at Grenada.

Lamar Life instructed their attorneys to foreclose at once account inability to take care of regular installments, along with Fire Insurance, and Taxes, and so notified 2nd mortgagees Grenada Bank, who in turn asked me to retire or they would foreclose also, by agreement, am arranging to sell to best advantage to Tom Meek, (backed by Grenada Bank), the equipment and current stock, Ford Motor Co. Having previously arranged with Meek for my dealership, permitting me to also tender resignation as their representative.

As you well know I have lost heavily for the past three years, and am simply right up against it for operating capital, in accordance with what I can get out of the business, I will of course settle with my creditors, provided they do not throw me in bankruptcy, current accounts only amount to less than a thousand dollars.

The three cars are here and I would suggest that you get the Plymouth and take it to Eupora as early as possible; this car is in fair condition and has good tires &c.

Can't you drive over Sunday afternoon and bring a driver? You could take the car then. We are all well, and with love to you both; hope to see you over as it suits your convenience.

Devotedly yours,
Dad
(signed) Alston McCaslin

The foregoing letter is first-hand documentation that Grandfather McCaslin managed to retain his Ford dealership, his stock, and other assets, until March 1934.[8]

Grandfather McCaslin soon lost all the rest of his assets except for his home and their one remaining automobile. We know from family tradition that Grandfather McCaslin, during the cold days that followed, would leave home each morning with an empty coal scuttle. He would find work somewhere, and return with food and a scuttle of coal. The family would eat, and then gather around the fire in the fireplace – until the coals were burned low. Then, they would disperse to their various bedrooms, and under layers of quilts or blankets, go to sleep. The next day, Grandfather McCaslin would go about doing the same thing, in order to put food on the table and coal in the grate. Later, for a short period of time, he began selling small pecan pies door to door. He was determined to stay active and to provide what he could for his family.

We have a color picture postcard of the "PUBLIC SQUARE, GRENADA, MISS.," postmarked March 17, 1934, Grenada. The Grenada Ford Company was located on one side of the square. The postcard is imprinted on the reverse side:

"PUBLISHED BY THE ECLIPSE, GRENADA, MISS."

The Eclipse was the elegant drugstore on the square that Grandfather McCaslin had built while his daughter, Louise, was a young child. As mentioned earlier, during early years of the Depression, he lost the Eclipse drug store, the publishing business, the bakery, the Railroad Café, along with other commercial holdings, including the mercantile store.

Contemporaneously, Frank Hamer, a former Texas Ranger, had trailed the notorious bank robbers, Bonnie and Clyde, across nine states before he was able to stage a deadly ambush outside Arcadia, Louisiana, in May 1934. Hamer and five other lawmen shot and killed Bonnie and Clyde as they drove through the trap. Bonnie Parker and Clyde Barrow were buried in separate cemeteries in Dallas, Texas.

Mother and Daddy's first residence in Eupora was a small apartment over the garage at the home of T. F. Taylor, Jr. – a white brick home on W.

---

[8] That Grandfather McCaslin retained ownership until this 1934 date is verified later in a 1938 newspaper article that follows. In 2002, I had the letter framed between glass as a gift to my brother.

Clarke Avenue, adjacent to the huge, three-story home built by T. F. Taylor, Sr. (The "big house," into which the T. F. Taylor, Jr. family moved after his father's death. To this day, this brick, Tudor-style home at 71 W. Clarke Avenue is the most stately and elegant in Eupora).

Mother said that they had very few wedding gifts, because they had not had a formal wedding. Their possessions were but a few pieces of furniture given them by each of their parents. Daddy surprised Mother with a baby chicken for Easter. He had the chick in a cardboard box, with which he had rigged an electric light bulb for warmth. During the night, the box caught fire. They awakened, choked and blinded by smoke. Daddy instructed Mother to go downstairs quickly to save herself, to get out of the apartment. Unable to see his hand in front of his face, immediately he thought of the two new pairs of shoes that he had purchased just that week. He reached into the closet, grabbed for a pair of shoes with his left hand, and with the right arm, raked up the entire rack of clothes on hangers and tore them from the rod. Then he stumbled out of the door, blinded by the smoke, down the exterior stairs, and out into the cold night air. When the smoke cleared from his eyes, he looked down. He had grabbed one each of the two new pairs of shoes. The only possessions salvaged from the flames that engulfed the building were the clothes that he had snatched from the clothes rod (for the rest of her life, Mother had a grave awareness for the potential of a house fire. During our teens and college years, if they were leaving town for a trip, she would leave notes throughout the entire house, cautioning us about safety, particularly fire).

Daddy's youngest brother, Henry, had attended Grenada College later during the Depression, but he desperately wanted to work for Grenada Bank. Mother told us that while Daddy was working at the Bank of Eupora, Henry came to town and came by the bank. He made the trip from Grenada solely to ask Daddy if, as promised, he had recommended him to Grenada Bank President Tol Thomas for a position at the bank. Daddy confirmed that he had. After talking briefly, Daddy told Henry that he would step next door to the drug store, to get coffee for the two of them, and asked Henry to answer the telephone in his absence. No sooner had Daddy left the bank and the telephone on his desk rang. Henry answered. Tol Thomas' voice was at the other end of the line, and, assuming that he was speaking with Daddy, Thomas thundered: "McCaslin, do you recommend that I hire Henry?" Naturally Henry replied: "Yes sir. He can keep a fine set of books!" Thomas then stated: "Tell him to go to the Shelby Bank. He's got a job." Henry was hired on his own recommendation, completely unknown by Tol Thomas.[9]

When the Bank of Eupora was established in 1898, it was the first "branch bank" ever to be established in the state, and one of the first in the entire nation. The idea of branch banking was conceived by the then president of Grenada Bank, Mr. J. Tol Thomas.

Our parents socialized often with the Taylors and the Fortners. They all were often together for dining, or attending football games in Starkville or Oxford, or trips to Little Rock, New Orleans, as well as two trips to Havana, Cuba. Epicureans that they were, they often drove more than an hour over to Greenwood for dinner at Lusco's, a distance of sixty miles. At that time, Lusco's was a grocery store. The restaurant dates back to 1932 – prohibition times. In those early days, one would enter the grocery store, walk past the shelves full of canned goods in the front of the grocery store to the back, then through a door with a loosely-drawn curtain. Beyond the curtain was the dining area, where tables of various sizes were sequestered behind wooden partitions. This back room, where alcoholic beverages were served, was hidden from the front of the store. The food was excellent, and customers drove long distances to dine at Lusco's.

Mother told of an incident that occurred there:

> We were dining at Lusco's one night, with T. F., Lavinia, Pete, and Virginia. The shrimp gumbo was one of the specialties. While eating the gumbo, T. F. winced noticeably, and retrieved the crown of a human tooth from his mouth. He was disgusted, and called Lusco, the owner, over to the table. After berating him for having allowed this careless thing to happen, our party left the restaurant. A little way from the restaurant, T. F. suddenly remarked, "Hey. That was *my* tooth!" With that statement, he turned his Cadillac around, drove back to Lusco's, and we all went back in. T. F. apologized to Lusco and we sat back down for our meal. I always respected T. F. for admitting to this error and for apologizing.

---

[9]　In later years, Uncle Henry smiled broadly when this story was re-told in his presence. Henry spent most of his career as president of the bank in Rosedale, Mississippi – he had it nationalized – and he was joined by his children after their college graduation. Henry Sr. retired in 1991, and Henry E. McCaslin, Jr. became President of First National Bank of Rosedale. At the turn of the 21st century, First National Bank of Rosedale was viewed as one of the best small-town banks in the nation.

Mother recalled Daddy's proclivity toward a good poker game. He played with a group each month in Eupora. Some of the men were from out of town and were professionals. Sometimes Daddy would win a small amount and some nights he would lose a little. Mother said that they had such limited pecuniary resources, she begged Daddy, on several occasions, to quit playing poker. He told her that he wanted to win big just one time, after which he promised that he would give up the game of poker, honoring her wishes. Early one morning, Daddy came home from the game. He woke Mother to show her the hundreds of dollars that he had won. Mother asked him if he now would quit, and he reaffirmed that he would. The next month, one of the other men called him about the game and he told them he had quit. They insisted that he had to return and allow them the opportunity to win back some of their losses. He agreed to do so, but only one time. It was a matter of sportsmanship. He played the scheduled night of that month; he lost a little; and he never played poker again. However, he did enjoy making a small bet on a golf game, or a football game, and he played Hearts or Canasta at the country club, following the round of golf.

By 1935 the nation had achieved some measure of recovery, but businessmen and bankers were resisting more and more Roosevelt's New Deal program. They distrusted his experiments, were shocked that he had taken the Nation off the gold standard and allowed deficits in the budget, and resented the concessions to labor.

In 1935, Daddy was transferred from Eupora to the Bank of Grenada branch in Cleveland. They became active members of the Presbyterian Church. We know little of their life or times in Cleveland except what brief notes Mother kept in her diary, which, from time to time, mentioned that Daddy was at a church meeting.

Daddy and Mother moved to Louisville, Mississippi, in the first half of 1936. Mother's childhood home, Ackerman, was eighteen miles southeast of Eupora by way of Highway 9. Louisville was located another fifteen miles southeast of Ackerman on Highway 15. As in Charleston, Eupora, and Cleveland, Daddy continued to serve Grenada Bank, now with the Louisville Branch. The close proximity to Ackerman allowed them to visit Mother's parents frequently. An envelope that had contained photographs was mailed from the photography company on July 31, 1936 to "Mrs. A.J. McCaslin, c/o Louisville, Bank, Miss."

Uncle Willie advanced his career with the beginning of his employment with Shell Oil Company in 1937.[10]

In 1938, the Memphis, Tennessee newspaper told of Grandfather McCaslin's causing a stir in "his brand-new" Model "T" Ford. The article (original copies of which we have framed) explained that Mr. McCaslin owned Grenada Ford Company from 1912 through 1934, and when he sold the business, the purchaser did not wish to buy the Model "T" parts. Consequently, he went into the parts business. From parts remaining in 1938, he had mechanics assemble a complete Model "T" from the stock, the cost of the labor being about fifty dollars, and enough parts remained to build two more.

Because Mother was thought to be expecting, her mother wrote to her in Louisville in August 1938:

> Sugar–
>
> How are you feeling? I'm sorry I could not offer a curing remedy for your ailment. You seemed more depressed than in pain, & I didn't know why until 8:00 P.M. when you said you didn't want to be sick. I wonder if you should not have some adjustments so as to get your organs just right, before you suffer another spell like the first one. If & when you arrange to be pregnant, you must also arrange to be very quiet, for at least 3 whole months and 6 would be better & really 9 months may be necessary for with your disorders, it's too easy for the same thing to happen over & over. Do you really think or hope you are pregnant? If so, don't tennis or swim or lift–stretch, etc., etc. There's worlds of things you should do and not do, but especially one in just your case must be very particularly careful. Fran said last winter she had a book you'd profit by, by studying it, that she'd lend you. I wonder if she did...
>
> Guess they are powerful busy. So am I. Had a few peaches to can, also a few tomatoes. Old Mary has an "eternity" case she has to stay with. She doesn't get except promise of Dr. James

---

[10] Uncle Willie was employed by Shell Oil Company until 1952 in various marketing assignments, principally relating to industrial products and their application, rising to manager of their Industrial Sales Department, Atlanta Division, for three years. In 1949, he was transferred to Houston, Texas, in charge of jobber sales for their Texas District.

to give her what medicine she needs... I ironed Willie's shirts
& washed....

Heaps of love to you, my darling
From Mother.

From the foregoing, apparently Mother believed that she had a miscarriage. But soon she was pregnant with Jay (who would be born eleven months later, July 19, 1939).

Alston Jones McCaslin III sustained a stroke in August 1938. Mother visited her beloved father-in-law frequently in Grenada during the two months of his illness,. Grenada Bank President Tol Thomas lived in the next block and he stopped by to visit every day, as he walked to or from the bank. Louise Vance wrote:[11]

In 1938, at the age of seventy-four, Daddy suffered a very severe stroke. He lost his speech, and his entire body was paralyzed, with the exception of his left arm, which he could move a little. The bedroom was turned into a hospital room, and we had helpers who would come and stay with him and help Mother with the nursing. His mind was alert, and he could communicate very well with his eyes. I can remember those vivid blue eyes flashing with anger or smiling when he was pleased. Mary Margaret had always been a great favorite of his, because she would always stand up to him and wasn't afraid to tease or love him. He often had said about her, "That girl has spunk." Following his stroke, while he was bedridden, Mary Margaret would come to Grenada and visit for several days at a time. I can remember her sitting by Daddy's bed, holding his hand, and talking for hours. He loved her visits!

---

[11]   Louise Vance, *THE ALSTON JONES McCASLIN FAMILY*, published 1988, pp. 104-105.

Alston Jones McCaslin III died in early October, 1938, six weeks before his seventy-fifth birthday. His obituary was published in the *GRENADA SENTINEL* as follows (Permission granted by the now *Grenada Star Sentinel*):

Death of A. J. McCASLIN
Saddens All Grenada

After an illness of two months, during which time he fought a grim fight against approaching dissolution, Alston Jones McCaslin, often called "Junior" by his friends and relatives, passed away early Sunday morning, October 9, 1938.

He was born in the McCaslin old home in the village of Graysport, Grenada County, November 28, 1863, his people being among the early settlers of that then important river landing on the Yalobusha River. Receiving such early education as that place afforded, he, as a young man, entered business, first there and later in Coffeeville. In 1904, he moved to Grenada, operating a bakery and establishing the Eclipse, at that time the most ornate soda fountain in North Mississippi, the fixtures of which have lasted until just recently when they were replaced with more modern fixtures. He was a pioneer Ford dealer and made and lost a fortune selling Ford cars. Not daunted by reverses in fortune, Mr. McCaslin, up until he was stricken, pushed on vigorously as if he was just embarking on his career, rather than bringing it to an end. He was indomitable in his determination to retrieve his lost estate and worked ceaselessly to that end.

On March 22, 1905, he and Miss Maude Windham were married. They have reared a fine group of young men and women, each of whom, in his or her respective field, is reflecting credit upon the training given in the McCaslin home.

Services from the Presbyterian Church, of which he was a member and an officer, were held Sunday afternoon. The Pastor, Rev. C. A. Pharr, conducted the services and later the services at Odd Fellows Cemetery, where Mr. McCaslin was laid to rest. The pall bearers were: Messrs. Clarence Burt, B. C. Adams, George Grant, George Granberry, Bob Vandiver, and Andrew Carouthers.

He is survived by his widow, Mrs. Maude Windham McCaslin: three daughters, Mrs. Alton Johnson of Buffalo, Texas, Mrs. Roger Dollarhide of Grenada, and Miss Louise McCaslin of Grenada; four sons, Alston of Louisville, Miss., Billy of Memphis, Byron of Rosedale, and Henry of Beulah; a brother, John McCaslin, and two sisters, Misses Willie and Hattie McCaslin.

Willie and Hattie were the two old maid sisters that Grandfather McCaslin had put through college.

Whereas we know from many family pictures that Mother and Daddy visited Mother's parents often in Ackerman, essentially little else is known of the two years that they resided in Louisville.[12] However, we have scores of family pictures made before and after Jay's birth. My brother, Alston Jones McCaslin V, was born in Louisville, Mississippi, on July 19, 1939.

Mother honored the paternal line in assigning her first-born son the family name. A score of photographs are of Jay as a baby, both at home in Eupora or while visiting at Grandfather Dobbs home. These are dated in Mother's hand. Uncle Willie, Frances, and William are pictured in many of the photographs. A few months after Jay's birth, the family returned to Cleveland, as corroborated with another envelope containing photographs which was addressed: "Mrs. A.J. McCaslin, 109 Leflore, Cleveland." Mother noted: "Dec. '39-Jan. '40."

---

[12] From the time of their marriage, Mother never was employed until after Daddy's death in 1953, when we moved to Gainesville, Georgia. In terms almost archaic to society today, she was a "housekeeper," as is designated on my December 1940 birth certificate.

Chapter Two

LIFE IN EUPORA

Eupora in 1940 was a small, sleepy, Southern town in Webster County, located some one-hundred and ten miles north of Jackson, Mississippi. The population was a few souls more than thirteen hundred. The town was established in 1889 on the Central Rail Lines, now Columbus & Greenville Railroad. Eupora was served by two major highways – U. S. Highway 82, East and West, and Mississippi Highway 9, North and South.

There were only four traffic lights in Eupora, three of which were on U. S. Highway 82, which thoroughfare divided the town in two. The "downtown" area, North Dunn Street, essentially was confined to one city block, with about fifteen stores on each side, although some commercial buildings were situated on adjoining corners at each intersection. The fourth traffic light in Eupora was at the north end of the single "downtown" block. Built on a slight rise of the hill, the buildings on the west side of N. Dunn Street were raised five concrete steps above the street – the "high side." The buildings on the east, the "low side," were at ground level. The city block of stores on N. Dunn Street was composed principally of characteristic establishments of a small town, viz: mercantile, hardware, two drug stores, barber shop, bank, and movie theater. On the east side of N. Dunn Street was the Jitney Jungle Grocery Store, owned by G. E. Childs and the Western Auto, owned by Oscar Miller, the father of Robert, both of which families lived on Adams Avenue. The Eupora Café was situated on the northeast corner of Highway 82. The large Buchanan & Son Mercantile Building was on the northwest corner of the intersection, across N. Dunn Street, facing the Eupora Café. J.R. Phillips Drygoods Store occupied the ground floor and our family dentist, Dr. Silas G. Maddox, had his small office on the second floor of this building.

The intersection of Highway 82 designated the beginning of South Dunn Street. On the east side of the intersection was the Ross Ford Motor Co. One building, Dr. Hugh Curry's medical office, separated the Ford place and the railroad tracks. Just across the tracks stood the Eupora Hotel.[13] Further down S. Dunn Street was the Farmers' Cotton Gin, then the Curry Medical Clinic, too small to be regarded as a hospital.

The Railroad Depot was on the west side S. Dunn St., situated between the railroad track and a spur track. The depot spread out perpendicular to S. Dunn Street, between the tracks, diagonally across from both Ross Ford Motor Co. to the north and the Eupora Hotel to the south.

The location of the railroad in 1889 was the genesis of the founding of Eupora later becoming the hub of trade, rather than the Webster County Seat of Walthall – which town, five miles north of Eupora toward Belle Fountain, had not grown beyond more than a few hundred citizens.

Adams Avenue originated at the railroad depot, forking off to the west of S. Dunn Street at a forty-five degree angle. Couched in an area between Adams Avenue and the railroad tracks was the Farmer's Co-Operative. (Our last residence in Eupora was on Adams Avenue).

At the north end corner of the "down town" block on N. Dunn Street was a coffee shop, adjoining the Eupora Theater, and directly behind these two buildings was the Baptist Church, with the church manse beside it. The Wofford family owned the theater. Eupora boasted two drug stores. One was the Embry Drug Company, owned by the Embry brothers, both of whom were pharmacists and neighbors of ours. Six doors removed was The Eupora Drug Store. The Eupora Bank and the barber shop were between The Eupora Drug Store and the theater. Across the intersection of West Fox Avenue from the coffee shop, the same side of N. Dunn Street, stood the marble-clad U.S. Post Office, situated on the corner previously occupied by the former Baptist Church. Directly behind the Post office on West Fox Avenue stood the stone remnants of a once beautiful and stately Presbyterian Church – the structure had long been abandoned and was enveloped with a collage of vines. Saplings and other vegetation had overtaken the yard once covered in grass. Located diagonally across from

---

[13]   *THE HISTORY OF WEBSTER COUNTY*, pub. by Webster County History Association, 1985, provides a history of Eupora, as well as many photographs.

the post office on N. Dunn Street was the Eupora Community Center (where, in 1951 and 1952, we first learned a few dance steps, to the music played from a large juke box stocked with early 1950s music). At the end of the block, N. Dunn Street ended at Clark Avenue, where if one continued to drive straight it became the driveway of Pete Fortner's brick home. At the top of the first hill on W. Clarke Avenue, on the right, was the resplendent home of T. F. Taylor, Jr., of whom we will say more later. Down that hill and at the top of the next, on the right, stood the Eupora High School building. The road turned south to become N. Joliffe Street, which led directly toward our home on Adams Avenue.

World War II began with the invasion of Poland by Germany, September 1, 1939. Jay was t six weeks of age. The war began to run rampant in Europe as America watched from across the Atlantic Ocean.

The 1940 Mississippi census found my family in Bolivar County, Cleveland City, April 6. The family was enumerated at 109 Leflore Street: A. J. McCaslin, age thirty-one; Mrs. McCaslin, age twenty-six; A.J. McCaslin, Jr., nine months of age; and Daddy's brother Byron, age twenty-seven. Clearly marked "R" for renter, the house cost thirty-five dollars per month (Suzanne and I rented our first apartment in 1965 in Decatur, Georgia, for eighty-five dollars per month, including all utilities except for the telephone). The category for employment states that Daddy worked for "52 weeks in 1939," and his total income for 1939 is enumerated as "$1,500.00." Close below the listing is the household of a primary school teacher who made "$900.00" per year. The mean annual income in the 1940 census was about nine hundred and sixty dollars, so Daddy's income was well above the average. On this date, April 6, Mother was one month along in her pregnancy with me. Perhaps unknown to everybody but her, I was present during the census, although not included.

A week later, April 13, the census taker enumerated Mother's parents in Choctaw County, Ackerman Town. Grandfather Dobbs was fifty-five and Grandmother Dobbs was fifty-four. Estel Bridges Dobbs' occupation is listed: "mail carrier, U. S. Post Office," and he earned "$1,800.00" in 1939. Only Mamie and Estel resided in the home. Grandfather Dobbs owned his home, valued at two-thousand dollars. It was built by Mamie's father, John Adams V. Their house was single story, frame, with a standing seam tin roof, and a wide porch across the front, and stood about four feet above ground. A breezeway ran from the front to the back, with rooms opening off of each side. (There is a hand-made coat rack on our breezeway today from the breezeway of the Adams home. The coat rack was made by my great grandfather John Adams, when the house was built in the mid-19ᵗʰ century).

On April 9, the Grenada County, Grenada, April 9, census lists Grandmother McCaslin. Her address was 515 Main Street. She was enumerated as fifty-four years of age. Listed are daughters Louise, age twenty-one, Adelaide Dollarhide, at twenty-three, Roger Dollarhide, "son-in-law," at twenty-seven, and Roger Dollarhide, Jr., age four. Grandmother McCaslin owned her home, which was valued at "$5,000.00." This was the two-story house that Mr. McCaslin had built for her in 1905. An early photograph of the McCaslin home is displayed in *THE ALSTON JONES McCASLIN FAMILY*.

Mother was always methodical in nature. She kept a diary most of her adult life, and many details were recorded contemporaneously. As an example, in one of her diaries, each day she recorded her activities and events in their lives from January 1 to April, 1941. She wrote of Daddy's driving to Cleveland in January to obtain an apartment into which they could move, in anticipation of being transferred again. Daddy's mother, referred to as Mother Mac (short for McCaslin), was visiting in Eupora. When the apartment did not materialize, Mother put Grandmother McCaslin on the bus to ferry her back to Grenada.

Mother decided to go to Ackerman for a visit. She took Jay with her, driving the eighteen miles through a heavy snowfall. Upon arrival, she found her father to be very ill. The snow continued to fall through the night. The next morning, Grandfather Dobbs' condition had worsened. The doctor was summoned and upon his arrival, he diagnosed the condition as acute appendicitis. Mother was instructed by the doctor to take her father to the hospital in Houston, Mississippi. On arrival there, Dr. Philpot operated immediately. It was discovered that the appendix had ruptured and was gangrenous. Mother wired Daddy and called her mother.

Mother then characterized the subsequent days: of returning to Ackerman, the cold weather, and the deep snow. Jay became sick with a chest cold, and Mother wrote, "I nursed him, *praying* that he would not get pneumonia." Grandfather Dobbs recovered slowly. Numerous other remarks in Mother's diary pertained to daily activities. Her entry for February 19 mentioned that Jay was seven months old and had cut his two lower teeth.

Having secured a place to live, Mother and Daddy moved back to Cleveland. On Thursday, February 22, 1940, the entry in the diary stated that Henry and Lorena McCaslin arrived from Beulah, as planned, and they all went to Memphis to see *Gone With The Wind*.[14]

On Sunday, March 10, Mother and Daddy joined the Presbyterian Church, where they earlier had been members. Jay was enrolled on the "Cradle Roll." First Presbyterian Church, Cleveland, Mississippi, signed by the pastor, R. A. Bolling. Jay was eight months of age. Later that afternoon, according to the diary, Henry, Lorena, Byron, and Mother Mac stopped by the house for a visit. They were on their way from Grenada to Beulah. Then, on Monday, the 11th, Mother and Daddy drove to Beulah to visit with Henry and Lorena.

(An accomplished author, in his proof-reading in 2011 of *LETTERS TO AND FROM A CHRISTIAN MOTHER AND MORE* cautioned: "The fact that you went to the corner store to buy eggs may be of interest to you and your family, but probably not to others." I beg the reader's indulgence again. Many notes of Mother's in her diary describe contemporaneously the close, familial ties of family members and the trials and tribulations of that post-Depression era. Therefore, I believe these details add substance to the narrative for a broader audience than just our family members).

On March 31, Mother noted that Billy and Dorothy McCaslin came for a visit. Then, on April 4th, Mother wrote that Henry and Lorena came over for a visit, but that Daddy had gone to a Sunday school party. Billy and Henry often traveled in excess of a hundred miles purely for a visit. A month later, in May of 1940, still in Cleveland, Mother was expecting another baby.

President Roosevelt had used neutrality legislation, attempting to keep the United States out of the war in Europe. Meanwhile, he sought to enhance the nations that were threatened or attacked. When France fell and England came under siege in 1940, Roosevelt began to send Great Britain all possible aid short of actual military involvement.

Then Daddy was transferred back to the Bank of Eupora. Soon after arriving, as affirmed in my birth certificate that follows, Daddy had assumed the position of bookkeeper, working with his best friend,

---

[14]   Three years of publicity had preceded Hollywood's release of this film. It was three and one-half hours in running time. Premiering in Atlanta on December 15, 1939, it set records for production cost of over four million, and was a box office record setter in its own time.

multi-millionaire T. F. Taylor, Jr. at the Taylor Lumber Company, Eupora. Among other holdings, T. F. Taylor, Jr. owned the lumber companies located in Duck Hill and Sturgis. Mother remained in Cleveland with Jay (for they did not physically move to Eupora until January 1, 1941). She chose to continue under the care of Dr. Hickman in Louisville, so she commuted from Cleveland as necessary for prenatal appointments, staying with her parents in Ackerman. Ostensibly, when the due date was near, she was in Ackerman. In her diary, Mother noted that she went into labor late in the evening of December 5. My birth certificate registers Mother's arrival at the hospital in Louisville at 1:00 a.m., prior to my birth at 6:00 a.m., December 6, 1940. My birth certificate reads in part as follows:

> NAME: Silas Dobbs McCaslin...Mother's Stay Before Delivery in Hospital, 5 hours; in the community, 5 hours... FATHER OF CHILD, Alston Jones McCaslin, Jr...32 years of age...USUAL OCCUPATION, Bookkeeper; Business, Lumber Co....MOTHER OF CHILD, Mary Margaret Dobbs, 27 years of age...Housekeeper, own home.

Mother was keenly aware of her maternal ancestry, having collaborated in the work on family history and genealogy with both her cousin Carey Cranfield Dobbs and her Aunt Arlin. Mother had an uncle, the brother of Estel Bridges Dobbs, named Silas Abner Dobbs; hence the Silas Dobbs name had been handed down, generation after generation. As noticed earlier, Mother's grandfather was Silas Barnabas Dobbs, and his father was Silas Mercer Dobbs, all being named after Silas Mercer's father, the Reverend Silas Dobbs (1794-1864).

The Reverend Silas Dobbs was son of Lodowick Adams Dobbs and grandson of Fortune Dobbs, the latter of whom was a patriot in the Revolutionary War. Lodowick Adams Dobbs served under Francis Marion, the Swamp Fox (who was fictionally represented by Mel Gibson in the movie, "The Patriot." Lodowick had a Revolutionary War flintlock, and it adorned the fireplace, beneath the Dobbs family coat of arms, for several generations. Ultimately it came down to Mother, and Jay and I grew up admiring that long, heavy gun. The long rifle had a hexagonal barrel and ornate brass work on the stock. After the deaths of Mother and then Gene, his third wife sold the gun to a local antique dealer).

Lodwick Adams Dobb's father, Fortune Dobbs was a kinsman of Arthur Dobbs (1689-1765), Colonial Governor of North Carolina. Of the many colonial wills that I transcribed in genealogical research, the last will and testament of Governor Arthur Dobbs is the most eloquent in expressing his Christian faith. The opening words of his will read as follows:

> IN THE NAME OF THE ALMIGHTY GOD, AMEN. I, Arthur Dobbs, of Brunswick, in New Hanover, Governor and Captain General of the Province of North Carolina, in America, enjoying a moderate state of health and having the blessing of the infinitely perfect and good God the Father Almighty, a perfect and sound mind and memory, do make this my last Will and Testament in manner following:
>
> First, I recommend my soul to the Almighty Triune God, Jehovah Elohim and his only Begotten son, Jesus Christ my God and only Savior and Redeemer and to his Holy Spirit Blessed forever; and my Body to the Earth to be decently and privately interred, in an assured and full hope of a Glorious and happy Resurrection with the Just, at the first Resurrection and a Blessed immortality in the Heavenly Kingdom of Christ the Messiah, until he shall deliver up his Mediatorial Kingdom to God his Father when he shall be all in all his Creatures; and instead of immoderate Funeral Expenses, I desire that one hundred pounds, Sterling Money, may be paid and distributed proportionally among the Housekeepers of the Parrishes of Ballynure and Kilroot in the County of Antrim, and Kingdom of Ireland, and one other Hundred....

The foregoing last will and testament is an example of the distinct Christian faith that most Protestant Americans had two-hundred and fifty years ago. Every Christian last will and testament began in a similar fashion, first asking for a "Christian" burial. Colonial American Christians essentially were honest and good folks; ethical and moral. They were well churched, they prayed, they catechized their children, and they read their Bibles. They generally strived to live Christ-like lives, aspiring toward obedience of the Ten Commandments as well as respecting the civil law. They knew fully what the Bible said about Heaven and Hell, and by and large, they planned to spend Eternity in the Heaven.

Mother and Daddy moved from Cleveland back to Eupora on January 1, 1941 – I was less than a month old. As earlier noticed, Daddy now had assumed the position of bookkeeper at Taylor Lumber Company, Eupora. Shortly thereafter, Daddy's position was expanded to partner with T. F. Taylor, Jr., and he began keeping the books and managing the Sturgis Lumber Company (a position which Daddy held until his death in 1953). He commuted to Sturgis, about thirty-five miles from Eupora. (Years later, when I was nine and ten and eleven years of age, on vacation days for me and in the summer months, I would accompany Daddy to Sturgis. He would let me drive the entire trip there and back, as he sat on the passenger side reading a current magazine, *LIFE* or *SATURDAY EVENING POST*). Jay went to Sturgis only one time. Daddy and I formed a strong bond. I was his little "tough guy," and Jay was more the studious type.

The close friendship that Mother and Daddy had with Lavinia and T. F. apparently became more personal. As we have seen, it was a friendship reaching back to 1932, when Daddy first arrived at the Bank of Eupora. He had mentioned T. F. in several of the letters that he wrote to Mother in 1933 and 1934, and the Taylors, along with the Fortners, had accompanied them on the trip to New Orleans for Mardi Gras in February 1934.

Representative of Mother's persistent journalistic prowess in her diary, the following details are transcribed as typical:

> I am starting this on December seventh, 1941. Life has been extremely interesting this past year. I wish I had a record of it. From now on I shall keep one of happenings of major importance.
>
> We moved back to Eupora on January 1st 1941. Took P. T. Sullivan's duplex. Spent the year at home trying to live within our budget...
>
> In April, Brother gave up his job and rejoined the Navy on request![15] He went to Pensacola for two weeks, then they moved to Corpus Christie, and have been there since. They were at home for ten days leave the last of October.
>
> George Hughes[16] left home in April for Washington, Bermuda, & finally England, where he has been since, as an attache' in the Embassy. His daughter, Judy, was born July 16.
>
> Little Billy McCaslin, Jr. was born July 8.

---

[15] A 1933 Annapolis graduate, Uncle Willie Dobbs would rise to the rank of Lt. Commander in his service in World War II, and later to Captain, USN retired.

[16] Hughes was the close friend of Uncle Willie and Mother's life-long friend, whom she had accompanied at the 1933 Annapolis prom.

Daddy developed arthritis & finally a stomach trouble. In November, he went to Dr. Colbert & found it to be gallbladder trouble & is now on a diet...

December 6, 1941. Si's birthday. Kitty and I took Jay and Si over to Helen's to find he weighed 21½ pounds. I spent the morning loafing up town with Jay. Wrapped Xmas pkgs. Polished shoes & finished William's bed socks.

Dec. 7. Sunday. We went over home early; attended church with Mother. Had fried chicken for dinner & chatted. Heard over radio that Hawaii was attacked by Japan. Home early. Radio thrilling with talk of air raids over San Francisco.

Dec. 8. Monday. Roosevelt spoke to first War Congress. Churchill also spoke. Planning on another supper for T. F. and Lavania. Doris Hayes is getting a truck driver to bring the oysters tonight. Saw Lady & she gave me some hand-me-downs for Si – from Little Billy. Radio still interesting about the war.

Dec. 10. Wednesday. Supper tonight. A huge sack of fresh oysters in shell. 5 lbs. Shrimp. Lettuce hearts with french dressing. A card from Mother Mac saying that Patricia had died (on Tuesday, I presume). It shocked me terribly. Wrote Mary and Mother Mac. The Taylors came over & we had a wonderful evening. They stayed til 10 p.m. talking about the war & what it might mean to us.

Dec. 11. Thursday. Doris & Tom Ross came to eat more oysters. Brother sent a gift for my birthday. Bath powder & cologne. So precious he is. Tom left the party and returned with a box of candy.

Mother mentioned in her diary the attack on Pearl Harbor on the morning of December 7. That was the most barbaric, one-day attack that our country had ever sustained by another nation, and it provoked the U.S. to enter the war. I had turned one year of age on the sixth, the day before. Four days after the dreadful surprise attack, the following announcement was made on December 11, 1941, by the president:

To the Congress of the United States:

On the morning of December 11 the Government of Germany, pursuing its course of world conquest, declared war against the United States. The long-known and the long-expected has thus taken place. The forces endeavoring to enslave

31

the entire world now are moving toward this hemisphere. Never before has there been a greater challenge to life, liberty and civilization. Delay invites great danger. Rapid and united effort by all of the peoples of the world who are determined to remain free will insure a world victory of the forces of justice and of righteousness over the forces of savagery and of barbarism. Italy also has declared war against the United States. I therefore request the Congress to recognize a state of war between the United States and Germany, and between the United States and Italy.

Franklin D. Roosevelt

The War Resolution

Declaring that a state of war exists between the Government of Germany and the government and the people of the United States and making provision to prosecute the same. Whereas the Government of Germany has formally declared war against the government and the people of the United States of America:

Therefore, be it RESOLVED by the Senate and House of Representatives of the United States of America in Congress assembled, that the state of war between the United States and the Government of Germany which has thus been thrust upon the United States is hereby formally declared; and the president is hereby authorized and directed to employ the entire naval and military forces of the government to carry on war against the Government of Germany; and to bring the conflict to a successful termination, all of the resources of the country are hereby pledged by the Congress of the United States.

December 11, 1941

The diary continues:

Dec. 12. Friday. Stayed home. Lavinia came by after lunch, bringing a yarn holder she'd gotten in Jackson for me & 12 glasses I wanted for Mac.

Dec. 13. Saturday. I mailed Kay's box. Cost 39 cents. Remember to make them light from now on. Bought a roast & chops for the weekend. Delores & Frank Reich came by on the way to Kansas. Si broke our pretty electric clock Brother gave me.

Dec. 14. Sunday. Stayed home all day. Listened to radio. Roast for dinner. Children well & happy. Looking forward to Christmas with joy & hope....

Dec. 15. Monday. To town to mail pkgs. & long distance cards. To Greenwood after lunch with Helen, Lady Mary, Virginia, Sara, & Katherine. This is the 150th anniversary of Bill of Rights. Marvelous Radio program with Roosevelt & numerous stars. Radio reports today 2700 naval men killed at Pearl Harbor last Sunday. Memo.: Jay says: "To morning, we're going to see Grandpapa. Si says: "Bye-bye," "Ma ma," "Da da," and goes like a firecracker. "Dow!"

Dec. 16. Tuesday. Stayed home all morning. Blocked two Red Cross sweaters! After lunch, Daddy came over to have his car worked on, bringing Mother. She & I chatted. She made some biscuits for me. The children contracted colds. Hazel Lee came by to ask me to go to Cumberland tomorrow for Red Cross knitting.

Dec. 17. Wednesday. To town at 10 a.m. Brought home some corduroy overalls for Si. Mac got some fresh pork from T. F.'s hog killing (This writer's note: a common occurrence of which more will be said later). Went to Cumberland with friends to talk to the women about Red Cross knitting. Home at 5 p.m. Children cross with colds.

Dec. 18. Thursday. Stayed home all morning & wrapped a few gifts. To town hurriedly before Kitty left, then home all afternoon. Lavinia's sister Dottie is here. We are eating spare ribs & tenderloin. Mac sent his mother the turkey Mr. Tom Taylor gave us (This writer's note: Tom was the brother of T. F. Taylor and the uncle of T. F. Taylor, Jr. Daddy would later serve as a pall bearer in Tom's funeral). Good radio programs. War news sounds better.

Dec. 19. Friday. Went by to see Dottie. Lavinia gave me a huge pork tenderloin. She is having the bridge club this afternoon. To town taking Jay & Annie Gaye with us & rode us around, giving Jay and Si some gifts.

Dec. 20. Saturday. Today she came by with a piece of fruit cake for us. Back to Lavinia's for a moment. Then home to stay. Cards arriving, but no news as yet from Kay or George. We plan to go home on Wednesday, then to Grenada on Thursday.

> Dec. 21. Sunday. Home all day. Radio good. Mac & Jay
> went to town and bought me a coke. I made some fudge squares
> & doctored Jay and Si's colds....

On Christmas Eve, it was reported how Admiral Chester Nimitz surmised the surprise attack on Pearl Harbor in saying that the Japanese military made three of the biggest mistakes an attack force could possibly make, or else God was taking care of America. When asked by the media to explain, he said, first the aggression occurred on Sunday morning when ninety per cent of the crew members were ashore on leave; therefore there were only thirty-eight hundred casualties rather than thirty-eight thousand. And second, only the ships in port were bombed while the dry docks were unharmed. Therefore, rather than having to tow the ships back to the U.S. for repair, they were repaired in the harbor in less time than the tow would have required. And third, five miles from the harbor, over a hill, were the fuel tanks that supplied fuel for the entire Pacific theater of war. The fuel tanks were untouched, when a single bomb from one plane could have exploded all of those tanks of fuel. Both of Nimitz's statements were true. It certainly appeared that God was protecting the U.S. in this attack.

Mother's diary continues, with similar entries made daily, pertaining to activities, the weather, etc. Detailed memoranda are given, particularly regarding things that Jay and I did and said. A trip to Ackerman followed on Wednesday the 24th. Mother said, "Uncle Si came and was darling. Left at dark." On Christmas Day, the following entry was made:

> Dec. 25. Thursday. Up at 6 a.m. Breakfast. Fed the children
> & off to Grenada. Stopped by Eupora, but reached Grenada
> before 10. Si went to sleep. Everyone was home but Mary.
> Grand toys for the children & wonderful dinner. Picture made.
> After 5:00 we left. Went by to see....
>
> Dec. 28. Sunday. Mother & Daddy came to dinner. Mac was
> sick -- stomach. Good roast. They stayed till nearly four o'clock.
> The children were good. Enjoyed the day, and I think Mother
> and Daddy did. Brought us eggs, cream, buttermilk, etc....
>
> Dec. 31. Wednesday. Stayed home all morning....nothing
> happened this New Year's Eve.

The carving of the faces of four distinguished American Presidents, namely George Washington, Thomas Jefferson, Theodore Roosevelt, and

Abraham Lincoln, in the face of Mount Rushmore, in South Dakota's Black Hills was begun in 1927 by Sculptor Gutzon Borglum and was finally completed in 1941, fourteen years later. The cost was one million (which sculpture today is priceless).

World War II was regarded as the worst war that the world had ever seen (counting only Americans, there were 405,399 casualties, second only to the Civil War). Auto production came to a halt, as Detroit tooled up for full-time war production. Automakers turned to the production of tanks, airplanes, trucks, and various machines headed for the front.[17] The "General Purpose" vehicle earlier was invented by the Bantam Car Company, which built over two thousand light four-wheel drives for the US Army before World War II. Ford and Willys-Overland produced seven-hundred thousand Jeeps during the war, beginning in 1942. "General Purpose" was truncated to "GP," then to "Jeep."

Mother's diary continues in 1942, recording current events:

> Jan. 1. Thursday. Stayed home all day. Let Kitty go early. Took a nap with the children. Mother and Daddy came by. Daddy feeling better. Very little news. Manila still holding out. Most of interest, sale of cars prohibited. Wonder if T. F. will get his. He & Lavinia flew to Dallas for the game today.
>
> Jan. 2. Friday. Manila fell. Occupied by Japs. But MacArthur still fighting. After lunch, got out and went by to see Annie Gaye. Then to town for groceries. After supper I wrote letters. Wish I could have news of George, but guess no one can say.
>
> Jan. 3. Saturday. Home all day....
>
> Jan. 5. Monday. Home all morning....Mac is appointed Air Raid Warden for South Eupora!....

The weather was brutal. The temperature dropped to five degrees. In spite of running the water, the pipes froze. Daddy got a blowtorch and thawed the pipes. By Monday the 12th, it began to warm some.

---

[17] By 1943, one hundred and twelve thousand mechanics had been lost by repair shops to the war effort. Cars went on sale again in 1946, but consumers had to wait until 1949 for an "all-new" model.

Jan. 12. Monday. Mother and Daddy came by today. Daddy[18] is feeling better, but his arthritis seems the same. Mother brought Mother Goose book for Jay....

Jan. 14. Wednesday. We are considering Ralph Hightower's house, but he has promised to rent it to Oscar and Sara. Saw Virginia at Lavinia's and it was mentioned. T. F. came home tonight & Mac spoke of our interest in the house....We have renters moving in Saturday....

Jan. 16. Friday. Today, T. F. told us to go on and buy it, but Ralph doesn't know what he wants to do....Ralph's house is shabby but could be cute. Wish we could buy it, just to be settled....

Jan. 17. Saturday. To town with Jay. The Kimbroughs came and paid $7.00 advance rent. Lavinia came over & we chatted. Made some fudge for T. F.'s birthday. To bed, after reading some.

Jan. 18. Sunday. Very warm. To Lavinia's to take candy and see Jim, who is here for weekend. Brother and Fran will be here next week, in route to Hartford, Conn....

Feb. 19. Monday. Mother and Daddy came. I gave Daddy three of Mac's old suits. Mother and I went to town & shopped around....

Feb. 26. Monday. To Lavinia's....A wire from Brother in French saying meet him in Ackerman tonight. I left soon after lunch to get Kitty. They are there at 4:30; Brother & I returned for Mac, but he couldn't leave for one of T. F.'s lumber yards at Sturgis burned. Home again at supper & chatted with Auntie and Spurgeon, Brother and Fran. Grand day at home. At 2:30 we all left. Fran rode with me to Mathiston, then on alone with kids. Turning cold....

Uncle Willie wrote Mother and Daddy from the "QUEBEC GARRISON CLUB" to advise of his military-related travel and present status as follows:

---

[18]   Genetically, Jay inherited the gene for colon cancer from Grandfather Dobbs, and both Mother and I had the gene for osteoarthritis.

Monday, Mar. 16

Dear Mary & Mac,

Did you receive the picture? I sent two home, one of which
is for you.

By plane from Miami to Quebec – total travel time 25
hours: Miami – New York, 8 hours; New York – Montreal, 3
hours; Montreal – Quebec, 1 hour; total in the air, 12 hours.
They say its wild here, but only 20 degrees F, snow 4 ft. deep
average; I've never seen so much snow in my life. All street
signs and adv. in French here, all the people speak French,
however one can get around O.K. with English. Lunch today
in this club – Englishmen's equivalent to our officer's clubs –
superior. This is wonderful country.

I'm to be skipper of a corvette: U.S.S. Haste. Can't say
much more about the details, you know, but it is really a very
fine and important assignment. Frances and Wm. remain in
Miami Beach. She may visit friends of ours in Boston for a
month in April & part of May. I expect to see them, of course.

This is my first letter home, so send it to Mama.

Love,
Wm.

In 1942 T. F. Taylor, Jr., became a multi-millionaire upon the death of
his father, T. F. Taylor, Sr., the latter of whom, as earlier noted, had been a
prominent and wealthy Eupora businessman.

The entries in Mother's diary continue, with daily schedules, visits
with various friends, the weather, &c. Skipping to 1943:

Feb. 4. Wednesday. Mac suggested we go to Winona for
supper. Helen & Jimmy wanted Pete and Virginia to go to
Greenwood. So we all went. Called Meredith. Ate steaks and
had fun....

Feb. 12. Thursday. Mother & Daddy came for the children
early after dinner. I finished packing & walked to town. Mailed
a few valentines. Mac got off & we came home & left after
boiling some eggs & eating a sandwich. Reached Cleveland
around 8:00. Went by to see Bill Sugg and Ellen while rehearsal
was finishing. Then to Beulah. Sat up late & talked. Friday

37

morn. Mac played golf & we talked...Then we all went to Cleveland to Byron's wedding & reception. Then drove to.... then spent the afternoon on the lake in Henry's boat. After supper, the four of us went to Cleveland to see a show, but ended up by going to Dr. Ringold's and finally to the Delta Club.

Feb. 15. Sunday. We all slept late, then got up, breakfasted, dressed, and went to church in Rosedale to hear Mr. Street. Lorena served a grand "anniversary dinner" and we left soon after dropping Mother Mac in Grenada. Reaching home, went by to give T. F. a check, then on to Ackerman for our children....

Feb. 20. Friday...The war news just gets worse and worse....

Feb. 21. Saturday...Went to Ackerman in time for dinner. William was there. Lamb roast. After dinner, I went with Mother to the memorial ceremony for Troy Biggens, first Choctaw County boy to be killed in action. Home early. Cooked supper at home....

Feb. 23. Monday. Jay now is 38 inches tall; 2 yrs., 7 mos. Si is 30 inches tall; nearly 15 mos. T. F. went to Memphis. Roosevelt spoke at nine p.m...Alas, tonight first shells fell on Continental U.S.A. at or near Santa Barbara, California. There was a black out for 4 hours & antiaircraft fire....

Feb. 25. Wednesday...Enemy bombers flew over Los Angeles & the anti-aircraft guns were in operation....[19]

Feb. 27. Friday...Fran came by with William en route to Clarksdale. Brother will be home Sunday. Hope we can see him. Fran brought me a cotton length & 4 napkins. To town in a.m. Coke with Lavinia. Jay went home with Mary Foy & I went after him. T. F. still sick. Letter from Henry....

Entries continue. The birth of David Alston Dollarhide; a week-long visit by Mother Mac; bridge games; sewing; Jay says: "Dress me off," "Dob" for Bob, "Muskins" for muffins.

Apr. 12. Mother & Daddy came on 12th; they spent the afternoon. This week I decided I was pregnant....

If Mother was pregnant, she must have miscarried; there were no further entries in her diary regarding the pregnancy. Also, there was

---

[19]   This actually was s rumor.

no commentary by Mother in her diary that would convey any sense of financial or emotional crisis in our home resulting from the ongoing war.

Parenthetic: William Faulkner was born in 1897 in New Albany, Mississippi. His family moved to Oxford, Mississippi, in 1902. He resided in Oxford from 1927 to 1931 during the time that Daddy was attending Ole Miss. Having earlier published several titles, which were financial failures, he released *Sartoris* and *The Sound and the Fury* in 1929. *As I Lay Dying* was followed by a best seller *The Sanctuary*, in 1931. *Light in August* was published in 1932. From 1929 to 1932, he had become the most extraordinarily productive of any American writer in history (extensive biographical information for Faulkner is extant).

Faulkner had worked throughout 1941 writing and reworking stories into an episodic novel about the McCaslin family, several members of which family had appeared briefly in *The Unvanquished*. Whereas several stories that would comprise *Go Down, Moses* had been published separately in magazines, Faulkner revised the parts that would comprise the novel, which spans more than 100 years in the history of Yoknapatawpha County. The book was published in May 1942 as *Go Down, Moses and Other Stories*.

Go Down, Moses was a collection of Yoknapaawpha County stories of which the novella, *The Bear*, is the best known. Faulkner was interested especially in multi- generational family chronicles, and many characters appear in more than one book. This was the case with Faulkner's use of the McCaslin family name in *Go Down, Moses.*

Go Down, Moses is viewed as one of Faulkner's masterpieces. The novel tells the story of the McCaslin family, beginning with the family patriarch Lucius Quintus Carothers McCaslin. Descendants were multi-generational and to our family, the story was unspeakable.

Mother told us later in life that about 1943 Daddy wrote William Faulkner, denouncing him for the use of the McCaslin name in a pejorative manner. William Faulkner's reply to Daddy's letter was couched in rhetoric. Essentially, he stated that he intended nothing deprecating in the use of the McCaslin

name; that he had chosen it, along with some other prominent
Mississippi names (such as Carothers), as representative of fine,
old Mississippi families, the use of which names most readers in
the State of Mississippi would easily recognize to be fictitious.

By 1943, our family resided in a rented house on S. Dunn Street. Our
friend Bryan McRee lived in the next house, which was separated from
ours by a large cow pasture. His mother, Mrs. McRee, was Assistant
Principal of Eupora Consolidated School (and later would be our fifth
grade teacher). Diagonally across the street from our house, a long, grassy
yard under a canopy of trees led up a steep hill to the fine brick home of
Judge Everette and Olive Eudy, which occupied two lots.

Along the side of our house, adjacent to the driveway, stood a tall
hedge bush. In reality, it probably was only seven or eight feet in height,
but to us it was imposing. It was from that hedge that Mother instructed us
to bring her a switch that would be the instrument to deliver disciplinary
measures when we had been disobedient or impertinent, which untoward
behavior was relatively uncommon. I learned the word "impertinent" at
a very early age – one of Mother's particular words, associated with our
occasional spiteful behavior. Jay and I would be told to go to the hedge
and select the "right size of switch," and we knew from experience, that
if it were too small or too limber, she would send us again, or even a third
time. My earliest memory of corporal punishment was followed by Mother
stating: "This hurts me more than it does you." (Although Mother almost
always made this comment, it was not until parenthood for me that I fully
understood the concept. At a later age, perhaps five or six, the switch was
replaced by one of our leather belts, which inflicted more pain. If we had
been grossly disobedient, Daddy would follow up with another spanking
when he got home. He used a 12-inch ruler).

Chapter Three

VISITS IN ACKERMAN
DURING THE WAR

Concurrent with the foregoing recollections are the many fond memories of Ackerman when we visited Mother's parents at the old Dobbs family home. Grandfather Dobbs, first employed in 1903 as a rural mail carrier, had retired from that work in the early 1940s.

Jay clearly remembered a visit at Grandfather's house in the summer of 1943. Spurgeon Adams, the brother of Grandmother Dobbs, came around on his motorcycle. He took cousin William for a ride and upon their return, Jay wanted to ride. Jay was wearing short pants, and as he climbed on the seat behind Spurgeon, his bare leg touched the hot engine, and a painful burn resulted. Jay began to cry, and Mother rushed into the house to get the necessary remedy for treatment. I have but a fleeting memory of the event. Yet, I have an obscure recollection, as early as the fall of 1943, of playing around and about the Dobbs home.[20] I was not yet three years of age, and Jay, barely five. I keenly remember Grandmother Dobbs cooking in the kitchen, and serving up scrumptious meals at the dining room table.

---

[20]   We have an oil-on-board painting of the old Adams-Dobbs home, painted from memory about 1960 by Uncle Willie. It was a gift to Mother. On the reverse of the board, Uncle Willie sketched in pencil a schematic layout of the home site, with the several buildings, including the ice house, the smoke house, and the barn. The home originally was that of John Adams, born 1847. He had it built for himself and his wife, Lucy Ann Mathis Adams. Mother told us that John Adams had a home built for each of his daughters as they married. Estel and Mamie lived in the house built next door, that her parents had built for Mamie. Upon the death of Lucy in 1917, Mamie and Estel moved in with her father, to care for him. John Adams died in 1920.

During these visits in the early 1940s, Grandfather would sit on the steps, and often call to one of us to come sit next to him. I sharply recall his scent – that of an older man. He told us tales, many of which were familiar, having been re-told to us by Mother. In fact, these tales were the basis for many short stories that Mother wrote and submitted to publishing houses for review, and hopefully for acceptance.

We would go with Grandfather to the watermelon patch to pick a fresh, sweet watermelon, which he would hoist to his shoulder, bring home, slice, and serve to us on the back porch or in the back yard, to minimize the mess. We relished the sweet taste, as we playfully "squirted" the watermelon seeds at one another, and the chickens gathered around to eat the seeds as they fell to the ground.

We often frolicked about in the hay in the loft of the barn, which was situated behind the house, and we ducked in and out of the old ice house and the smoke house. We frequently roamed the thick woods beyond the watermelon patch behind the house, finding various things that interested boys, both plant and animal species.

Visits in Ackerman during the summer usually included a trip to Choctaw Lake, a public recreational area. The lake was situated about halfway between Ackerman and Louisville. A large wooden lake pavilion was located some two hundred feet up the hill, nestled in the woods. A broad porch extended across the front of the pavilion and from a rocking chair one could wile away the morning or afternoon looking out at the lake. At the edge of Choctaw Lake was a man-made sand beach, with a pier extending out about fifty feet to a stationary dock that supported both a three-foot and a ten-foot diving board (the picture on the cover of this book shows the Choctaw Lake in the background). Another twenty-five feet out in the lake rose the wooden platform to which the older kids and adults could swim, and from which they could dive or use as they sunbathed.

While the parents generally relaxed in wooden lawn chairs on the shore and engaged in conversation, the children would play in the shallow water, roped off at a depth of three feet. Many family photographs were made of these occasions.

Cousin William Adams Dobbs, Jr., was our first cousin. His father, Uncle Willie, as earlier noticed, was a 1932 Annapolis graduate, and was promoted to Lieutenant Commander in World War II while serving in the Pacific. William and his mother lived with our grandparents while Uncle Willie was at sea, and William had early memories of Ackerman. Jay and

I later had similar experiences, but William was two years older than Jay. William reflected on distinct memories of his early years of 1943-1944:

> I spent some time there during the war years, and attended the second half of first grade and the first half of second grade at the local school. That is where I learned to read, using Dick, Jane, Spot, & Puff as characters in these elementary readers. I participated in a Christmas program there, by reciting a poem, which name I lost (this writer's note: *Jest 'Fore Christmas*, by Eugene Field)...."Father calls me William, Mother calls me Will...long about Christmas, I'm as good as I can be...." It was a hit and I was asked to provide an encore performance the next day in the cafeteria....
>
> When I visit Ackerman, I make it a point to go to the First Baptist Church, because it was there that I first met Jesus. That spot on our planet marks the beginning of my conscious spiritual life. I will always be grateful to Grandfather Dobbs for taking me there, not only on Sunday mornings, but also on Wednesday nights for their prayer meetings. What a blessing that was for me, to hear and see these faithful people singing praise to God and asking, in all humility, for His blessing. That single experience has had more influence on me than anything else, and it has carried me through sixty years. It was the beginning, which gradually led to other beliefs, such as the Bible is the Word of God. I have come to know this primarily by preparing and reading the lessons at church over the past twenty years. As a student of science, and you know this too, we can compare the knowledge we have accumulated over the past four hundred years or so to the truths proclaimed in the Bible, and see the difference in their importance to us as persons, as children of God. Our scientific knowledge as St. Paul says, will pass away, leaving only Faith, Hope, and Love. There was another moment when I read I Cor. 13, and it struck me as the most profound that I ever read. I don't remember when it was, but my insides leap for joy every time I hear it said that "If I give my body to be burned and have not love...." What a wonderful truth that is and are we not privileged to have heard it?!
>
> Back to Ackerman: What follows is less important. You mentioned watermelon. Do you remember there was always the question: when cut, would it be a red or a yellow watermelon?

On their back porch or in the yard, we used to have watermelon seed fights. At that age I never wore shoes, except on Sundays and in the dead of winter. Two of my school mates didn't own shoes. They lived on Highway 9, and had an open well in their backyard. Two of my friends were Rosemary Love and Beth Ramsey.

Grandfather taught me many things. How to fish, for example. He told me to watch the cork. I remember watching the cork so intensely that I was unable to sleep that night for nightmares about water. One night he took me fox hunting. He always carried his dogs in the trunk of the car. They would willingly jump in because they knew that fun was in store for them. The fox hunt consisted of a group of cars parked at a bonfire, around which the men sat, as they made coffee and cooked bacon. They would turn the dogs loose and listen for the result. Occasionally, someone would jump into a car and drive off to see the fox, which presumably was in a tree.

Grandmother seemed always to be working, and she was a whistler. Grandmother was a Martha, not a Mary. She had a large flour barrel, and made great biscuits.

Mr. Dobbs used to take me on his mail route, which he usually completed at midday. After lunch, he would take his rifle and shoot squirrels. Mrs. Dobbs would cook them for supper and we ate them with biscuits and gravy–they tasted like chicken and were delicious. Every time I see a squirrel now, I look at those juicy hind legs....

As early as 1943, I recall how Grandmother Dobbs would walk out into the back yard, grasp an unsuspecting chicken around the neck, twirl it around in the air, and wring its neck. The headless chicken would fly away, land, and run about wildly, with Grandmother Dobbs chasing after it. When she caught the chicken again, she would take it into the kitchen, dress it, and prepare it for the frying pan. Jay and I witnessed this common activity many times in our youth, in Ackerman as well as in outlying areas of Eupora.

It was customary for Grandmother Dobbs to cook huge meals, including fried chicken, beef, potatoes, and several vegetables. Always, there were the biscuits and gravy. The family would sit down to dinner in the dining room to enjoy the feast.

We usually drove back the twenty miles to Eupora after these visits. But occasionally Jay and I would remain there for a day or so longer. Many of our photographs of Ackerman include our cousin William and his parents. The earlier photographs were taken about 1943, when William and his mother lived there.

Mother recalled a premonition that she had and the sad events that hit the family in 1943:[21]

> I had one of my supernatural experiences that I don't tell often because it sounds like a tall tale. It was in August of 1943, and everything was fine; everyone was in good health. Of course Mother and Daddy had their problems, but they were getting along as well as they had for several years. Everything was just normal and good. No reason for alarm or nightmares. But, one night, it was very hot, and I was sleeping in a spare room that we had, by myself. And, I waked up – it was not a dream – with a strange thought or feeling. There are no words to describe this experience sensibly. I waked up with a load, a burden in my hands. It was just as if I was holding Death, Death, in my hands, and could not rid myself of it. It was frightening and strange. I had never had anything happen like that before. And I was not particularly fearful of death, and certainly had no reason to be fearful of it at that point in my life, and yet here it was. Just present and heavy and ominous. And I rationalized it and thought: "What in the world; how ridiculous!" And all those things that you have when you have a premonition or a bad dream. And I put it out of my mind and went on back to sleep. Sometime later, I waked up again with the same sensation. And this happened three times that night. And by the third time I really was frightened and just panicked.
>
> I am not really one to have nightmares, and I don't dream very often. Well I guess I dream, but very seldom do I wake up remembering a dream, or having had a dream. And when I do, they are good dreams. I very seldom have a dream that

---

[21]   For Christmas, 1979, we gave Mother a tape recorder with the request that she record, at her convenience, memories of her early life. One recording, on May 2, 1980, the twenty-first wedding anniversary of her marriage to Eugene Ward, was only three months prior to her heart attack that resulted in her death. Her taped memories principally were a strong testimony to the Christian faith of both her and her parents, and they provide detailed, first-hand, verbally recorded family information which, in having, we consider a rare privilege. Witness the following.

is not pleasurable to recall. One of my teachers at Mississippi Southern, a psychologist, told me one time, that if everybody was like me, all of the psychologists and psychiatrists would be out of business. And this is true. I've just never had that kind of fears and bad experiences in my mind. But this was one that really hit me. Well, you know how we are able to put things out of our minds and to rationalize things and laugh about them and decide that they are unimportant. So this is what I did. As I said, not ever having had this type experience before.

Well one day Mother Mac was visiting in Eupora and we were playing bridge next door at Lady Mary's. Just making conversation, I told this experience. Mother Mac carefully laid her hand down on the table – I can see her right now – and looked at me, and she said, "Mary Margaret, don't laugh about that. That means something. I don't know what, but it means something, and it could very well mean your own death. So don't you laugh about it!" She went on to say, "I would take it to mean something very serious. I would take it to mean, teach your children. Teach your children. Because, no one can do it as well as you, and you may not be here to do it." Of course we all were serious for a minute, and then laughed and turned that off. But this was in August.

And it was in the last of October when Auntie and Spurgeon Adams had the automobile wreck and both were killed. Of course I thought about my dream, or premonition. And there were five people killed in that wreck. Spurgeon had taken a black family down into the Delta to work out some legal problems. He was so good, and loved the black people so much, and was always helping them. And so some of this family were killed. I counted Auntie and Spurgeon as two of the people who had died. And again, since the dream occurred three times, I didn't want to think about the third person, for logically it would be three. But, I don't know. I just didn't put that much importance on it, really, even after Auntie and Spurgeon died. But, then Mother died three months later. And after she died, being three very precious, dear people, close to me, as close as anyone could be in family relationships, I certainly did look upon it as a warning from the Lord, a true premonition, a vision, telling me something like this was going to happen.

Then of course I have had similar experiences since, and you wonder. When you tell someone about it, they would say, "You didn't understand what it meant, so what good was it?

What was the reason for it? It didn't tell you anything until after the fact." Well, I think that this is the point. When we have a premonition like this, even though we don't know at the time what it means, and what is going to happen, after the happening proves this premonition or this warning to have been true, then we can see, we can know, that the Lord knew about it beforehand. That He was in it. That it was His will and His purpose, however bad and terrible it might be in our lives. It was His will. His work. His doing. And the fact that we were told or warned about it ahead of time proves, you see, that the Lord knew about it, and was preparing us for the experience. At least this is the way that I have always interpreted these things. And, as I talk to you on future tapes, I will tell you other experiences like this that I have had.[22]

As earlier noticed, T. F. Taylor, Jr., and his wife, Lavinia Foy Taylor, were the Mother and Daddy's closest friends. (In 1941, Daddy became a business partner with T. F. He was the son of T. F. (Tom) Taylor, Sr., and the nephew of William (Bill) Green Taylor.

Bill and T. F. Taylor, Sr., were pioneer citizens of Webster County. The brothers established a business in 1902 which grew to be the largest poultry produce market in the State. Bill Taylor died in early October 1943. All of the pall bearers in his funeral were family friends. Among them were Bob Sugg, A. J. McCaslin, H. H. Ross, Eddie Embry, and C. P. Fortner.

Bob Sugg, an attorney, was the father of our best friends Rob and Charles, who lived two houses from us. Bank president, C. P. (Pete) Fortner, and Herman Ross, the owner of the Ford dealership, were friends and neighbors. Eddie Embry and his brother, Ralph, were pharmacists. (The families of Ralph and Eddie Embry would be our neighbors in 1946, upon our moving to Adams Avenue. The two Embry families lived across from each other on Adams Avenue. Ralph's daughter, Harriet, her younger brother, Shorty, and Eddie's daughter, Iantha, would become close friends of ours. Harriet and I would begin the first grade together. The side yard of the Eddie Embry house, a vacant, residential lot, would double as our football and baseball field. Emmy Embry was the younger sister of Harriet

---

[22]   This recollection was at the end of the tape. There were no others made. Mother died four months later, August 1, 1980. Could it be that the Lord was allowing her to make this recording to warn us of her pending death? That in itself another premonition? The secular world calls this ESP.

and Shorty and in college would become the friend of Daisy, the wife of Paige Cothren).

My third birthday, December 6, 1943, was a clear, balmy day. Mother set up a card table in the front yard and decorated it, placing the cake in the center, before the arrival of the other neighborhood kids that were invited. After I opened my presents, we had ice cream and cake. Then we played in the front yard, where Mother served us lemonade. Our birthdays in later years differed little from the other birthday parties that we attended. Birthdays were simple, consisting essentially of the cardboard horns and hats, the dessert, and the opening of presents. Afterwards, we played with the new toys received. (That was uncomplicated and inexpensive compared to children's parties in the 21st century. Driven by the ever-present sin of pride and parents' wanting to best the last sensational party given for another child, it now is common to witness the renting of a pony to ride; having a clown to perform antics and hand out helium-filled balloons; or hosting a paid magician; or more extravagant: bringing in a zoo of small animals for petting).

Our parents needed nothing more than a card table, and if indoors, chairs for the small number of children. "Musical Chairs" was quite popular followed by "Gossip." How extraordinarily gossip distorted truth in childhood, yet even more so in adult circles.

An entry in Mother's diary, dated December 20, 1943, first spoke of her brother:

> Dec. 20. Monday. This year, Brother was on the Atlantic, Capt. of *N.S.B. Fessenden*,[23] on a huge convoy to Casa Blanca. He left around the first of Dec. & will not be back until mid-January. Frances decided to stay in Jacksonville for Santa Claus, so I decided to stay in Eupora. Invited Mother & Daddy to spend Saturday with us. I decorated a lovely little Spruce tree & the boys were thrilled...On Thursday we went to Greenwood with

---

[23] The DE-142 *U.S.S. Fessenden* was an Edsall Class Destroyer Escort, named for William P. Fessenden, Secretary of the Treasury under President Abraham Lincoln. Captain William A. Dobbs, put the ship in commission in June, 1943, and was her commanding officer for two years. It had a displacement of 1590 tons; a length of 306 feet, and a speed of 21 knots. The armament consisted of torpedo tubes, 1 twin 40mm MK1 AA, an 8x20mm MK 4AA, 1 Hedgehog Projector MK10, 2 depth charge tracks, 8 "K" gun projectors complement. It was powered by Fairbanks-Morse Model 38d81/8 geared diesel engines.

T. F. and Lavinia. Had a good time...Friday night the kids went to bed early & Santa came with a bang. A job!....

Mother & Daddy came about 10:00 bringing chicken and dressing & a lot of things. We had a wonderful Christmas Day, in spite of it being at my house instead of Mother's....[24]

Among the photographs mentioned earlier are scores made in Ackerman with Uncle Willie in his dress blue Navy uniform, home on leave. Jay, Cousin William, and I are virtual rug rats in these pictures, some of which show us feeding a cow or holding a kitten. The pictures have enormous sentimental value to us but need not be reproduced here.

The last letter that Grandmother wrote to Mother was postmarked "Ackerman, Dec. 30, 1943," and addressed to "Mrs. Alston McCaslin, Eupora, Miss." (Notice carefully the day and time sequence). The letter first refers to Christmas memories, then pertains to Uncle Willie at war:

Mary Darling:

We did so much enjoy Christmas Day with you & family. It took us way back. Tis really true, there's quite a letdown feeling after it's over. I could not ever quite understand why, however, there's so much "build-up" in preparing for the one day, both in that & actual work. It ends abruptly, though memories fill the mind, seems there's that wish to prolong the joy. The static was less & music finer this year than a long time. Each program was so fine & the more repetitions the better I enjoyed each one.

The outing has not hurt us in any way. I still have my cold – it's the hanging on kind. When I go out doors, I wrap up in everything I can find for the terrible penetrating weather we're having now is nothing but flu & pneumonia weather. Dad is wearing his high-top rubbers. So don't mail others. Just bring them. Also, I left the green glass bowl.

---

[24] Dateline April 19, 1978; a newspaper article verified that Capt. William A. Dobbs (U. S. Navy ret.) and his wife are native Mississippians....He served on active naval duty over five years during WW II, placing in commission and operating as commanding office three ASW and AA warships in the Gulf of Mexico; Caribbean Sea; North, Middle, and South Atlantic, Antarctic and Indian oceans, and the Mediterranean Sea. The last six months of WW II he served as commodore of Escort Division 59 in the Pacific.

Letter from Frances said she'd be here some time Friday. We had a cable gram from Willie to Mrs. W. A. D, Ackerman, wishing us all at home a Merry Christmas. Mr. Graves phoned it to me. He said, "I don't know where this is sent from. He doesn't say." I told him that was alright. The message was the thing that counted.

I'll bet he's had plenty choppy sailing & they all will be so happy to come to port, which I hope is soon. Dad & I are sending letters so that soon as he does get near, he can hear from home. The way you and he love & think of home makes us the happiest couple anywhere to be found. You can't quite yet understand, but when your boys grow up and get away, then you will. And they are fast growing up, too. The years get shorter. Bless their precious hearts, they already come home, but it will deepen & be of a more serious kind.

Their Christmas seemed as perfect as children could wish and the grand assortment of toys should provide amusement & joy for a full year....

A few weeks ago I had a short but very realistic dream about Spurgeon. Every day it pops into my mind before I know it....

If Mac gets Saturday holiday, we'll expect you both early. Dad gets the day off. He has no shells to hunt with; he is feeling better by far than this time last year. Is taking "Dr. I. Q." vitamins....

Will get this mailed.

Love to each from
Your Mother.

P. S.

Sugar,

Frances called saying they had no gas for any trip & that the trains and busses were still too crowded to get on one and that it looked as if coming was impossible. Had hoped someone would be driving this direction, but not one had she found. She insisted we spend Sat. New Years day there & to be sure to let her know. Said come Fri. night, but I said, at once, we couldn't plan for that, tho maybe we might make it a day visit. She said if we did, she wanted to call Aunt Ruth & have her too. Wonder if we should try to go. Lots of driving for Dad in one day.

He said he'd have the gas, maybe. Wish you all could go, too. If we just had a 2-seater!! One thing about it, I've got the meat & some canned stuff for her. Haven't slaughtered the beef yet, tho Dad will try to get it over with this week. Folks are taking Christmas this week. He didn't think they would. The less some work, the better they feel about it.

I'm sending this that you might try to get me some cheese, if possible. Dad has some ration points, but Ackerman grocery men can't get cheese. Lots of folks are wondering why. You possibly can't either, now. I can eat it, when I can't eat meat, and my diet has to be limited for a while yet. Long as I'm dosing for cold, I keep my digestion upset if I take on greases or too many sweets.[25] A couple of pounds, if you can get it. I will get points for you.

And, I failed to pay for "apple print." You owe us nothing on anything but for gifts, and don't mention it.

Mother

The entry in the diary reads:

Dec. 31. Friday. Daddy telephoned that he was taking Mother to the hospital...later, Daddy phoned. Mother was resting....

Mother wrote a letter to her parents immediately upon receiving the telephone call from her dad:

Friday night, Dec. 31

Dearest you two:

You are the most unpredictable two guys I ever knew. Expecting you to be dashing off in one direction, you go in the other, on a very different reason.

---

[25] It will be noted later, in Mother's own words from the 1980 tape recording, that her mother had indulged in eating some fresh oysters from the Coast which she fried. It was the result of that greasy food that exacerbated her ulcer, leading to a perforation.

Of course, I am very anxious about you, Mother. But I am reassured by the knowledge that you are at the right place, and waiting <u>very</u> impatiently to have news of you.

We were planning to have Mac drive us over to Ackerman tonight (tomorrow he will work as usual). The children were disappointed, as was I on getting your letter, last night, that Frances was not coming. But things have a way of working out. Twas best for your peace of mind that she canceled the visit herself, before you had to do it. Also, just yesterday, we rented our apartment to a girl whose husband is going to the Army & she wants to move in tomorrow. So she & I spent the afternoon scrubbing in there & have a lot more to do tomorrow....

I'll try to get you some cheese, but may not be successful....

Frances telephoned me this morning shortly after Daddy called. She offered to come up & keep the place going till you got back, & I didn't know what to tell her. She'll write, & if you can use any "offers" from her, do so. It is helping & accepting help freely, that develops the tie of kinship with people. She will be happy if she can be of any help. In any way. So take her up, if you can, as you would me. There is a certain joy and satisfaction in being of help that increases ones love & interest. So, please, don't say "No no. We don't need you," if you can use her, or if anything she suggests is reasonable and workable.

Mother, I feel like your recent cold weakened your system to the extent that your stomach couldn't help getting upset. But, also I am afraid you have been worrying too much these past few months. Just plain worry, I believe, can cause the stomach trouble, and this is to beg you <u>not</u> to worry. About anything. It is just <u>useless</u>. It helps nothing, & is not the right attitude at all. And you can absolutely overcome it if you will practice. I used to worry myself. About next year; next month. Whether our house would burn down. Whether we would have a car wreck, etc. Whether I'll be a war widow before long. The future health and security of my kids. Oh. I could name dozens of reasons for worry. But I just <u>don't</u> do it.

If I go to the other extreme, I may get to the point of not even caring how dirty my house gets or whether I ever have a new dress or not. Of course, I don't believe I could <u>ever</u> be that carefree. I never did like tramps, so I am not afraid of becoming one.

But I don't worry about the serious things. God has always taken wonderful care of us, & what He has in store for us is the best, anyway. "All things work together for the good of those who love the Lord...." When I need bravery or courage or calm, I ask for it & I get it. And every night, I ask His help & guidance. I pile up all the worries of the day & give them over into His infinite care, & fall off to sleep as peacefully as a child. I know I will have my share of trouble & sorrow. But, I prefer to live a full, long life with those things, than not to live at all. They are the due of each human being. They are to strengthen & develop our characters & to keep us closer to God.

Right here the phone rang & twas Daddy. And as I waited, I could hardly hold the phone for shaking. But, I <u>knew</u> it would be good news. It just <u>had</u> to be. Such is my faith in God's goodness.

I didn't realize how much the above preaching was more to <u>myself</u> & to bolster my own feelings than for you.

It makes me sick to think how Mother suffers. I wish it were possible for me to be on hand at such a time, to help someway. But, bless both your hearts. You just have to nurse each other it seems. But I can't think of two sweeter nurses.

In my excitement over the phone call, I have already forgotten the room number. But I am sure you will get this.

Back to my preaching. Please, Mother, don't worry about Brother. The submarine menace is just about ended, sure enough. Let's be just thankful he is not <u>across</u> to stay. Or on one of our subs, or in the Army in Italy.

Let's <u>believe</u> in his ability to bring his ship safely home at all times. Let's <u>believe</u> that we are taken care of, & if we are busy <u>believing</u>, our minds will have no room for worries.

And for <u>all</u> our sakes, don't worry about money. It is wonderful to have a good doctor who doesn't overcharge. I hope he will always charge you as heretofore–reasonably–as he <u>should</u> people in moderate means. Don't tell him tho', but if it cost $500.00 to stop your stomach ache, we'd get it stopped, & not mind the cost. So forget that aspect.

And everything else that causes you a moment's fret. Relax & get well & hurry home.

Was surely thrilled to hear Daddy say you were sleeping. Please, Daddy, write a card every day, and if you want me to go to Ackerman to check up on things, I'll be glad to.

I feel sure you have someone taking care of things. Your friends are numerous. But I'll be glad to go over & stay if necessary.

If you need any money, check on me at the Bank of Eupora. (Even as late as the 1960s, you could write a personal check on a blank piece of paper and your bank would honor it; that was before checks had account and routing numbers; your bank knew you).

If you need anything I can give or do or lend, call on me.

Your loving daughter,
M.M.

Chapter Four

GOING HOME TO TAKE MOTHER

Grandfather Dobbs wrote a postcard to Mother on December 31, but it was postmarked "January 1, 1944." The card told of the positive progress of Grandmother Dobbs:

Friday, 8:30 p.m.

Mother is resting well and has been relieved of pain. Do not think operation necessary.

Love,
E. B. D.

Mother mailed her letter the next morning – Saturday. The letter arrived January 3, too late for her mother to read.

Mother later received a letter. Her hand-written note attached states, "A letter from my daddy written January 1, 1944, two days before my mother died, January 3, 1944." The letter told of Grandmother Dobbs' improvement:

Room 502
Baptist Hospital
Memphis 10

Dear Jane,

Thankful to report Mother feeling fine.

Twill be a day or two before she can be x-rayed, but if she continues to improve, should be able to go home in a week.

Love to the kids, and you all.
E. B. D.

Mother added a note to Granddaddy's letter concerning the state of her mother's health:

Mother did <u>not</u> "improve." This letter was stamped Jan. 2, 1944. Daddy must have mailed it the night before, because early in the morning of Jan 2, he called me to come to Memphis. I did not get there in time to see Mother (probably the Grace and Mercy of God to me!). She died at 1:30 a.m. on January 3, 1944. Daddy and I rode home together that day. Mother Mac was keeping my boys...

"Jane" was Daddy's special nickname for me.

Grandmother died of peritonitis, secondary to a perforated ulcer (a rupture of the intestine caused by an ulcer).

Mother later reflected on her mother's illness:[26]

Mother had ulcers, and had had for over ten years. Mother was the most calm, serene, strong person. She could go to someone's home who was sick, and go in the sick room and nurse them and calm everybody there, and in the face of death of a friend or a neighbor, she was the one who was called upon. And everybody looked upon her as the strongest person. And yet, she had ulcers. I think what it was, Mother was able to be outwardly calm, and she certainly had a deep abiding faith

---

[26] The 1980 tape recording is inscribed in her hand entitled: "Memories." At the end of the tape, Mother states that she will make future recordings, but when she did find the time to use the tape recorder, she utilized her time doing something else, which to her was more important. She recorded Bible lessons, the tapes of which we also have, and which we value highly. She began the May 2nd tape recording by telling how happy she had been in her marriage to Gene, and how highly respected he was in Gainesville, particularly within the medical community. She speaks of what Mother Mac had told her, after she had gotten to know Gene well. "I have never known a sweeter man in all my life – in all the world, bar none – as Gene Ward." Mother speaks of how dearly Gene loved Granny, and how Granny loved him. Mother said, "Granny referred to him as her 'son-in-law,' which was a great tribute."

in the promises of God. But, she was so tender-hearted, that she grieved inwardly over the world and unbelieving friends and relatives, and certainly over her children – Brother and me – and at this time, Brother was at sea, captain of a ship in the Atlantic, chasing submarines. And, we didn't hear from him for months at a time. And Mother grieved about him and every other mother's son in the war. And then, too, Auntie and Spurgeon, Sara Margaret's parents, had been killed in October of 1943 in a terrible automobile accident. And Mother grieved about their deaths. She was so close to her brother, Spurgeon. They were almost like twins. He was so considerate of her and loved her so much. And we saw so much of them. They lived in Ackerman, and we visited often. They would drop by frequently, a couple of times a week, in the late afternoon or evening. Daddy, Spurgeon, and I, and another would play bridge. We just had a wonderful relationship with them. At their death, it was such a horrible, terrible thing. They both were broken up terribly. Mother just had a hard time getting over that.

Then that fall, she had a bad cold that hung on and on, and she was determined to get over it. And yet, she was supposed to be better, as far as her ulcers. She had been to the doctor in Memphis back in the summer, and he had told her that if she stayed on her diet she would be alright. This was the first Christmas that we did not go home. We had always gone to my home in Ackerman on Christmas Eve, and on Christmas Day, we would drive over to Grenada and have a Christmas Dinner with Mac's family, and all the brothers and sisters would be there. On this Christmas, with the children, we elected to stay at home. We lived in Eupora. We planned for Mother and Daddy to come down. They came down and spent Christmas Day with us, and that is the last time I saw my mother. Later on that week, we were going to go spend New Years weekend with them. But, on the last day of December, Daddy called, and was on the way to Memphis to take Mother to the hospital. She had had an attack the night before from a ruptured ulcer in her colon. I was told that unless this trouble was corrected by surgery, within eight hours, there was very little chance for survival, because of peritonitis. That night, when Mother was so sick, Daddy had called the doctor who said they had to go to the hospital. It was cold, and Daddy went out and there was no gas in the car. He had to wake someone up to open the gas station. It just took time. And then the long drive to Memphis. By the time he got there, it was too late for surgery. Mother lived for two or three days. She died on the 3rd of January, 1944. Daddy had kept in touch by telephone, and he called me and said that I needed to get up there; that Mother was just as sick as anybody could be and still live. Mac and I went to Grenada to leave the children for Mother Mac to keep. I missed the train at about 3:00 in the afternoon. I think it was Sunday. We went dashing to the train and it had just left. I then checked with the bus line, and there was one leaving in about an hour. Then, we were late getting to the bus station and I missed the bus. Finally, I got a bus about 10:00 that night, and got to Memphis about 1:30 in the morning, and I went to the home of my friend who lived there. I had called her and told her of the situation. I knew if I went directly to the hospital I wouldn't be able to find Daddy, and Mother would be asleep and so on. So, I went to my friend Thelma, and she fixed me some supper and put me to sleep. This was Thelma and Hans Kohler, friends from Ackerman who had moved to Memphis, and later moved to New Orleans. Hans had grown up in Ackerman.

The next morning the phone rang and it was my daddy. He said "Mary, I'm going home." I said, "Daddy, what are you going home for." And he said, "To take your mother." I said, "Daddy, did she die?" He replied, "Yes." And I said, "But I want to go with you." He asked how I had gotten there, thinking by car. He said, "Come on. Of course, you can go home with me." So Thelma took me over to the hospital and Daddy and I drove home. I asked him how he knew that I was at Thelma's. He said, "I just knew. I just guessed it. I called, thinking you would be there." We drove home. On the way, my daddy, who adored Mother, asked me to do something for him. I said, "Of course Daddy, what." He said, "I want you, at Mother's funeral, not to shed one single tear." And I said that I didn't think I could do that, because tears are very easy for me. I cry at sweet movies, and stories, and novels. I just knew that I couldn't do it. And Daddy said, "Yes you can. I want you to do this for me, and as a witness to our friends and to our faith. So, just don't cry. Don't shed a tear."

And amazingly enough, this is what I did. I really don't see how I did it. I held on to my daddy's hand very tightly, all the way through. And the service was so beautiful, that I was able to do it. But it still, in my memory, was a marvel and a miracle to me.

Brother was at sea, and Daddy was unable to get a message
to him. This was right in the middle of the war. We didn't know
where he was. Through the Red Cross, Daddy finally got a cable
to him, in which he said, "The sunshine has gone out of my life."
He then told him that Mother had died. I know that this was a
terrible experience for Brother - not being at home....

Mother's diary entry was as follows:

Jan. 3. Why oh why did they not know her trouble? I was
writing to her when Daddy called. She suffered all this day. I
wrote to Fran & Brother. Fran phoned me and Sara Margaret
phoned me. I had no help....

Van H. Hardin, Pastor, Ackerman Baptist Church, preached the funeral
for Mamie Adams Dobbs, at 2:00 p.m., Tuesday, Jan. 4, 1944. The sermon
was as follows:

Scripture: Jno. 11:20-28a.

God never smiled upon a world of strife with sweeter
fragrance from a soul than from this one that we have known,
loved, and delighted in her Christ-like presence. Like the
sparkling dewdrops that wait to meet the glorious beauty of the
morning sun and the flower that turns its lovely face to follow
its warming rays to the eventide, so was she. I do not believe that
there was ever a time in her life that she failed to hear the call of
the Master, but that in her own quiet, serene way, she went out to
meet Him. There was not the prodding that must come to some;
there was not the desolate hand of the dire necessity that must
scourge some to the fold of Masterful obedience. But instead,
hers was a noble and willing heart that thrilled to the Message
of the Master. Even as Martha's heart went out to her Lord, just
so did she go out to meet Him too. This was so characteristic
of a life that was so consecrated to such a noble purpose. The
loving touch of kindness, the tender words of comfort, and the
unending hours of intercessory prayer were known by all that
had need of the helping hand. His Spirit is hers because she
went out to meet Him; she knew Him, and she followed Him.

It was her chosen lot to share the sorrow, heartache, trouble,
pain, and joy of all whom she met. How well qualified she was

to exemplify these Christian virtues. And there was a secret to this abundant life that she knew so well. Many years before she had heard Jesus say, My child you know that "I am the resurrection, and the life; he that believeth on me, though he die, yet shall he live; and whosoever liveth and believeth on me shall never die. Believest thou this?" How blissfully sweet was that trusting answer when she said, "Yea, Lord, I have believed," and having thus spoken she went away.[27]

In pain she came to bless the earth; in pain she went away. But in all that was the lot of human kind there was the light of the divine. Christ planted a song in her heart that all the tempests of life could never drive away. She sang of the joys of eternal life. She gave voice to the light of hope when others of less faith would have despaired. Even during the last fleeting hours on earth while the skilled hand of the surgeon was striving in vain to retain her here, there played upon her lips a song, one that might well have been from the heavenly chorus. We will not forget.

When Christ went away long years ago, he said unto us, "My children I go to the right hand of the Father that I may make a place for you." And what a place he must have prepared for her. How quietly He came and called her from the midst of a world of chaos and suffering to rest eternally from the burden of life's load.

No minister in all the land ever lost one more interested in his personal welfare and in the work. The world never knew of the secret prayers uttered in his behalf. In the midst of faults and failures, in trials and many dark hours her prayers were there and the burden was made lighter and a faint heart was made stronger. Her words of encouragement were rays of light that we shall never forget. Not many nights ago many of us sat together around the banquet table and how we thrill in the memory of the kindly words spoken. How much they have helped, no one will ever know. As we were about to go, she led us in singing, "Bless Be the Tie That Binds," and little did we know how strong those ties were until the arms of separation were tugging at them. They are stronger now than ever before. The valley of the shadows can not tear them asunder.

---

[27] Ironically, this same Scripture, John 11:25ff, was selected by Ben Haden as the text when he officiated at the funeral service of Mother on August 3, 1980.

May the Holy Spirit, the Comforter of broken hearts, bring solace and loving care to all that weep. To this loving husband, to this faithful daughter, to the brave son so far away, to these loyal sisters and relatives, we lend our hearts in unending sympathy in this sore trial. As she would have done let us rely upon our Heavenly Father for comfort and strength to face the days ahead. God bless and keep you very close.

(Prayer) Heavenly Father we turn our hearts toward thee and lift our eyes through tears to give thee thanks for this noble soul that fought life's battles so bravely. Even Master do we praise thy Holy Name for the supreme faith that was so evident in every phase of her life. Lord if it were not for such refreshing souls so permeated with the spirit of Heaven, life's desert ways would be dreary indeed. Our memories thrill in the unending challenge that leads us on through weary ways to accomplish more for thee, O' God, in Thy earthly vineyard. Lord bless the sainted influence that lingers near us like the fragrance of precious ointment, that lifts our soul when we would falter, that gives us strength when we would faint, that drives away fear with undaunted courage and lends sustaining faith to meet our trials. We press on toward the mark of the High Calling of God with lighter tread because this lovely life has gone on before. Help us Master in our pressing human needs and we shall remain ever thankful; in the name of the Father, and the Son, and the Holy Spirit. AMEN.

This service was conducted in the "new brick Baptist church," completed on April 12, 1908, which replaced a frame structure, built over 20 years earlier. Mother's maternal grandparents, John and Lucy Adams, were charter members of the Baptist Church in 1885. John Adams was on the building committee for the wood frame church building completed in 1886. He was the chairman of the building committee in 1908. Mother recalled an incident: "When the Baptist Church was being built, John Adams gave all of the lumber – he owned timber land and a lumber mill. As chairman of the building committee, he also supervised the construction. Mr. Heflin, the brick layer, was at work on the church. John Adams visited the site one day and said, 'Mr. Heflin, that wall is not plumb.' Heflin, bullheaded, replied, 'I've built it, it's fine, and I'm not going to rebuild it.' When he finished, John Adams put his foot against the long wall and pushed it over. Adams then said: 'Mr. Heflin, I guess you'll have to rebuild the wall. It was not plumb.' Heflin went about cleaning the brick and rebuilding the brick wall."

A newspaper column in "The Plain Dealer," Vol. 56, No. 24, January 1944: provides the following (Permission granted, "The Plain Dealer" now a subsidiary of the Winston County Journal, Louisville, Mississippi):

BELOVED LADY PASSED AWAY

The citizens of Ackerman were shocked and grieved on Monday morning when the news reached here of the sudden death of Mrs. Mamie Adams Dobbs at the Baptist Hospital in Memphis at about 1:15 a.m. Few knew she had been carried there early Friday morning. Although she wasn't in the best of health, no one realized she was in so serious a condition.

She was born Feb. 18, 1886. Her parents, Mr. and Mrs. John Adams, were early settlers of this section of the country, who helped in many ways in the building of this town. Here she grew into womanhood. After completing high school, she attended Blue Mountain College, graduating with honors. In 1907 she was married to Mr. Estel B. Dobbs, thus uniting two of our most prominent families. Four children were born to this union. Two died in infancy.

With pride we look back over her years of usefulness to her family, her church, and community. She served faithfully the Sunday school, the W.M.U., and all of its auxiliaries in numerous capacities. It would be impossible to enumerate the number of books she taught in the W.M.U. as only she could teach them. Eternity alone can tell the good she has done. On account of her health, she would have to give up her work at times, but when she would gain enough strength, come back and do what she could. At the time of her death, she was Counselor for the Young Women's Circle. It will be hard to fill her place. Although Mamie, as we called her, was talented and gifted along many lines, she, like her Lord and Master, walked humbly in His steps daily.

Mrs. Dobbs was always on the side of right and justice and helped promote all moves for the betterment of the town and community. She served as president and secretary of the 20th Century Club many times. She also held offices in the Federated Club work and through her literary ability won for her club many awards.

She is survived by her husband, E. B. Dobbs, her son, Lt. Comdr. W. A. Dobbs, now on the high seas in the service of his country, and her daughter, Mrs. Margaret Dobbs McCaslin, of Eupora, and three grandsons, two sisters, Mrs. W. C. Gillis, Ackerman, and Mrs. Ruth Stewart, Jackson.

Funeral services were conducted from the Ackerman Baptist Church, Tuesday afternoon, Jan. 4, 1944, at 3 o'clock by her pastor, the Rev. Van Hardin, assisted by the pastors of the town. Interment followed in Enon Cemetery. The following out of town people attended the funeral: Mr. and Mrs. Silas Dobbs, St. Louis, Mo., Mrs. Willie A. Dobbs and son, William, of Jackson, Mrs. Clyde Elizabeth Dobbs Lyle of Meridian, Mrs. C. P. Fortner and Mr. and Mrs. A. J. McCaslin of Eupora.

The next entry in her diary pertains to beginning the task of sorting through her mother's things:

Jan. 5. Back to Ackerman after dinner...Cleaned out some dresser drawers...Took William to Dr. Hickman for checkup. Waffles for supper. Wrote to Brother....

The entries in the foregoing diary abruptly stopped at this point. (His being even more of a romantic than I, I gave Jay all of Mother's diaries that had been stored in a trunk for thirty years). Mother had lost her mother. Grandmother Dobbs' death was one of the most traumatic events in Mother's life. Yet, life went on, without tears.

A letter from Frances Dobbs, the envelope postmarked "Tuscaloosa, Jan. 11, 1944," consoling them on their loss:

Dearest Dad & Mary,

Just a line from here to say I'm on my way, but also that I'm thinking of you and missing you and hoping that I haven't irritated you by seeming light & giddy-headed over our great loss. My relationship was to me an unusual one, just as your relationship was to you. There was nothing casual about my love for Mother, and I will miss her every day that I live.

Will let you hear the minute Willie gets in.

So, bye bye,

Frances

A letter from a family friend, postmarked Blue Mountain College, January 15, reads as follows:

Dear Margaret,

I was so sorry to learn of the passing of your dear, sweet mother recently, and I want you to know that you and all her loved ones have my sincerest sympathy in your great sorrow and loss. I know you miss her unspeakably, and I know from my own experience just what it means to lose a precious mother. But I know that you hold in memory much that will ever be a precious legacy to you of her life and good work in this world, and that you will be comforted too by the sweet and precious promises of His Word. There are so <u>many</u> comforting passages that have ever been a comfort to me, four of which I give below. Psalms 46:1; Deu. 33:27; John 14:1-3; and I Thes. 4:13-18.

We remember you lovingly at Blue Mountain College, as also your dear mother and aunts, who all were "B. M. C. girls," and we grieve with you in your sorrow. May God bless and comfort your hearts as He alone can.

Most sincerely, your friend,
"Miss Bessie"

All of grandmother Dobbs' sisters had gone to Blue Mountain College. And, as mentioned, as each got married, their father, John Adams, had built them a home in Ackerman.

Mother's brother was at sea at various times, first as Captain of the *U. S. S. Fessenden*. Frances and William lived much of the time of the war in Ackerman, with Grandfather. For security reasons, Uncle Willie could say little to his family in his correspondence about his duty assignments (throughout his life, Uncle Willie was proud to have served in the U. S. Navy. He rose rapidly, through war-time promotions, to the rank of Lieutenant Commander and later had a convoy in the Pacific. As a civilian, he wore white buck shoes year round, and often white trousers and a blue blazer. In his lapel button hole was a small, unpretentious metal bar. I once asked him what the bar represented. He replied, "The bar signifies that the ship that I was commanding, the *U.S.S. Fessenden*, sank a German U-Boat, in September 1944, just east of the Cape Verde Islands – the islands that are located off the northwestern coast of Africa"). Uncharacteristic to

64

previous years, Uncle Willie wrote from New York to inform Daddy of his recent port:

January 27, 1944
Dear Mac,

I was just about halfway on the return trip here from Casa Blanca when Mama's death occurred. Frances has been of wonderful help to me these ten days while the ship was in the Navy Yard for work & repairs. I know you have been a fine, stable influence to the family while I couldn't be there. Frances and I will appreciate your future advice and guidance in any problems that may arise. I hope you feel free to advise Frances in matters that she cannot fully cope with in connection with management of our affairs. She may ask you sometimes; and since I may be away for years, yet, except for the merest moments at home on visits, your advice on many things would be appreciated.

I sent a package home today of some darning and whatnot, and in it is something Frances will be delighted to offer you tastes of until it is exhausted.

I want to visit at home a time or two this spring and will look forward to seeing you and family then. I wish we had another boy to match your fine little fellows. I am very glad that Wm., now, will be able to visit Jay & Si, and they can visit him so easily, and they can grow up knowing each other so much better than ever before.

I talk like this war is going to last forever, and it does seem like we are making very slow progress. I really don't see how it will end – the minimum I place at 3 years hence...frankly I don't like it at all. I believe we could have ended it by end of '44 if we'd been at the job properly since 1940.

Regards,
Wm.

Uncle Willie indeed did come home for a visit in the spring. Frances was pregnant soon after his visit, and Mother recalled that Grandfather would bring hot coffee to her in bed, before she woke up.

In the middle of the large pasture separating our house from the McRee home was a shallow pond, no more than two feet in depth. We did not stray from the yard, except to go into the pasture. When I was three years of age, in the summer of 1944, Jay and I were playing out by the pond, about 100 feet from the house. The cows in the pasture would wade out into the shallow water to drink. Mother cautiously watched us from the kitchen window. She had instructed us never to go into the water. On this day, she saw me strip down to my briefs and discerned what I was about to do; the forbidden act of going into the pond. She dashed out of the house and ran across the field, calling out to me to stop. Hearing her frantic call, I took my briefs off and threw them well out into the pond. Then I waded into the shallow water, stark naked, as Mother rushed up in the knee-deep water and grabbed me out of the water. When she asked me why I had disobeyed her and had gone into the water, I replied, "I had to get my britches!" That mischievous act resulted in my having to fetch a switch from the hedge bush, and necessary switching followed. (Society today has stripped from parents the measure of corporal punishment, which always had been according to the Biblical standard). The idiom "Spare the rod and spoil the child" is based upon Proverbs 13:24: "He that spareth his rod hateth his son: but he that loveth him chasteneth him early."

I distinctly remember that as young children, Jay and I always had to take an afternoon nap. We did not always sleep. Instead, we often laughed until our stomachs ached, and we acted boisterously by jumping on the bed, or by pillow fighting, for which behavior Mother would admonish us. But the scheduled nap time served Mother in providing her a break from watching us. She probably napped in her room, too, if we were not unruly.

Daddy acquired the "Cadillac truck." It was a novelty, and he kept it parked in the driveway at home. Of course Cadillac did not make a truck. Actually it was a long wooden-bed Ford truck, with a Cadillac engine. In the summer months, when Daddy came home from work, he would load us up on the flat, wooden bed of the truck, and then slowly drive around town and pick up our friends. After a short excursion, he would return each child to his house, and the parents would thank him for the diversion. Daddy sold the truck after a few months.

Louise Vance told of a visit of ours in Grenada when I was about four, and Jay five. Members of the family were sitting on the porch at Grandmother McCaslin's house (she was Mother Mac to her children and Granny to the grandchildren). Louise said that Mother was engaging everyone with one of her intriguing stories, and as everyone listened, Granny noticed that Jay and I were throwing rocks at a passing bus traversing down Main Street. Granny called to us to stop, and then said, "They're going to ruin the McCaslin name."

Daddy wrote Mother after returning from Dayton, Ohio, telling of the trip:

June 14, 1944

Dear M. M.,

T. F. and I arrived home Friday night, after having a nice trip in his new Chrysler "Saratoga" and a most pleasant visit with John and rose Mary Hunt in Dayton. Also had cocktails at Ed Kuntz's home, who is worth about 30 million.

I failed to get anything for Jay and Si, attending T. F. I spent the entire time in hotel rooms, business meetings and places to eat. We did not attend a theater or enter a store.

Sunday morning, I drove over to Ackerman for several hours. Frances said the kids had been extremely good.

Bring me a box of mild Havanas, mild, mind you....

When coming through Duck Hill last week, I found Sam with an ice box full of tasty Cheddar and a good Wisconsin. Got about two pounds of each, and together with the Holland cheese I picked up in Greenville, have been on an almost entirely cheese diet, with here and there a can of fruit.

Best regards to the Hughes! Wish I were there.

Devotedly,
Alston

Mother's parents were on a tour of the West and sent colorful post cards to Jay and me.

Grandfather Dobbs sent two picture postcards of a red diesel engine roaring down the track entitled: "Aboard *THE REBEL*. The cards were, dated Oct. 5, 1944, one addressed to Master Jay McCaslin, states:

Dear Jay,

I am here in St. Louis and will see the big ball game today. Am visiting Uncle Si and Aunt Dimple, and having a good time.

Lovingly,
Grandpapa

The second postcard was identical and was addressed to Master Si McCaslin:

Hello Big Shot.

Hope you are well and enjoying life as much as I am.

Love,
Grandpapa

Frances Dobbs left William in Ackerman with Sara Moss and went to Starkville to have her baby – her parents lived in Starkville. Frances did not want to take William out of school. While in Starkville, Catherine was born on February 13, 1945. Then, Frances had a ruptured tube and was transferred to Memphis for emergency surgery.

In Mother's own words (this being a continuation of the 1980 tape recording):

> But then, Daddy lived at home by himself all of 1944 and 1945. We would go over and spend the night. Many times I would cook fried chicken and have a real happy visit with Daddy. He had a precious old woman who came and kept house, so that he was able to manage. But he went down in health. He had been suffering from arthritis terribly since January or February of 1940. When Jay was six months old, Daddy had an emergency appendectomy, and had never been well after that. He always said that he believed the doctor sewed up a pair of scissors in him. But he had real bad arthritis from then on, and went to Hot Springs about twice a year to take the baths. He never did talk about it very much. I told Henry Jennings (our family internist) recently that my daddy suffered from arthritis. I have no idea what kind it was. He apparently didn't want to talk about it, and I didn't want to pry. Just to look at him you could tell that he had pain. Most of what I knew about it was what Mother would say.
>
> But he had suffered all these six years, with terrible arthritis....

By 1945, we had moved around the block to Adams Avenue, and there we still lived a mere one city block from S. Dunn Street and downtown. Adams Avenue originated at the Eupora Railroad Depot.

Our house on Adams Avenue backed up to a service lane, but beyond the lane was a vast pastureland where cows grazed in solitude. The block on which we lived was not your typical square city block, but rather rhomboidal in shape. The block occupied almost that entire south side of town. I estimate that it was at least a mile around the perimeter of the block. Our house on Adams Avenue was due west of our earlier residence on S. Dunn Street, the latter of which was across the street from Judge Eudy's house, at the corner of S. Dunn Street and W. Gould Avenue, a few hundred feet from Deadman's Curve. Around that deadly curve, on the left, was Sheriff Snyder's home. On turning right on Adams Avenue and coursing back down the hill was the Sugg's house, next to the Elks Taylor house, and then our house. Lady Mary and Elks Taylor were fine neighbors – no relationship to T. F. Taylor. Their daughter, Carolyn, was Jay's age. Lady Mary was a talented artist. Mother acquired two of her oils of primitive Mississippi scenes (in the 1960s and 1970s, her works were well highly collectable).

We lived in a duplex in the home of the widow Mrs. Wall. She was the aunt of T. F. Taylor, Jr., and the sister of T. F. Taylor, Sr., and Bill Taylor. She must have been in her seventies, and she was small, with a stooped frame. Although frail, she was spry and got around just fine. We shared a screened-in front porch with Mrs. Wall.

On the way down Adams Avenue, toward town, was the home of Mrs. Julia Berryhill. Her house was the third from the Railroad Depot. Dr. Berryhill had been a pioneer medical doctor in Eupora (he died in 1950 at age ninety-one, having been the first physician in Eupora). His widow was ninety years of age. Occasionally Mother would walk to town with me and usually would stop and talk with Mrs. Berryhill, when she saw her on the porch. Mother said that Mrs. Berryhill loved me. I would climb the steps to her porch on her invitation to come join her on her porch swing. My legs were so short that they stuck straight out, and Mrs. Berryhill would begin swinging away, thrusting her feet straight out too.

On one particular occasion, Mother said that as we were swinging, Mrs. Berryhill asked: "Si. Can you get down off an elephant?" I replied, "Yes." She then said, "You can't get down off an elephant. How would you get down off an elephant?" Mother said that I looked up at her, as we were swinging, frowned at her as though she were ignorant, and said, "I could climb down; I could slide down; I could jump down." Mrs. Berryhill then said, "You can't get down off of an elephant. You get down off of a goose."

With that, Mother said that I screwed up my face, looked her directly in the eyes, and replied, "Well maybe <u>you</u> can't get down off an elephant, but I sure can!"

On April 12, 1945, while at Warm Springs, Georgia, President Franklin D. Roosevelt died of a cerebral hemorrhage. Vice President Harry S. Truman was sworn in as President.

Jay and I were invited to an Easter egg hunt on Main Street, across from the Curry Clinic. I rushed around with all our friends, looking for the hand-painted eggs, and I happened upon the Golden Goose Egg, the prize which earlier had been disclosed. It truly was a goose egg, painted with gold paint. The grand prize was a baby rabbit. A tiny, brown, wild rabbit. Jay and I were both thrilled, and we took it home in the shoe box provided. Daddy was pleased that we had won, too. We played with the rabbit for several hours on the carpet. Then we tucked him into a nest of cotton in the shoe box and we went to bed ourselves. The next morning, the rabbit was gone. He had chewed through the cardboard box. We never found our bunny rabbit.

We got our first dog, a pedigree, black Cocker Spaniel. Few people had a purebred dog in those days. We named him Jiggs, after the beloved comic strip character. Jiggs was but a small puppy when he came to live with us. By the end of a year, he was practically full grown. Many of our family pictures show us posing with Jiggs.

One day we were in front of a lady's home, next door to Buddy Reed's house down Adams Avenue. There was an antique brown, glazed, clay pot under the water spout of the hydrant in her front yard. Jiggs was thirsty and plunged his head down in the pot to lap some water. We then discovered that we had a problem. Jiggs' head was stuck. He began to thrash about violently, and so doing, waving the pot to-and-fro. Panicked. After every effort failed to pull the clay pot from Jiggs' head, we picked up a brick and smashed the pot, the very moment that the lady came out of her front door. Mother got a telephone call from the lady, who irately expressed her discontent over "those McCaslin boys who broke my antique pot."

In keeping with a habit of most all of the dogs in the neighborhood, Jiggs chased cars, running alongside of the slow-moving car and barking at the tire. Drivers were seldom distracted, having grown accustomed to this nuisance. Eventually, Jiggs was run over by an automobile. The injuries were critical, but he survived. However, his right hind leg was crippled, and he walked with a limp.

There was the incident of Jay's catching a bird that had inadvertently flown onto our screened back porch. We found a birdcage in the Embry's garage, in which we put the bird. We kept it for some time, finally releasing it again to the wild.

> Parenthetic: Suzanne Brooks Campbell was born on June 25, 1945, in Maryville, Blount County, Tennessee, to Trigg Preston Campbell and his wife, Inez Glenn Brooks. (Suzanne was a junior at Agnes Scott College, Decatur, Georgia, when I first met her. The details of this chance meeting are provided in *LETTERS TO AND FROM A CHRISTIAN MOTHER AND MORE*. We have been married now for 49 years).[28]

Choctaw Lake was located a few miles from Ackerman. Jay and I learned to swim in Choctaw Lake the summer of 1945. Mother had been promising that Daddy would give us swimming lessons. One day Jay and I were frolicking in the shallow of the lake, inside the rope. Mother asked him again when he would give us a swimming lesson and he turned to us and said, "Let's go, boys." We followed him as he walked out to the end of the dock, well past the shallow, and to the deep area, where we had never ventured on our own. He turned to me and said, "Are you ready to learn to swim?" When it was acknowledged in the affirmative, he took me up under my arms, and to my surprise, swung me twelve or fifteen feet out into the deep water. When I came to the surface, sputtering, I began to dog-paddle back to the dock. I remember experiencing sheer panic, but I was so proud to have swum back to the ladder on the dock. Jay had begun crying from absolute fear of the unknown. Daddy followed then, throwing Jay way out into the deep. He dog-paddled to the surface and back to the ladder. Following this initiation, we returned to the shallow water, where Daddy gave us our first lesson of the "Australian Crawl." We were both confident swimmers by the end of the summer. We never had formal lessons, yet became excellent swimmers of good form, merely by imitating Daddy and other accomplished swimmers.

---

[28] We met on a blind date in early September 1965 and I proposed marriage to her that very night, eight hours after meeting her, but she laughingly waved the proposal off, assuming that I was joking. We were pinned one week later on our second date. One month after our first date, I proposed again, this time with diamond ring in hand. We married in Maryville, Tennessee, December 20, 1965.

Dr. Hugh Curry was approximately the age of Daddy, and he and his wife, Virginia, were very close friends of my parents. Hugh had joined his father (Eupora's second medical doctor) in the practice of medicine. Together they established the first medical clinic in Webster County, the Curry Medical Clinic. After his father's retirement, Hugh was the only physician in town. He amassed significant wealth from his practice, and his elegant brick home was next door to Virginia and Pete Fortner's home on Clarke Avenue.

Dr. Curry's son, Kim, was four months younger than I, and we were good friends. Kim always had the finest toys and sporting equipment. He had a Bowie Knife – it was so fine, and so expensive looking. In fact, Kim had everything that a boy could ever dream of owning. But, he did not flaunt it. His material possessions all just seemed perfectly natural and normal. And I don't recall that there was ever any envy on my part – just that I was impressed with whatever new thing he had, and happy for him. (The year after we left Eupora, when Kim turned 15 and got his driver's license, his parents bought him a new, blue Chevrolet pickup truck with dual exhaust and glass packs). Back beyond his home was a creek that ran under a bridge on Highway 9. Kim and I frequently went to the creek to romp about, looking for snakes and turtles. If we found nothing of interest, we would whittle.

The Currys were faithful in their church attendance. However, Dr. Curry cursed like the proverbial sailor. Public cursing then was essentially limited to words that can be found in the Bible, and then usually only privately. In fact, most of the nation was absolutely shocked when "Gone With the Wind" was released in 1939 and Clark Gable uttered the famous line with the first curse word ever uttered on the motion picture screen.

Everyone knew that Dr. Curry cursed, and everyone simply accepted it. All of the people in Eupora were his patients, and they held Dr. Curry in high esteem. They adored him. However, Kim acquired the habit – the same profane language – at a very young age. Environmental, as the psychologist would rule. Kim's cursing was alarming to both adults and children, but necessarily tolerated by all, under the circumstances. What could you do? What could you possibly say?

One of Mother's stories about little Kim occurred at a Mississippi State College football game in Starkville that we attended. He was about seven or eight years of age. Sitting in the concrete stadium of Scott Field in clear but forty-degree temperature, having noticed clearly that Kim was shivering and his teeth audibly chattering, and after wrapping a wool blanket about his shoulders, Mother asked: "Kim, honey, are you cold?" Kim's reply was a vivid expression of his acute, thermal discomfort, and it was punctuated with profane words. Mother was astounded yet amused with Kim's language. But, what could you do? Environment had trumped morality.

In the mid-1940s, my parents had a white, enamel-covered metal "ice box" in the pantry – a modern sequel to the small oak ice boxes of the 19th century. Our pantry was a room about half the size of our kitchen, connecting to the kitchen by way of the screened-in back porch. Every day, the "Ice Man" would come around to deliver ice. He transported the ice from the Eupora Ice Company downtown in a horse-drawn wagon. The wagon was full of blocks of ice of about one cubic foot in size, draped with a heavy canvas tarpaulin, the cold water dripping out below the wagon from the slowly-melting ice. He would use a pair of large calipers to grasp and lift the block of ice from the wagon, placing it into a canvas bag, which had straps attached. He then slipped his arms through the straps, swung the bag up to his back, and walked to the rear of the house, into the pantry, placing the canvas bag on the floor. Again, with the calipers, he would lift the block of ice from the bag and place it in the upper portion of the ice box. The ice kept the contents of the separate box below cool. There was always an ice pick with which one could chip off ice to put in drinks. The last of the ice would melt in about two days, and would be re-delivered by the ice man.

Boys, more so than girls, roamed around freely on their bicycles. One could pedal one's bike from one side of town to the other in five minutes. One day I rode my bike down to the Eupora Ice Company. I was there to get an ice cone, as soon as the workman had time to make it for me. As a man purchased a block of ice, and it was loaded onto the deck of his pickup truck, he handed the proprietor money and from the cash register, change was made. As it was handed to the purchaser, a half dollar fell to the deck, rolled a few inches, then slipped through the crack. The deck purposefully was laid with spaces between the boards to allow the water from the melting ice to drain off. The ice man shrugged his shoulders and grimaced, then gave the customer another half dollar, and the customer was on his way. I asked the ice man if I could go under the deck and get the half dollar. He said: "You are welcome to anything you find under there, but I don't know how you will get there." There was a brick skirt surrounding the platform. But I knew of access. I was a fairly slender eight-year-old. The steps leading from the ground up to the deck had spaces of about eight inches between them. I easily slipped through two of the steps. It was cool. And wet. Cold water dripped from the deck above. The ground was covered with clean, daily-washed pea gravel to absorb the dripping water. The deck measured at least ten by twenty-five feet and stood about three feet from the ground. I crawled along under the deck on my hands and knees on the sparkling-clean pea gravel. I was absolutely astonished on discovering a veritable treasure trove. Coins of every denomination were simply lying on the surface. I did not dig. It was dim, but light enough to see bright new coins and even the corroded coins. I must have been the first kid ever to go there. When I crawled out the way I came in, both of my pockets were bulging with coins. I had retrieved about twenty-five dollars total. I quickly pedaled my bike the two blocks home and burst into the house to tell Mother. Once I explained that I had permission, she was quite pleased with my discovery and my effort. The coins soon went to the bank, deposited in my modest savings account.

Many were the hours that we spent in the Farmer's Co-Operative, climbing about atop the stacked sacks of fertilizer, jumping from one to another. There were stacks of other farm supplies through which we would race around in the isles of the warehouse. The proprietor never seemed to mind. We often bought necessities there; usually a cold soft drink and a *Moon Pie*. The front counter at the Co-op was filled with things such as Penny candy, wax coke-shaped bottles with colored sugar water, and the soda pop machines that contained glass, bottled drinks, from which one might choose a *7 Up, Dr. Pepper, Orange Crush,* or *Coca-Cola*. Some of the boys preferred *R.C. Cola,* because it contained a couple of ounces more for the same price. Then there was the freezer with the sliding glass lid, which contained treats such as ice cream sandwiches and Eskimo Pies.

Poignantly recalled – as early as five years of age – is <u>finally</u> being granted permission by Mother to "go barefoot" on the first of warm, spring days (we would not shed our shoes until permission was granted by someone's mother and reiterated by our own). Oh, the exhilarating experience of running through the cool, green grass of the fields and pastures on that first day. (Today this reminds me of the great liberty that God graciously and lovingly gives His children, to enjoy those things that are not forbidden). We would lie in the deep grass and look at the canopy of blue sky above, which was punctuated with occasional cloud formations. I was consumed with the enormity of it all. As taught at home and in Sunday school, we were aware of and awed by God's creation. Furthermore, on occasion, my brother and my friends and I would climb on top of a huge barn, which structure was perched at the top of the highest hill, behind Sheriff Snyder's home, practically in the shadow of the city water tank. We would walk out on the rusty, corrugated tin roof, barefoot. The town of Eupora stretched out across the horizon. We would lie down on the roof and stare at the sky, again recalling the vivid Sunday school lessons that declared that the creative hand of God had made the world, all that was within it, and the heavens above. We idled away hour after hour suggesting what animal or face each cloud formation resembled.

After that first day of summer, we wore shoes only to church on Sunday. Our feet quickly acquired calluses, and they were dirty from early morning until the bath at night. This Southern custom for children, both young boys and girls, continued year after year.

Heretofore we spoke of the large J. R. Phillips Drygoods Store on Main Street, across Main Street from the Eupora Café. Upstairs, occupying about one third of the space above Phillips Drygoods Store, was the office of Dr. Silas G. Maddox, who was born in the 1880s. In the early 1940s, Dr. Maddox was our dentist, and the only dental practitioner in town. He was in his late fifties. You would enter from the back side of the J. R. Phillips building, climb a long flight of wooden stairs to the second floor, and turn right. The doorway to the reception room was at the far end of the hallway with Dr. Maddox' name etched in the frosted glass in the top half of the door. The windows of his treatment room looked out over N. Dunn Street, where it intersected with Highway 82. It was a view of the heart of the town of Eupora. Vivid in our memory was that Dr. Maddox did not administer local anesthetic for preparation and placement of fillings. He reserved anesthesia only for extractions. Consequently, people were inclined often to prefer extractions in lieu of a restoration. The details of dentistry as practiced by Dr. Maddox were clear in our memory – the up-right, adjustable dental chair (dentistry in early years was universally practiced standing up); the white porcelain spittoon, with the small chrome water pipe swirling water in a circular fashion around the interior of the ceramic bowl (spittoon); the round, porcelain bracket table, with the piecrust-type edge, to keep the instruments from rolling; the use of a small, glass mortar and pestle to mix the silver amalgam. The anesthetic carpule had two rubber stoppers, one at each end. We longed for the scent of the cavity varnish, swabbed into the cavity before the filling, for the scent declared that the procedure was almost over. Dr. Maddox willingly gave us some of the discarded anesthetic carpules. One rubber stopper could be pushed with a small round stick to one end of the carpule, with the second inserted at the other end. Then while grasping the glass cylinder, with a stick, the rubber stopper at the far end could be jettisoned, with a quick push against the other. We had loads of fun shooting those small rubber stoppers at one another, or bouncing them off of the wall or ceiling. They would shoot a much greater distance than the typical pea shooter, that latter of which we frequently whittled out of a section of sugar cane.

Our telephone number was 2102. In a town of thirteen hundred, why such a high number? Certainly the prefix had not been needed in small towns. Jay and I knew the telephone numbers of all of our friends, as well as those for many businesses, owing to the uncluttered and clear mind of a child. The telephone itself was the old, heavy black enamel-over-pot metal style, with a circular, white dial. The receiver rested in a cradle and the telephone sat on a bedside table in our parents' bedroom, and thereby was accessible from either the front or the back of the house. The handset was tethered to the base by a three-foot cord, so one could not wander. We could make a phone call, but we certainly did not engage in long conversations. Our friends were two doors away or across the street, but certainly no farther away than a five minute walk. Why would one want to talk on the telephone, when one could engage in conversation face to face? (Today conversations by "land lines" are being supplanted by cell phones, and texting and emails are relegating hand-written letters to the veritable trash can of antiquity).

About 1950, we bought a new white Frigidaire refrigerator. It was in the kitchen, to the right of the doorway leading to the back porch. The Frigidaire had a refrigerator below and a freezer above, cooled by an electric motor. Hence, the advent in our home of metal ice cube trays with levers. Daddy put one of the two large, oscillating Westinghouse fans on top of the refrigerator, and the temperature in the kitchen was usually quite comfortable.

Mother's new Bendix washing machine was delivered and placed in the pantry (as earlier stated, the pantry was accessed through a door to the right after going out on the porch). The Bendix was in the corner formerly occupied by the ice box. When the Bendix completed the washing cycle and began the spinning cycle for wringing the water out of the wet clothes, it would vibrate so much that it would translate across the floor. To prevent the machine from moving during operation, Daddy soon had a square hole cut in the floor of the pantry, a concrete footing poured on the ground below to the level of the floor, and the Bendix was literally bolted to that concrete foundation. The front door of the machine was set at an angle, and there was a small, round glass window in the door. Daddy would put his soiled golf balls in the Bendix to wash them and they made an awful noise. Mother strongly disapproved of this task.

Fresh milk was delivered daily by the milk man by horse and wagon. The tall quart bottle with the slender neck, sealed with a paper cap, came from a nearby dairy farm. The milk was bottled soon after milking, and it was ready to deliver. In the few hours it took to be delivered, the cream would have risen and occupied the entire area of the neck of the milk bottle. The cream was decanted first and saved for cooking. We could purchase butter milk, chocolate milk, and butter from the milkman. He left the bottles on the top step in the shade. Mother knew about when it would come.

Our eggs were delivered often by a farmer, and the eggs were fresh, having been laid only a few hours earlier. For a while, there was a particular farmer who brought the eggs on Saturday, when he knew that Daddy would be at home. Out of appreciation for the dozen freshly-laid eggs, Daddy would offer him a shot of whiskey, which the farmer never refused. Such could not be bought legally. After a time, he began coming twice a week, with only a half-dozen. Daddy still would give him a shot. When he started coming every day with only three eggs, the courtesy ended. It was back to the one-dozen delivery each week.

The U.S. mail came by train three times daily in large, locked canvas bags unloaded onto the wagons at the depot. Then those bags would immediately be transported two blocks to the post office. Whereas rural mail delivery was made outside of Eupora, our mail was posted at the Eupora U.S. Post Office. Daddy stopped at least twice daily to check his post office box. I remember being with him often as he would stand at one of the waist-high, marble-topped wrought iron tables to sort through his mail, discarding expendable stuff into the tall grey metal trash can. There were brass spittoons strategically placed throughout the post office lobby. Posted on the bulletin board were the pictures from the FBI of the "Ten Most Wanted Men," as well as other criminals.

Trash was picked up regularly. The man drove a green, wooden wagon, drawn by a huge brown work horse. The man had a primitive, hand-hewn wooden peg-leg, held in place by hand-made leather straps. He had been a trainman. He would climb down from the large, high-sided wagon, limp around behind one's house, empty the trash can into his container, and return to the wagon to dump it. His family had little in material things, and they lived in a modest house around the block. No one thought less of them – that was simply the job that he had. And he seemed grateful to have a job.

There were some boys, all brothers, and as they got older, they all became bullies. Abbot, the oldest of the boys, was about three years older than Jay. Abbot did not like any of our friends.

Daddy was over six feet, athletic, and physically had persuasive powers. Once, when Jay was ten and I was nine years of age, the town bully, Abbot saw us as we walked home about dark from the Saturday matinee picture show. He was thirteen. A foot taller than Jay, he tried to pick a fight. Abbot's younger brother would position himself on his hands and knees behind Jay, and Abbot would push Jay backwards over him. He pushed Jay around and slapped him in the face. When Jay refused to fight, Abbot took his lighted cigarette (yes, at thirteen years of age) and burned Jay on the arm. We ran home, scared to death and crying. As we entered the house, upset as we were, Daddy asked for an explanation. Jay told him what had happened and showed him the burned place. Daddy said, "Come on, boys," and we went to the car. Daddy had a spotlight on this particular Cadillac (which even today is common on police cars). He drove around the block to Abbot's home, pulled into the driveway, and turned into the grass in the yard with his bright lights shining on the front of the house. He turned the spotlight on, directed it right at eye level on the front door, and honked the horn. When Abbot's father came and opened the door, he shaded his eyes from the glare of the headlights and spotlight with his hand and asked: "What is going on?" Daddy called to Abbot's father to summon Abbot to the door. Daddy stepped out of the car and walked up to the small porch, saying to Jay and me: "Come on boys!" Abbot appeared, cowering behind his father. Daddy reached by Abbot's father, grasped Abbot by the hair of the head, and lifted him about ten inches off the floor. Abbot hung there, perfectly still. The look on his face reflected that he was terrified! Daddy began talking. "Abbot, if you ever bother my boys again, I'll be back. In fact, if you as much as see them walking down the street, I suggest that you cross to the other side of the street. Do you understand me?" Abbot answered affirmatively. Abbot's father said, "You hear that now, boy!" Daddy released his grip on Abbot's hair, and he dropped to the floor. He then turned and walked back to the car. Daddy switched the spotlight off, backed out of the yard, and drove home silently. As we walked in the house, Daddy said, "Let me know if Abbot gives you any more trouble."

Abbot's father had not asked Daddy what Abbot had done to us, but I'm sure he found out after we left the house that night. Abbot, and his younger brothers, never as much as spoke an ugly word to us again. In fact, they were right nice to us from then on.

Mother had thought it important that her boys, and their friends, be given the opportunity to become Cub Scouts. She qualified as an official Cub Scout Den Mother. We were fitted with the royal blue uniforms and soon began having our Den Meetings in our living room. Jay and I earned numerous merit badges, which Mother sewed on our uniforms. We wore our Cub Scout uniforms proudly. We worked our way up from Webelos through the ascending ranks of Wolf and Bear to Lion.

During those days, we enjoyed "camping out," usually during the summer months. Of course, we had our official, genuine U. S. Army pup tent, acquired at the Army and Navy Store. Our first outings were in the back yard, and we often found refuge back inside in our own bed before 9:00. Later, we stayed until midnight, then later, all the night. And a year or so later, we ventured into the pastureland in the center of our block, probably two-hundred feet behind our house. Our church group took a couple of camping trips farther out of town, deep into the woodlands. I can still remember waking up to the smell of bacon frying in a pan over an open fire and arising early to assist in preparation of the rest of the breakfast.

We grew up with trains being commonplace. The old steam engine locomotives passed through Eupora three times daily in the 1940s. Often, we were down the tracks somewhere, perhaps playing on a bridge, or in a creek below, as the train rolled into town. Fortunately I never witnessed a trainman's being injured, but peg-leg men were not uncommon. On one occasion, the train engineer invited Jay and me to come up the steel ladder into the engine room. The experience was exhilarating to us. The engineer coached us on the operation of this ominous monster of a machine. The diesel locomotive replaced the steam locomotive about 1950.

We frequently played around at the railroad depot, and watched as the train arrived. Merchandise was unloaded from the box cars onto the mobile railroad depot wagons, and other items were loaded onto the box cars for shipment, including the U. S. mail. Once unloaded, the merchandise was moved about on the wooden wagons, which had iron wheels, the tongue of which wagon had a handle designed for pulling and guiding the wagon. When things were idle at the train depot, we would pull one another about on the large, heavy wagons. No one seemed to mind; at least nothing ever was said.

We often would occupy ourselves on long summer days looking for four-leaf clovers. The clover usually has three leaves, and I suppose the four-leaf clover is a mutant or aberration. They were extremely hard to find. The clover also produced small white flowers, with about a four-inch stem. We would pick the flowers and patiently tie them together in a long strand. Then came the fun. One of us would sit on the curb on each side of the street, with the clover chain lying on the pavement. Other friends would be sitting, innocent-looking, beside us. Kids sitting on the curb was a very common scene. As an automobile would appear and slowly come down the street, at the last second, we would suddenly lift the chain to about a three foot height. The driver would frantically slam on the brakes, to avoid hitting what appeared to be some type of dangerous line or barrier, even though it was held by children. Gradually, adults caught on to the prank and would speed right on through the clover chain, smiling and waving, carrying most of it with them. We then would patiently begin constructing a replacement.

The June bug was a shiny green flying bug, about the size of a nickel. They were plentiful in Mississippi during the summer. One would carefully catch a June bug, tie a sewing thread to its leg, feed the thread out as it flew away, and then allow it to circle overhead. Often, someone else's June bug would fly by another thread, and they would become entangled. We would sort this snare out and launch the flights again.

Robert Wayne Miller and his little sister, Mary Jane, lived directly across the street. They were the adopted children of Oscar and Sarah Miller. Ostensibly, this is the house that Mother wrote about in her diary much earlier, the house that they had hoped to rent. Obviously the Millers had rented the house (which Mother had regarded as "shabby but could be cute"), and Mother and Daddy obtained the duplex in Mrs. Wall's home. Mr. Miller owned the Western Auto Store, and Sarah was the principal of the high school. About every second year, for Christmas, Jay and I would get a new bicycle, purchased from Oscar Miller.

Earnest Edgar (Mac) Coleman lived in the house to the right of the Millers, next to the Embrys' house. Mac Coleman was the Town Marshall, of whom more will be said later. He had a gold badge and a handgun, but dressed in street clothes. Rob and Charles Sugg lived two houses up the hill from us, with Carolyn Taylor's house in between. Carolyn was the only child of Lady Mary and Elks Taylor.[29] Carolyn was Jay's age. She often was around as we played neighborhood games, but she was not in our clubs. They were for boys only. Bob Sugg was a prominent lawyer.[30]

Life in the neighborhood with Rob and Charles Sugg, Robert Wayne Miller, and others was never boring. Were we mischievous? Occasionally. Usually trouble followed when one's challenge was buttressed with "I double-dog-dare you." Those were challenging words that would provoke a kid. Seldom did one have to resort to the greater challenge: "I triple-dog-dare you. But, essentially, we were good kids. As a matter of fact, Mother, Sarah Miller, and Lorraine Sugg conducted weekly Bible studies for us and our friends. Already Jay and I had been reared in the Christian faith at Mother's knee, having daily devotionals at breakfast and Bible verses to memorize.

In the warm summer nights we romped around at dusk catching "lightening bugs," which we would place in a mayonnaise jar, the lid of which was perforated with holes punched in it with an ice pick. The parents were relaxed in their heavy, painted metal lawn chairs, carrying on conversation, usually in front of the Elks Taylor home.

President Truman made some of the most crucial decisions in history. Soon after V-E Day, the war against Japan had reached its final stage. An urgent plea to Japan to surrender was rejected. Truman, after consultations with his advisers, ordered a uranium atomic bomb (Little Boy) to be dropped on Hiroshima on August 6, killing one-hundred thousand people, and a plutonium atomic bomb (Fat Man) on Nagasaki three days later,

---

[29] A special to the *New York Times*, in October 1982, was a piece was entitled **"AGE ISSUE IS FOCUS OF RACE"** The writer spoke of the obstacles of young Haley Barbour (who one day would be the Republican Mississippi Governor) in his campaign against the renowned Senator John C. Stennis. Lady Mary Taylor of Eupora, Miss., a few minutes after she and Haley Barbour had a cordial conversation about her daughter and grandchildren, stated: "We like Haley...." She then announced that her daughter, Carolyn, had earlier been out with Haley. But since Lady Mary had known Senator Stennis for many years, she said that they would stick with old friends.

[30] Robert Perkins Sugg was Attorney for Town of Eupora, 1940-1950; Webster County Prosecuting Attorney 1949-1971; Justice of the Mississippi Supreme Court, 1971-1983.

killing over seventy-five thousand people. It was another week, August 14, before the Japanese announced its surrender, which was not entirely unconditional, because the Allies had agreed to allow the country to keep its emperor. The formal signing by Japanese representatives of the "Instrument of Surrender," took place on September 2, in Tokyo Bay, aboard the battleship *Missouri*. The Allied delegation was headed by General MacArthur, who became the military governor of occupied Japan. Soon after this date, Uncle Willie came home.

The precise date of the end of the war is not agreed upon. Generally speaking, the end of World War II was the signing of the armistice, August 14, 1945. However, some are of the opinion that it came with the formal surrender of Japan on September 2, 1945. (It is the general consensus that the San Francisco Peace Treaty, signed with Japan in San Francisco in 1951, finally resolved all of the issues).

Mother loved gardening. Following the end of the war, many people had "Victory Gardens" in recognition of the defeat of Japan and Hitler.

During 1945, the first computer was built; Hitler committed suicide; and the United Nations was founded.

Memories of Christmas are keenly recalled. Mother would draw a Christmas scene with our names on them which she would have printed and send to family and friends. (Beginning about 1949, she wrote a Christmas poem for the card. Mother had a poetic nature. She would wake during the night, turn on a light, and write the poem that had come to her in her sleep, knowing that she would not remember it at daybreak. Beginning in the early 1940s, Mother would write her letter to Santa Clause early in December and would speak out loud to us as she wrote and listed the various things that we wanted Santa to bring from the North Pole. Later she began typing her letters. One of these typewritten letters reads as follows:

> Eupora, Miss.
> Nov. 24, 1945
> Dear Santa Claus:
>
> I hope your are planning to come to see us this year. Jay and Si have been pretty good boys. When they are bad, they are sorry. And, they are trying to be real sweet just now. These are the things that they want you to bring them if you will:

A new gun apiece, new bedroom slippers, a toy, a box of modeling clay, if you think they are big enough not to make a mess with it. They need a new belt apiece, and maybe some tinker toys – but not if you don't think they need them. And some kind of a game or something like that. I think they will be glad to get anything you bring them, Santa Claus. Just be sure to come – go to see all the little children that have been good.

If it is not asking too much, Santa Claus, I wish you would bring them some new bedroom slippers and things like that that they need. They love new clothes as well as toys.

I promise you that they will be good boys.

Thank you Santa Claus,
Mrs. McCaslin

When young, every Christmas Eve, Jay and I could hardly manage to sleep a wink. We were relatively certain what Santa would bring, and the myriad of wrapped presents under the tree was far more than adequate to sustain restlessness for us. At four, and five, and six years of age, we would tiptoe into our parents' bedroom as early as midnight to ask them what time it was, or if we could go into the living room. They would turn us back to our room. This routine would continue every hour or so until about 4:00 or 4:30 a.m., and finally, they would permit us to go into the living room and turn on the lights; but they would sleep until about 6:00. We had plenty to play with, but opening of the presents waited until our parents joined us with a freshly brewed cup of coffee in hand. By then, we had already begun to assemble things out of the *Erector Set*, the *Lincoln Logs*, and the *American Bricks*. And we often got a new box of *Pick-up Sticks*. There were wrapped presents from family and friends, but predominantly from our parents. After opening our presents, we were well stocked with necessities of clothing – socks, shoes, a belt, shirts, and so forth. The remainder of the day was spent outside with our friends, trying out our new things such as a bicycle, a *Red Rider* BB gun, or cap pistols in their leather holsters.

Grandfather Dobbs had apparently had been diagnosed with a tumor and would require surgery. (From her 1980 tape recording) Mother said:

> And then in March 1946, he went to Memphis to have a prostate operation.[31] He drove his car up there. He stayed several weeks in the hospital....

Granddaddy still remained at Methodist Hospital, recuperating from surgery. Mother wrote her father, the envelope postmarked "Eupora, Mar. 28, 1946." The letter provided him with an update of family matters as follows:

> Wednesday night
> Darling:
>
> Got home O.K. & have been writing to Brother & Mother Mac.
> When I got here, Mac had already gone to Ackerman for the kids, so I phoned Sara & told her all about you.
> Jiggs was waiting for me on the front porch. I didn't tell you, because I knew you'd feel so bad, but I thought Jiggs was dead. He disappeared Saturday night & wasn't seen again till after I left Monday afternoon. I just knew he had been killed, because he had never gone away from home like that. But, he was here & frisky today. It seems he had just suddenly decided to take a jaunt. Boy! Was I glad to see that puppy.
> I had <u>no</u> manuscripts waiting, as I thought I would have. I have a hunch I will have another acceptance this week, or something. And today on the bus I heard a nice looking veteran say he was from Charleston, Miss. So I spoke to him about the crippled boy & this fellow assured me that Billy Price could do (& probably would do) my illustrations. I gave the boy all the information necessary & he is going to see Billy Price for me.

---

[31] Over forty years later, cousin William Dobbs told me that Grandfather Dobbs had colon cancer, which in this letter is called "prostate surgery." William held the PhD in biophysiology, but more, he was older than Jay and he clearly remembered the diagnosis of Grandfather Dobbs. Brother Jay was diagnosed with colon cancer in early December 1987. Surgery followed three days later, then radiation therapy which later resulted in total remission of the cancer; 18 years later, Jay developed lung cancer.

This veteran & Billy's older brother are good friends. So, I feel good about that.

I truly feel, honey Pop, that we are now due for a happy period of success & (maybe) prosperity–of a sort. Course it will be slow, but I think we are capable of doing big things together. It may be my jubilance over your promised good health that has me so optimistic. That, alone, is enough.

I had a nice letter from Arlin – very similar to yours of this morning.[32]

It is raining here now & I am very tired and sleepy. So will say g'nite with all kinds of love.

M.M.

Hope you are sound asleep. Tell that doctor to go light, if he can!

Mac will come up when you say so, & maybe me too.

M.M.

Grandfather Dobbs received the following letter from Mother, at the Methodist Hospital, Memphis, on March 30, 1946:

Saturday morning

Dearest Daddy,

Herman called early this morning to tell me that you would not be ready to come home tomorrow. So I thought that I would send another note to you.

Hope we hear today that you can come Monday. Mac is going to bring Billy's car home, so the back seat of it will be more comfortable than our car. We don't know yet just how we will go up. It seems silly to take our car up there, just to get there. Maybe, oh, I don't know. Mac will decide.

Everything here is all right. Puppy has had a bath and looks so pretty. He is staying home too. I believe someone had him put up for those days that he was missing.

---

[32] There are dozens of letters in our files from Grandfather Dobbs's sister, Arlin Dobbs Wright. Many were written to Mr. and Mrs. E. B. Dobbs and many were to Mother and Daddy.

Mildred will help me three days a week. She is a good girl, but her husband will interfere with my calling on her just anytime. Three days a week, though, will be a great help.

> Wish you would talk to the doctor about your diet; how much meat you can eat, about drinking, too; and all those things. Ask him too, which vitamins you should take. Get all the information that you can from him about your future intake. Am sure he knows more than Dr. James, so find out everything you'd like to know...
>
> I must stop now. Hurry and be ready to come home. Talked to Dr. Hugh Curry and he was glad that you were doing well. He said you needed to be in the hospital Christmas, but he was afraid you'd balk.

Love,
M. M.

Chapter Five

LOSS QUICKENS
FAITH IN GOD

Granddaddy remained at Methodist Hospital longer than expected. Mother's letter to him, postmarked Eupora, April 5, 1946, advises him to be patient:

Thursday night
Dearest Daddy:

I called Dr. Mason tonight & he told me you had a heart attack. Oh Daddy, darling. Take care of yourself. I know you are so very tired of that hospital and ready to come home, and everything. But days now will mean years, to you, in longevity. Please be content to stay there and do as the doctors say. They (the doctors) know better than we do what can be hurtful to one's insides. Please be good & patient & take it easy. You needn't be in such a hurry to come home, cause when you <u>do</u> come, I intend to keep you down & quiet and restful for a good while. The "coming home" will not mean a quick fishing trip. By gun, your nurses there may be nicer than your nurse here. So you'd better stay while you have a good excuse.

I haven't written because I thought every day (since Sunday) that I would hear that you were ready to come home. I am very sorry that I haven't had any letters there for you all these days, and I will write each day now till I <u>do</u> hear from you....

Dr. Mason said you would probably not be ready to come home till Monday or Tuesday. The trip there & back in one day is such a hard one, & I can't spend the night, because of the kids. So I will not come. You don't need to see me to know how much

I care about you. You are just as important to me as any human being there is, & your comfort and joy are <u>more</u> important than that of anyone else.

I'd be up there everyday, if it were feasible. Lavinia offered to keep my children, but she couldn't do it. They are too much for anyone who isn't used to boys. Maybe if you will be very good & are ready to come home Monday, maybe we can all drive up Sunday & I can stay over & drive Billy's car back when you are ready.

At any rate, I'll see you soon. There is no special news with us. I have not accomplished anything. Have been sewing and mending this week. Must stop now & write another letter or two. Be happy, darling. I love you terribly much.

M.M.

Granddaddy was released about a week later. Mother (in the remainder of her 1980 tape recording) spoke of her daddy's return and his fragile condition:

He then came home. I brought him over to Eupora, set him up, and nursed him all those months, until he died, October 26, 1946. But, in the interim, between March and October, he was back and forth in the hospital in Memphis. I would travel back and forth. For a week or two, he would be better, and then start going down again. He simply never did recover from that operation. I guess his whole physical condition was just so run down. He may have had cancer. Back in those days, it was a hush, hush thing for people to have cancer. He died at home, and I was present. He is the only person that I have ever seen die. It was about 4:00 in the afternoon that he died, yet for weeks before that, I had known and he had known. And we talked about it. And I have always felt that that experience with my father, nursing him and watching him weaken, knowing that he was going to die, was the greatest spiritual growth experience that I had ever had up until that time, or since, in such a short length of time. (Author's note: *this statement is the basis for the title of this chapter*). We talked about the Lord. One afternoon, I said something about the children, Jay and Si – whom he adored, particularly, because he saw so much of them. He said how much he loved them, then he turned to me and said, "I love

88

you better than anything or anyone in the whole world, with one exception." I thought he was going to say, "Those boys." When I said, "What is that exception, Daddy?" He pointed upward and said, "The Lord. I love the Lord best." And, I think it was two or three weeks before he died. He would have little spells in which he was irrational and would say strange things. But the things he said when I thought he was being irrational made so much sense. And one day he told me that he had had a vision. I asked him to tell me about it. He said that around his bed he had seen a little white picket fence, and his mother was standing at the gate. And she told him that he would never leave that bed. He told me that he knew what that meant. And when I would give him a sleeping pill at night – he had one every night – he would hold the pill before he put it in his mouth, look at me, and his eyes would twinkle, and he would say, "One of these nights I am going to take this and I am not going to wake up." Of course I would say, "Oh Daddy! Don't talk like that." Then he would say, "Well that is true. And I am ready." He told me one time, "The Lord has really answered my prayers. I have always had a fear of dying suddenly and violently, and I have prayed all my life that the Lord would not let me die that way, and he certainly has answered my prayers. He's given me plenty of time to think about it."

And we would talk about the books that he had read and the magazine articles he had read. He would go out on the porch to sit and read. It was just precious. And we read the Bible and talked about it. I just look back on those days as being such a privilege, such a glorious, precious privilege. I had a good cook and housekeeper, so that I did not have to do too much of that kind of work. Just nursing him and bathing him and feeding him and taking care of him was difficult physically. But, I was young, and every moment was precious because I knew that it would not go on for long.

I loved my daddy so very much – and Mother, too – but Daddy and I had a relationship that was just precious and rare. We understood each other and appreciated each other in a way that was just marvelous and wonderful to look back on. And he was just so brilliant and so articulate and so witty. Just a darling guy....

Estel Bridges Dobbs died in Eupora, October 26, 1946, in his sixty-second year, in the home of his daughter, Mary Margaret Dobbs McCaslin. He was, for some seven months, a victim of that dreaded malignancy, cancer.

THE CHOCTAW COUNTY PLAIN DEALER, on September 15, 1946, published the following (Permission granted by *The Plain Dealer* now a subsidiary of *The Winston County Journal*):

TRIBUTE TO MR. DOBBS

When the messenger of death came to Mr. Estel B. Dobbs, although expected for many months, yet it was with deep regret to the many friends, and especially it brought to his Sunday school class a feeling of sadness. It is with much sorrow we chronicle the passing of one so true to his home, his community, his church and his God, at the age of sixty-two years.

He hearkened to every call his church made upon him. Tasks that others shirked, we knew Mr. Dobbs would give his time to, and give his best. As teacher of the T.E.L Sunday School Class he was faithful and true, where his place will be hard to fill.

To his children, Lieutenant Commander Willie Dobbs, Decatur, Georgia, and Mrs. Mary Margaret McCaslin, Eupora, Mississippi, we commend his memory – beautiful and worthy to be emulated pressing onward and upward towards his ideals as he found in Christ Jesus. To his loved ones and all who mourn his going we would say:

> I cannot say, I will not say
>   That he is dead. He is just away.
> With a cheery smile and a wave of the hand
>   He has wandered into an unknown land.
> And left us dreaming, how very fair
>   It needs must be, since he lingers there.
> And you, oh you, who are left behind, yearn
>   For the old time step and the glad return.
> I think of him as faring on, as dear
>   In the loves of there, as the loves of here.
> I think of him as the same, I say.
>   He is not dead, he is just away.

May God bless and comfort each of you and may you rejoice with him that he is with your Mother on the Beautiful Isle of Somewhere. God doeth all things well.

Humbly submitted by the T.E.L. Class of Ackerman Baptist Church. Mrs. Alice Prewitt, Mrs. J. D. Weeks, Mrs. Wilton Walters.

Estel Bridges Dobbs is buried beside his beloved wife in Enon Cemetery, Ackerman, Mississippi.

Our later visits in Ackerman included time spent with Sara Margaret and Fenley Moss. Sara Margaret was the daughter of Spurgeon Adams, and he was the brother of Mamie Adams Dobbs. Fenley was a rural mail route carrier, just as Grandfather Dobbs before. Folks residing in town picked their mail up each day at the post office, whereas country families had mail delivered each day. The mailman was somewhat like a family member, trustworthy and highly respected. It was an esteemed occupation, highly sought after.

Mother endured emotional strife following the death of her father. With her brother living in Decatur, Georgia, the responsibility fell upon her shoulders to dispose of her parents' personal and household belongings. She had grown up with all of those "old things" and regarded them as commonplace and of little value. Their two-bedroom duplex apartment on Adams Avenue was small, and Mother had inadequate space for anything else. And her brother had no need for furniture at the time. Mother gave away all of the family antique furniture to friends in Ackerman.

Only a year or so later, she realized with regret what a terrible mistake she had made, and she began collecting antiques that were similar to the pieces that she had given away. She purchased many beautiful pieces of furniture from Mr. Beard in Macon, Mississippi. And, she had him refinish antiques that she bought elsewhere. One article of furniture that she had retained, and which she valued highly, was a small mahogany table, on four turned legs, with slipper feet, connected with stretchers. The table was made by hand in the early-19th century for Mother's grandfather, John Adams, and is still in the possession of our family. Uncle Willie had a banjo wall clock that also belonged to Great Grandfather John Adams. As earlier noticed, Mother had the Revolutionary War flintlock rifle belonging to our ancestor, Lodowick Dobbs.

Mother wrote scores of short stories and poems in her hand; then, typewritten, she submitted each to various magazines or publishing houses for consideration. She mentioned her writing in the letters to her father earlier. Her writing principally was during the period from 1945 to 1949. Often she wrote under the pseudonym of Fortune Dobbs, but also used Mary Dobbs, Mary Margaret McCaslin, and Ben Hur Lampman,. We have copies of many of these manuscripts, as well as her correspondence with the editors of various publishing houses or magazines to which she submitted her works – the many letters of inquiry, replies, and rejections of her poems and short stories. The names of the various magazines were many, among which the following: *LADIES HOME JOURNAL, COUNTRY GENTLEMEN, GOOD HOUSEKEEPING, CHRISTIAN HOME, CHRISTIAN LIFE, COSMOPOLITAN, REDBOOK, COLLIER'S, MCCALL'S, READER'S DIGEST, VICTORIAN MAGAZINE, WOMAN'S HOME COMPANION, CHRISTIAN HERALD, MOTHER'S MAGAZINE, ESQUIRE, ARGOSY, ATLANTIC, MADEMOISELLE, WOMAN'S DAY, AMERICAN.* Among the publishing houses were the following: SIMON AND SCHUSTER, E.. P. DUTTON & CO., DAVID MCKAY CO., G. P. PUTNAM'S SONS, LITTLE BROWN & CO., THE DIETZ PRESS, ZONDERVAN PUBLISHING HOUSE, RANDOM HOUSE, VIKING PRESS, and THE CHILDREN'S PRESS. Mother was a prolific writer.

We have a copy of *THE Atlantic*, February 1945, in which is published, "OLD BILL BENT TO DRINK," by Ben Hur Lampman, another of Mother's pen names.

From the foregoing correspondence, it should be noticed that Mother credited her father for many of the stories. It must have been his tales on which she relied to base many of her poems and short stories. The following are Mother's contemporaneous notes on some of the manuscripts that she sold:

PIECES SOLD

A PRIVILEGE OF PARENTS, 1000 words. $10.00. Sold March 1, 1946 to MOTHER'S MAGAZINE, David G. Cook, Ed., by Mary Dobbs.

ALBERT'S SHOOTIN EYE, 1750 words. $17.50. Sold April 6, 1946 to HUNTING AND FISHING. Bernie Roth, Ed. by Fortune Dobbs.

DAYS TILL, Article, 220 words. $5.00. Sold March 10; received check April 20, 1946.

TO TWO TO SIX, Irene Parrott, Ed. by Mary M. McCaslin, 1946

BALDY, 4600 words. $50.00. Sold May 4, 1946 to AMERICAN FIELD, W. F. Brown, Ed. by Fortune Dobbs.

The American Field Publishing Co., 222 West Adams Avenue, Chicago, Ill., on April 30, 1946, is comparable to other correspondence she received for pieces that she sold. They wrote regarding future plans for publication:

Fortune Dobbs
Eupora, Mississippi
Dear Mr. Dobbs:

Appreciate your thoughtfulness in sending us *BALDY* and we are very glad to accept your offering
Enclosed is our check for $50.00 covering the manuscript. Publication date at this writing is indefinite.

With best wishes,
Sincerely yours,
W. F. Brown, Editor

From the paltry payments of the foregoing, except for *BALDY*, it is obvious that she was motivated from the pride of journalism, rather than the lure of compensation (with inflation, $50.00 in 2014 would be $610.00).

ALBERT'S SHOOTIN EYE, by Fortune Dobbs, noted above, was published by *HUNTING AND FISHING*," in the September 1946 issue.

In the same loose-leaf notebook which now contains her manuscripts, Mother took notes, principally expressions that Jay and I made, anecdotes, and stories that she heard. All these notations she intended to weave into her own stories later. A single illustration of her notes:

RIDDLE FOR JUVENILE: When are pajamas scared? When they are 'fraid' (frayed).
Mother says it to Si, and he is baffled, then tells Jay that his pajamas are scared, and Mother overhears Jay say, "That is a riddle."

She compiled ideas, short stories, dialect and non-dialect narratives, and poems. As earlier noticed, she credited her father with many of the stories. She was prolific in her writing during our youth. She seemed to leap at every opportunity to spin a yarn, which she intended to incorporate into her writing later. Additionally, the notebook was used like a diary, where she took notes on daily events. One such story follows:

> Halloween party. Bought masks and fixed costumes. "Bad fairies" turn over lawn furniture. Mommie explains that it is just the bad boys playing pranks. So Si and Don and John bust the pumpkins and put them on Nancy's porch and put dirt in her well. Playing pranks. Si comes home and tells Mommie and she made him stay in his own yard for a week.

SUMMA TIME is one of Mother's short stories in which she writes of several events in the lives of her children. The children's stories are biographical and begin with a birthday party for Jay in Eupora on his sixth birthday. Subsequent chapters of the short story center around a visit to Grandfather's house in Ackerman, during the summer of 1945, a year and a half after the death of Grandmother Dobbs. The titles of the chapters sketch our adventures during 1945. The characters (CY being her pen name for me) and content of the 62- page manuscript are as follows:

S U M M A T I M E
A Story of the South
by
Mary Margaret McCaslin

CHARACTERS

JAY: who is SIX and has a little brother named CY.
CY: who is FOUR (nearly five) and has a big brother named JAY.
JIGGS: who is a black Cocker Spaniel – and NOISY.
MRS. CHICKEN: who is a big fat hen whom you cannot trust.
MOMMIE: who is mommie.
CAROLINE, KAY, AND ROB: children on The Street.
TOBY: from MATLANTA.
GRANDADDY: who is MR. ADAMS, and MISTUH ESTEL –
    but mostly GRANDADDY.
SAM: who is Bandy-legged and Good.
ROCK: a hound dog.

CONTENTS

Mother took a correspondence course in 1946 on short story writing from The University of Chicago, for which she got college credit. We have sundry correspondence between her and an official of the university.

An example of her correspondence with publishing houses is the series of letters from the Bentel Agency, in Hollywood, California, the letters dated from August to November 1946. Illustrative is a followup reply, dated September 6, 1946, from *The American Field Publishing Co.*, Chicago, Ill., which confirms the ongoing plan for future publication:

> Miss Fortune Dobbs
> Eupora
> Mississippi
> Dear Miss Dobbs,
>
> I wish I could give you a definite date for the issue in which your story *BALDY* will appear, but it's still some time in the future. I am hoping, however, that it will not be too long before we can let our readers enjoy *BALDY*.

We noticed but still haven't read your *ALBERT'S SHOOTIN EYE.*

Any time that you have a story you think suited to the *AMERICAN FIELD*, we shall welcome the opportunity to give you a prompt report on it.

Most sincerely yours,
W. F. Brown
Editor

Dr. Benjamin Spock (1903-1998) published *The Common Book of Baby and Child Care* in 1946. Spock's controversial work quickly became a bestseller.[33]

During summer months or on weekends, we often walked everywhere, unless it was more expedient to ride our bicycles. But we were not allowed to have our bikes at school. During our early school years, we walked to school every day, both ways, but uphill only going to school. We walked, rain or shine, and through snow and sleet. Actually it was only about the distance of four city blocks. We merely crossed Adams Avenue, took the sidewalk between Marshall Coleman's house and Harriett Embry's house, which led down a long inclining side-walk, ending at the steps leading up to the elevated railroad tracks, then down the steps on the other side. Next, on the way up the hill on the right, at the corner of U.S. Highway 82, was Mickey Ross' house.[34] Mickey's father was Tom Ross, owner of the Chrysler, Dodge, and Plymouth dealership; Tom's brother, Herman Ross,

---

[33] It sold more than thirty million copies in the first three decades, and it changed the way American parents reared their babies, promoting advice garnered from his ten years of pediatric practice and psychoanalytic training. Among his extremist recommendations: permission to use pacifiers and to maintain flexible feeding schedules, which were radical ideas in that day. Those actions led to permissiveness by the parent that resulted in undisciplined behavior. His popularity led him into teaching and to political activism, and his influence contributed to the social and moral transition that took place in the 1960s. Two generations were reared under the authority of Spock's liberal doctrine. Prior to his death in 1998 at age ninety-four, in an interview on network television, he grievously confessed that he had erred in his liberal thinking, expressing remorse for the harm engendered upon children for fifty years.

[34] As a bedtime story, in the late 1970s I would tell this to my younger daughter, Nancy. She loved hearing it over and over again. One time I slipped in saying: "up the hill past Mickey Mouse's house...." Nancy interrupted me immediately to say: "Oh Daddy, Mickey Mouse did not live near you."

owned the Ford dealership in Eupora (Tom and Herman were friends of my parents). After crossing U.S. Highway 82 (one of the four traffic lights in Eupora), we continued on up the hill on N. Joliff Street past Mr. and Mrs. Love's house; she was my second grade teacher. Occasionally after school, Mr. Love would be sitting on his front steps. He had a few tricks, the most magical of which was pulling a nickel out of my ear, which he then would give me to keep. We crossed the last intersection and arrived at the school grounds with the basketball gym the first building on the left (where later we saw in 1948, free of charge, the Harlem Globetrotters practice), and finally arriving at the grammar school building. Parked on the curb was a long line of yellow buses, on which the children from the country were transported to school. Ours was a consolidated county school; children were bused many miles from their parents' home place out in the county to attend school. After school, the buses again were lined up to convey the children home.

The Nuremberg Trials began in November 1945. They were a series of military tribunals conducted by Allied Forces in Nuremberg, Germany, following World War II regarding the prosecution mainly of political and military officials of Nazi Germany. The trials ended October 1, 1946. This was complicated stuff that our parents talked about.

Mother saved some of my report cards (the report cards that I have are for third, fourth, fifth, sixth, seventh, and twelfth grades. Why she did not save all of them I do not know). My teacher for first grade (1946-1947) was Mrs. Mary McLemore.

We have several letters written to "Mary Margaret and Mac McCaslin" from Dr. Carey Cranfield Dobbs, who was both the first cousin of Mother's father and the first cousin of Mother's mother. Carey Cranfield Dobbs held the PhD. and earlier had been a professor of science at Delta State College. He both recognized and praised Mother's gifts of communication and composition. In 1947, the time of the letter below, Carey Dobbs was a college professor in Philadelphia, Pennsylvania. A bachelor for many years, he traveled extensively during periods that were available in his college teaching schedule, especially in the summer months; pursuing genealogy. Working with Aunt Arlin, he compiled important genealogy records of the Mississippi Dobbs. In his letters, he reminded Mother of the extensive notes that he had compiled, and a draft of a family history that he had completed, and in the particular letter that follows, he appealed to her passion and skill of journalism (the subject matter gives perspective to his high regard of Mother's scholarship in writing, a journalistic gift):

> October 10, 1947....I wonder just how serious you were when you said you would help me get the family notes in order. I promised to make the first draft as you very well recall. To my surprise, I have received my package of notes from Arlin and I hope by the last of next week to have all of my notes in shape and I shall be ready to send them down to you for your final corrections, getting them ready for the publishers. I took the liberty of asking Arlin if she would offer any criticisms or any more material to this that I am getting in line. In other words, I would like to send the material first for Arlin's criticisms, corrections, and additions, and then have her send it all over for your final getting together...(Arlin was Carey's cousin and Mother's aunt).
>
> October 23, 1947....Now about the publication of the family tree. This is a detail to which I have not given a great deal of thought. As I told you, I have about worn myself and several boxes out lugging notes around and it was my idea to write up all of these notes and get them ready for publication or distribution in some manner for anyone who is interested in them. I am also enclosing a letter from Arlin that will give you her views. I am also enclosing a sketch on Uncle Silas and this isn't as good as I would like. I would appreciate it if you would take the time to write this information up in better shape, filling in more details....If you will go with me insofar as criticizing the rough draft that I shall send you as to sentence structure, good expression, and English, I shall take it from there. It may cost $500 to have it published in book form...but if I should make a contribution to this generation and the generations to come, life will not have been in vain...I have a very efficient secretary and we have gotten together a large part of the manuscript and I would be pleased to send this down if you will take the time to read it, criticize and get it in shape that we can make the final copy for the publishers...
>
> Arlin has been a source of inspiration for many things in my life. I would have never gotten into this genealogical game had it not been for her....
>
> I do not recall Judge Eudy, but I do think he has good sense if he passes out compliments to you. I would have liked

to have been around to come forth with a loud, "Amen!" to any nice or complimentary thing that is said of you, Mac, or the children. I think you are tops. I have always appreciated you more than I have been able to express in words or deeds. There is just something fine about you both that is indescribable and inexpressible. I guess it is all because I think so much of each of you. One thing more, and that is that you have lovely children....

October 27, 1947...If you are ready to start your criticism of the first draft, I shall be very pleased to mail some material down to you...

November 1, 1947. I assure you that I greatly appreciate your interest and your standing by and helping me see this ancestor business out to the end...I am sending you a letter that I have just received from Northern Ireland. Nothing of interest except that I am trying to establish the Dobbs line on the other side....

Carey accepted the chair in science at the University of Havana, but died suddenly, shortly before he was to depart for Cuba. In Mother's 1971 seminal work, *DOBBS FAMILY HISTORY*, she gave posthumous credit to Carey for his contribution to the Dobbs genealogy.

C. S. Lewis (a Christian writer Jay and I would later come to greatly admire) made the cover of the September 8, 1947, issue of "TIME." with the legend: "His heresy: Christianity. (*Religion*)" in which he is treated in a lengthy essay that runs over several pages. *TIME* places Lewis among those "heretical" modern intellectuals like Eliot and Auden, who espouse a traditional Christian faith. The essay covers his personal history, place in Oxford, his fame, as well as his well-known writings like the *Screwtape Letters, Narnia*, etc.. The cover portrait by Boris Artzybasheff is brilliant and bold (Jay and I both acquired original copies of this 1947 magazine in 2004).

My cousin, Spurgeon Adams Moss, was born in December of 1947. Jay and I enjoyed frequent visits in Ackerman. We kind of "grew up" with Spurgeon. He and his parents, Sara Margaret and Fenley, occasionally came to Eupora.

Daddy would stop by Embry Drug Company every morning for a visit. While there, he usually would purchase a few packages of *Wrigley's* chewing gum and a *Tampa Nugget* cigar. That was the limit of his smoking - only one cigar a day. And, he generally smoked the cigar during the morning.

Cuban cigars were the best, bar none. Often, Daddy would acquire a few Cuban cigars, usually from T. F. Taylor, Jr., and he relished the luxury.

During 1947, Chuck Yeager broke the sound barrier; the Dead Sea Scrolls were discovered; and Polaroid cameras were invented.

In 1948, everyone owned a home ice cream freezer. Ours was wooden, with the mechanism that clamped tightly across the top, the gears engaging the tall steel drum inside. When the handle was turned, the drum spun in the ice/salt mixture, which lowered the temperature, and the cream slowly chilled to transform into ice cream. It was the responsibility of Jay and me to freeze the ice cream. Jay would turn the handle until his arm hurt, and then I would take over. Although younger, I seemed to work harder and longer in this task than big brother. Daddy dubbed me, "Sibo Caesar, Ice Cream Freezer." That nickname hung on for several years.

Daddy's enthusiasm and love for swimming and diving led him to join T. F. and many other citizens in the purchase of municipal bonds dated December 1948 in support of the construction of the Eupora Municipal Swimming Pool, complete with an office and dressing rooms. (We have the original bonds, held by the Bank of Eupora). The pool was located across the street from our school. Although small, the pool boasted a diving board. We swam there daily in the summer months.

On a number of occasions, just after daybreak – before Daddy went to work – he would take me to Love's Lake. This lake was on the two to three acre farm of Mr. Love, outside of Eupora. The Loves were the parents of Mr. Love, whose wife was our second grade teacher. In the middle of the lake was a platform with both a low and a high diving board. There I learned to imitate Daddy's diving style, and I honed this skill on the low diving board at the City pool. "Practice makes perfect." And, in practicing various dives, one often goes awry and the occasional, hard, and accidental slapping of one of my ears against the water took an early toll on my hearing. Frequent visits to Grenada and Greenwood afforded Jay and me the opportunity of swimming in much larger municipal pools, which had high diving boards.

All of us boys were good at throwing rocks, and we threw rocks because it was fun and it was a way to develop precision. We never intended to hurt anybody, but we were serious about improving our accuracy. There were some bullies who would throw rocks at you with a malicious intent. Fortunately, one had time to observe the flight of the rock, and could easily step aside. A bully who lived diagonally across Adams Avenue failed to pay attention to the trajectory of a rock one of us threw back, after he had tried to pelt us with rocks from his driveway. The small rock fractured his upper central incisor – the resulting appearance of which was quite common in those days for boys.

Once we acquired small boxes and cut holes through them for our arms and head. We then hinged a smaller box to the top, over the head hole, and cut small openings, through which to see. The box came down below the knees. The only parts of the body left unprotected were your lower legs, and your arms. With this quasi-"suit of armor," we were like gladiators, and we would fight each other with wooden swords, jousting around in fun. Soon, we decided that we could have a rock fight, with this protection. It worked. We tried not to hurl a rock at one's feet or arms.

We depended upon our B.B. guns – the *Red Rider Rifle*. The name was routed into the wooden stock, below which name was the carving of a mounted cowboy (*Red Rider*) in full stride, twirling a rope overhead. We were very accurate with that popular child's rifle. All of the boys that I knew had one. We learned to gauge the trajectory of the B.B., and would raise the barrel appropriately, to compensate for the fall of the projectile, which adjustment of the aim to the tip of the barrel was probably about six or eight inches in height at sixty feet distance from the target. There was absolutely no harm seen with using the *Red Rider Rifle* in one's yard. The B.B. would not even shatter a windowpane, unless shot from a close distance. But it could leave a ding. We never owned a pump pellet gun. Parents regarded them as dangerous, just as they did a 22 rifle. (While on the last of three family trips made in consecutive summers with Suzanne's mother, Mother, and Gene, while in Kentucky in 1979, I acquired an original *Red Rider Rifle*, in very good condition. I still have it, and occasionally utilize it to irritate pesky squirrels in our yard that dig in our flower pots and beds, burying their nuts, which activity engenders memories of childhood).

We would wile away the hours carrying our *Red Rider Rifles* around the neighborhood, and to the adjacent woodlands. Many were the hours that we spent playing Cowboys and Indians or Army. We also hunted squirrels and rabbits, but they were virtually impossible to kill with a B.B. gun. Our weapon inflicted very little pain to those animals, and usually they were only annoyed or scared by our assault.

Our favorite game was the Blue Jay – they were mean birds. We regarded them as a nuisance. When Jiggs would catch a Blue Jay, many others would gather to the call of distress. The Blue Jays, sometimes as many as twenty in number, would dive from about thirty feet at Jiggs like Japanese fighter planes, shrieking loudly as they attacked. Jiggs would be crouched, with his prey between his front paws, and he would follow the flight pattern of the birds with his head as they swooped down within inches of his nose. I wondered what Jiggs was thinking.

Sparrows were so plentiful that they were regarded by us as expendable. They were our dominant prey, and being smaller, they were more challenging targets. But, we would think twice before shooting Red Birds or Robins. They were colorful songbirds. Red-headed Woodpeckers: now they were interesting and generally seen only very high up, pecking away at a rotten tree trunk. They were a challenging target. Crows were large birds, and difficult to fell. On a couple of occasions, I even brought down a bird in flight; as I recall, once it was a Dove, and the other time, a Black Bird. To accomplish such, you had to judge the trajectory of the falling B.B., as well as estimate the lead time in front of the flying bird. Accomplishing this was no small thing.

Our parents were not concerned about this activity. Almost all of the older boys hunted with shotguns and rifles. It was just understood that younger boys engaged in target practice and hunted with B.B. guns. However, there were limits, one being that we not damage private property. One time I was out behind the house, shooting my B.B. gun at some target, perhaps a sparrow. It was dusk, and, next door, Elks Taylor switched on his floodlight on the back of his house. I was at least ninety to one hundred feet away, as I took aim at the light bulb. I raised the barrel the needed six to seven inches to compensate for the trajectory and squeezed off the trigger. A split second later, the shattered fragments of the light bulb rained down in the disappearing glow of the light filament. Suddenly, my heart raced, and I suspected that my face flushed in fear or embarrassment. I experienced the sense of both surprise and guilt. Stunned, I went in the door to our back porch, propped the gun up, and walked into the kitchen, unaware that Daddy had been looking out of the kitchen window precisely as this act had occurred. He turned to me with a firm facial expression and said, "Don't you have an apology to make to Elks Taylor?" I replied, "Yes sir." Straightway, I went next door and made amends. Mr. Taylor thanked me for my honesty and forgave me, on the spot. Daddy was satisfied with my explanation upon my return.

Robert Wayne Miller, as well as Rob and Charles Sugg, had electric trains. Brother John Sugg was much younger. They had the extra room in their homes, whereas we did not, and a lawyer and Western Auto store owner had the wherewithal to provide a Lionel train set. Kim Curry's Lionel train layout was as elaborate as they came. Therefore, Jay and I had the benefit of growing up playing with trains, without the accompanying cost to our parents. Hours of time were consumed, as though they were but minutes, as we would rearrange the tracks, change the sequence of the box cars, and engineer these toy trains around the complex track systems. One time John Sugg, the baby brother, came into the room while the train was racing around the track. Smoke was coming out of the smokestack. John ran for a cup of water. Returning to the train, he poured the water on the locomotive, thinking that it was on fire. In reality, the smoke was generated purposefully, a tablet having placed a tablet in a compartment of the locomotive. It was a special effect that was seldom used, but available. No permanent water damage resulted to the locomotive, but it did cause quite a mess.

Due to damage to the concrete sidewalk from the growth of roots of the trees, it became necessary for the city to replace several sections. Only minutes after the workers left, we came out of hiding and gathered around to press our hand prints into the cool cement, and to carve our names (some 40 years later, I detoured through Eupora on our way to New Orleans from a McCaslin family reunion at J. P. Coleman State Park. I showed the section of concrete sidewalk to my two young daughters, and they each placed their little hands in the prints that I had left as a child).

As earlier mentioned, the Eupora Presbyterian Church, at one time, had been a beautiful structure, prominent in the church history of Eupora. But all that remained was the decaying building, still beautiful in its marble architecture, but overrun by vines and small Oak, Mimosa, and Chinaberry trees. The church was situated behind the post office. I don't know what happened to the church. Daddy had come from a long line of Presbyterians, and Mother's parents and ancestors had always been Baptists.

We were members of the Eupora Methodist Church. This was T. F. Taylor, Jr.'s church and his father's before him. Daddy must have chosen the Methodist church out of business considerations. I suppose most of the very prominent families in Eupora were Methodists; it was the church to belong to, socially speaking. Jay and I were baptized in the Eupora Methodist Church, and we attended every week. Mother taught the Morris

Bible Class for eight years. Our Sunday school lessons were accompanied by the colorful handouts featuring Bible characters that all of the children received each week. Mother, with difficulty, had to manage keeping Jay and me still during the services from her perch in the choir loft located behind the pulpit. This feat she accomplished by eye contact and subtle facial gestures.

Mother always had daily devotionals with us, if not at the breakfast table, then in the living room before we left for school. She counseled us daily in the Christian walk, emphasizing the importance of memorization of Scripture verses, prayer, and the value of daily Bible reading. From my earliest memories, we were brought up "in the nurture and admonition of the Lord." (*Eph. 6:4*).

Although reared at the knee of a Christian mother, it was not until eight years of age that I became a believing Christian. Mother had taken Jay and me to a tent meeting revival in Macon, Mississippi, to hear a heralded evangelist. Macon was fifteen miles from Eupora. The message of the evangelist brought to me the clear realization that I was a sinner, that Christ was the Son of God, and that He had died for my sins. I rose from my folding chair, walked down the sawdust aisle at that tent meeting, and confessed Christ as my Savior. My Christian conversion was a miracle. (This experience had a profound effect on my life thereafter. Then everything that I heard in church became more meaningful. Also, beginning then, more so than ever before, I became a person of prayer).

Usually on Sunday morning, Daddy headed for Grenada to play golf. In his absence, soon thereafter, Mother, Jay, and I joined the Baptist congregation, where the preaching was better and fellowship more meaningful and sincere. As noticed earlier, Mother's family had always been Baptist. We all three were very active members. The Eupora Baptist Church occupied the first block from N. Dunn Street, behind the Eupora Theater, and it was directly across the street from the shell which remained of the Presbyterian Church. The Methodist Church was in the next block, at the top of the hill, on the same side of the street as the Baptist Church. The Baptists had only recently built a new building. The peak of the roof of the sanctuary was surpassed in height by no other building in town. Atop the peak were three speakers splayed, over which system church bells were sounded on Sunday and were heard all over town. During Christmas season, Christmas carols were played over the speakers, and on one occasion, I was enlisted to sing a Christmas carol to the whole town!

Although I had been baptized earlier on joining the Methodist Church, I was baptized a Baptist. Baptists do not recognize baptism of other denominations. The immersion took place in the baptismal pool immediately behind and over the choir loft. Jay and I had to wear "old clothes" to church that Sunday night, rather than something that would need to be dry cleaned.

We never missed Sunday school, morning church, or evening church. We returned on Wednesday night each week for Prayer Meeting.[35] I believe that Jay and I were good kids; to reiterate, we were brought up in the nurture of the Lord at the knee of a strongly-professing Christian mother.

Life in a small town is an exceptional experience (I later was convinced that kids who grew up in urban or suburban areas were denied a certain connection with nature that kids, especially boys, from small towns simply took for granted). We could walk out of the front door of our house and be on the edge of town in the woods in ten minutes – on foot. If we ran, five minutes. We could go anywhere and do almost anything – anything that we regarded as permissible – and our parents never worried about our safety. We would be gone for hours on end, without any concern by Mother. Of course, upon our return, she would always ask where we had been. In the winter, darkness summoned our need to go home. In the summer months, we judged it to be time to go home by the level of the sun.

Those were the days when no one ever locked the front door of their house or the doors of their car. One would think nothing of leaving the keys in the ignition of the car, with all of the windows down. Valuables left visible in a car were perfectly safe. Only banks had burglar alarms. I cannot recall the occurrence of any crime in Eupora whatsoever.

Everyone in our small, deep South town seemed to have essential Christian morals, and they simply followed the Ten Commandments. There was no theft, no public sign of addiction to alcohol, no murder. To my knowledge, Eupora was crime free. Jay and I knew of no one that was divorced. There were two cases that Mother and others had whispered

---

[35] Children of most Baptist families attended church weekly, the same as in earlier generations. Suzanne and I followed the same pattern with our children. In a July 2001 Newsletter, Dr. James Dobson quoted research that stated:...if a child hasn't been introduced to Jesus Christ by the time he or she is 14, there is only a 4 percent chance that such conversion will happen between ages 14 and 18, and a 6 percent chance that it will occur in the remainder of life.

about, but we as kids knew nothing more – we were sheltered from this subject.

We did know of an illegitimate boy who lived with his mother. Everyone knew who the father was. That boy would come around frequently for financial handouts from his white father, a prominent family man in our neighborhood. The boy also was viewed as a "dope addict," and the source of the cost for his prescription drugs was assumed to be provided by the father.

Moreover, no one knew of any couple that was living together out of wedlock. Not in the small town of Eupora! If anything of that nature was occurring, our parents were successful in totally shielding it from us children; from any hint of it whatsoever. Moreover, such lifestyle would render shame from any community.

Blue Laws pertained to resting from the six-day work week on Sunday – the Lord's Day – and people strictly conformed with them.[36] All businesses were closed in Eupora on Sunday, except The Embry Drug Company and the Eupora Drug Store. Although open, only the light from the pharmacy in the rear of the store shone through the front window; the pharmacist always available to fill prescriptions to assuage the pain of injury or infection of an emergency by providing the necessary medical supplies. Mr. Embry was the father of Harriet and Shorty and younger sister, Emmy.

In the late 1940s, the Embrys were among the earliest of Eupora families to have a television set. Lavinia and T. F. Taylor had the first television in their three-story home (as mentioned earlier, a fine, Tudor-style brick home built by T. F. Taylor, Sr., that until this day is still the most stately of any home in town). Jay and I watched the inauguration of five-star General Dwight D. Eisenhower as President on January 23, 1953. Jay, Foy, and I were in the downstairs family room while our parents watched the same event on a television set in the library on the main floor of the Taylor home.

---

[36] Blue Laws were statutes regulating personal and public conduct, particularly on the Sabbath. Such was the designation because the Blue Laws (which originated in Virginia in 1624) reputedly were printed on blue paper in the colony of New Haven (1638-65). All of the Puritan colonies of New England enforced strict observance of the Sabbath. Moreover, in some colonies, expenditures on clothing and personal adornment also were limited by statute. After the American Revolution, blue laws generally fell into abeyance or were repealed, but many such statutes remained on the books, particularly in small communities. In the 1960s, observance of Blue Laws was gradually abandoned.

T. F. and Lavinia earlier had lived in a single-story brick home next door; and it was their garage apartment in which Mother and Daddy lived and from which they were driven during the night by the fire. In the mid-1940s, upon the death of T. F. Taylor, Jr.'s mother, Lavinia and T. F. Jr. moved next door to the big house.

Poker Man's Palace was unique to our town. It was located in the deep woods just beyond the rhomboidal city block that we lived on. It was a complex of gullies as deep as six to seven feet in the red clay, meandering around among the tall pines. Hardly a month would pass that we were not there at least two or three times. Outfitted with our authentic U. S. Army green drab equipment, that our parents had allowed us to purchase at the local Army and Navy Store, we roamed the woods with our *Red Rider Rifles*, looking for prey, be they birds, squirrels, snakes, or rabbits. We were quite knowledgeable about snakes, and no one ever was bitten, that I knew of. Frequently we captured those of the harmless species such as the garter snake the brown snake, or the black ratsnake. Yet we knew well to maintain a safe distance from the Eastern Coral Snake, the Copperhead, or the Diamondback and Timber Rattlesnakes. The latter, poisonous ones we mortally wounded in the head by pelting them with the needed number of shots from our Red Ryder B.B. guns. Girls never went with us to Poker Man's Palace.

In the red clay gullies of Poker Man's Palace we occasionally found Indian arrowheads. Tomahawk heads were rare, but fragments of clay pottery quite common. We would dig thoroughly in an area, if the findings were promising. Fundamentally necessary for each of us was the World War II Army shovel that we carried on these foraging trips. The handle was about twenty inches in length and the blade folded back on the handle, but by twisting the locking ring it could be adjusted to a forty-five degree angle to act as a hoe, or extended out as a shovel. These shovels were an absolute necessity for camping and for our outings at Poker Man's Palace. The WW II Army drab canvas ammunition belt had numerous small pockets with a cover that snapped into place, and it was handy for storing our caches. To the belt we attached our U.S. Army Canteen (filled with water) enveloped with the heavy, Army drab canvas cover, the authentic Army bayonet, and the folded shovel.

Often one of our classmates, while in grammar school, would come to school with one or more arrowheads in his pocket, which he had found on his own home place in the county. Jay and I would arrange to buy the arrowheads; after all, we were city boys (in the town of thirteen hundred). Mother would give us money to pay for them the next day. The price asked for a nice arrowhead would be a dime, or fifteen cents. Our collection is entirely from Mississippi Indian mounds, and probably Choctaw or Chickasaw in origin.

One of Daddy's friends, Ovid Senate, lived with his family in a fine, old turn-of-the century frame house a few miles out on Highway 9, on the way to Belfountain. We visited at the Senates' home on occasion. His were the *first* pair of binoculars that I ever used! On his farm, directly across the highway from his house, rose an immense Indian mound from the middle of the field. Jay and I dug in that mound at every opportunity, and many of our arrowheads were found there.[37] [38] Choctaw Indian mounds were common in Northern Mississippi. The mounds that one could see from the highways probably accounted for only a fraction of others that were out of view.

---

[37] For many years, it has been a Federal crime to dig in Indian mounds – a serious offence, like killing an American Eagle today. In my childhood, there was absolutely no concern, if one had the permission of the land owner.

[38] My nephew mentioned in May 2001 of recently finding an arrowhead while hunting. I told him of our collection and he was very interested. He had never known that his father and I had any, and he asked if he could have them to begin a collection. Brother Jay and I quickly concurred (arrowheads not being something in which my two daughters would have interest).

Chapter Six

OUR PRANKISH YOUTH

On the way to Poker Man's Palace, we walked past the city water tank. It stood on Eupora's highest hill on the edge of town, two-hundred feet from the rhomboid block, on the other side of which block we lived. Actually, the water tank was less than a thousand yards from our house. Town Sheriff Snyder's home was on the back side of our block, and the rear of his house faced the water tank. At the foot of the water tank was a shanty where a kind, poor family lived, often occupying themselves with work in their garden. Jay and I, with several of our friends, ventured past the water tank one day, as we had done scores of times. On a double-dog-dare by a friend, I determined to climb the water tank. The ladder extended up one of the legs of the tank, and the ladder was open and completely without protection. Jay followed a few feet behind me. As we ascended, barefoot, the town spread out in a panoramic view. We soon could see the roof of our house, and then, as we climbed further, we could view the entire countryside. It was only by the grace of God that neither of us fell. When we reached the underside belly of the tank, we circled around the platform (which did have a guard rail) that encircled the base of the water tank. We stared into the distance with awe. Below, the family members tending to their garden below, were reproaching us, telling us to come down before we fell, and continually calling for us to "be careful." Therewith, the family more vociferously called to us to climb down slowly. We were so engaged in this thrilling experience that we did not realize that ten or fifteen minutes had elapsed. Mrs. Snyder had seen us from the kitchen window of her home and called Mother on the telephone. Suddenly, there was Mother, standing alongside the family below, demanding that we climb down, cautioning us

109

to use great care. Later, Mother told of the telephone call from Mrs. Snyder, which went like this: "Mrs. McCaslin, Si, and I think Jay, have climbed the water tank, and they are running around up there. But don't worry, as hard-headed and tough as Si is, it won't hurt him if he falls." The punishment that followed for this mischievous (and illegal) deed was an unprecedented whipping, followed by isolation from my friends for several days. I never even dreamed of doing that again.

Sports in the neighborhood were always engaging. The Embrys lived literally a stone's throw from our house. Harriett and Shorty Embry lived directly across the street from their cousin, Iantha Embry. Adjacent to Iantha's house was a vacant lot large enough to accommodate a house. It was there that we played baseball. Boys and girls joined in the game. However, only the boys would play tackle football, usually in season on the same vacant lot. Occasionally, someone sustained a broken arm from the football game. It was rough.

The radio usually was playing at home or in the car. Mother, Jay, and I loved the gospel songs. Among the most prominent were the Blackwood Brothers. The quartet had formed in 1934 in Choctaw County and they were in their prime ten years later, after having been so prominent, singing live on the radio. Mother learned that they were coming to a church in Eupora and told Jay and me. We all were excited about hearing them in person. We went to a small, wood-frame church on the edge of town that night. The place was packed, with people even standing up in back and some in the side aisles. The three of us were the only white faces in the crowd. That made no difference. We recognized many of the folks. In our small town, we often played all over the neighborhood, and we knew many of these kind people. The singing continued for over an hour. Afterwards, many of the members talked with us and thanked us for coming.

I broke my arm under unusual circumstances. We had heard from a reliable source – as usual, an older friend – that one could climb to the top of a tall tree, grasp the small trunk with both hands, and leap outward. The tree was supposed to bend over and gently sway downward, lowering the sportsman to the ground. In a field adjacent to the sidewalk leading to school, we searched for an appropriate, tall tree. It had been raining earlier, so our quest took us trudging through the mud in the field. There we found the ideal tree, with a girth at waist level of about six inches. I was first. I scaled up the tree like a primate. Reaching near the top, some twenty feet above the ground, I grasped the tree with both hands, then leaped outward, trying to make the tree trunk below bend outward and downward – just as we had heard that it was supposed to do. The tree was too stiff, or I was too light in weight. A wise friend on the ground suggested that we get an ax and cut through part of the trunk, which sounded like the solution. He was off in a run, returning in a mere five minutes or so with a rusty old ax. Jay and friends took turns chopping through the six-inch trunk below. I waited, excited about this new adventure. The tree trunk simply did not bend under my weight, as anticipated. They continued to hack at the trunk with the ax. On the final blow, the trunk shifted off of the stump and dropped three feet straight down into the mud. With that violent downward thrust, the small limbs on which I was standing broke away, and I hung perilously with my hands, as the tree began to fall forward. I was met very quickly by the ground, and I had extended my left hand to break the fall. Immediately my lower arm felt strange. Numb. When I lifted it slowly out of the mud, it was apparent that my left wrist was no longer straight. Rather, my hand was at a right angle to my arm. Again, by the grace of God, I had not permanently injured myself.

As I walked the four or five hundred feet home, I was scared more about what Mother would say or do than I was of the severity of the injury. Jay's assessment of my trouble was not reassuring – reaffirming in his words that the trouble was not being the broken arm, but the eminent untoward reaction expected from Mother. We arrived home, she asked how it happened, and with my reply, she replied: "You what?" I needed to say nothing more. She just cried. She continued to cry as she loaded me into the car and took me to the Curry Clinic, articulating her fear that I had sustained life-long damage to my wrist. There, Dr. Curry x-rayed my wrist, set the two bones while I sat there and observed (traumatic injury is accompanied by physiological anesthesia). He then fashioned a cast by wrapping gauze, soaked in damp plaster of Paris slurry, over cotton batting, as I looked on. The plaster began to set, giving off mild heat to my left arm from my finger tips extending all the way up to my upperarm. He gave me one of the post-operative x-rays to keep (which I saved for many years). My arm healed in about six weeks! Then it required at least another two weeks for the dry, scaly and peeling skin to be replenished by healthy skin.

We seldom got into any trouble with Mrs. Wall, even when rainy weather necessitated our playing on the porch, which play generated loud noises and clutter. There was an injury that occurred when I was nine years of age. Jay and I each had a small steel fishing tackle box in which we kept various essential things valued by a young boy – of course fishing gear, a pocket knife, pieces of wood to carve, etc. The boxes were open beside us, as we played on the floor of the porch. Jay somehow had angered me (oh so common with a brother). I stood up, grabbed a folded canvas director's chair, and jokingly held it over my head, as though I were going to whack him. Jay looked up, knowing that I was teasing, but then yelled, "Spider!" I looked up, and there was a huge spider crawling down the chair toward my hand. I jumped backward in horror, slinging the folded chair aside, and my bare, right foot came down on the edge of the fishing tackle box. Pain shot through me. I had cut my foot badly, literally fileting the skin off the side of my big toe, and cutting deeply into the ball of my foot. Blood gushed. Mother heard my scream. She cried, then it was off to the doctor's office, again. An hour or so later, and following about ten stitches and a large gauze bandage, I was back on the porch playing with the others again, as though nothing had happened.

We always had golf balls for play at home. Daddy gave us his used or damaged ones, and we had found many others at the Grenada Golf Club in the rough, just off the fairways of the golf course. Sometimes we even waded out into the shallow lake traps and found dozens of golf balls, many of which were like new. Daddy had purchased a new set of golf clubs, and we had his old set. We often would practice our driving from the back yard, hitting out into the large field behind our house. On this particular day, Jay and I took a number of old balls and a couple of clubs and went over into Lady Mary Taylor's yard next door. Our plan was to practice our driving. First, Jay lofted one or two shots across our yard, the street, and into the huge yard behind the Embrys' house, where we played baseball and football. I was anxious to have my turn with the golf club. I lined up to hit the ball, knowing that Jay was standing behind me but certainly not knowing how close he stood. On my back-swing, my club head met with an obstruction. It was Jay's head. I hit him hard. I was at first irritated that he messed up my shot, but as I saw blood pouring down his forehead and eyebrow, I was terrified. He was bleeding profusely from the scalp, just inside the hairline. He started crying and ran across the yard, into the house, still crying loudly. Less than a minute later, Mother and Jay appeared and came down the front steps. She was holding a blood-soaked towel against his head wound. I was really frightened – even though it was an accident. I had hurt my brother, and I hurt for him! Mother was not crying this time; she was mad. As she walked toward me and reached the car, I stood, frozen, by the pile of golf balls, still with the weapon in my hand. Mother cut her eyes toward me, then pointed directly at me and said, "I'm taking Jay to the doctor's office for stitches. I will deal with you later." (Jay jokingly derided me all of his life, saying that I hit him on purpose. He had a scar from the laceration, but it was in his scalp, just inside the hairline. Had he not teased me among friends, one would never have known of the mark left).

Creeks. Surely, God created creeks as an environment intended for the enjoyment of little boys. We would spend endless hours in the creek bed, searching for snakes, turtles, tadpoles, frogs, or crayfish (crawdads). I don't ever remember any girls having any interest in creek beds. However, they were curious to see our cache, but easily scared if we jokingly thrust one of the captured creatures in our hand toward them. Kids five or more years older than we were used to swim in the creek, at a turn where it deepened. There was a rope permanently suspended from a large tree limb above, with which they used to swing out and drop into the deep water.

By 1948 when Jay and I had reached that age and had learned to swim, Eupora had built a small, fine municipal pool with accompanying dressing rooms across from the school. There Daddy taught me how to dive – first the swan, then the jackknife, then those with a half or full twist, and later cutaway back dives and flips. I never had a formal lesson but became a good diver merely by improving what Daddy had taught me. I landed on my side so many times that I developed impaired hearing, strangely the lower range in one ear and the high range in the other. I could hear everything, but not keenly.

We discovered that redeeming coat hangers at the local dry cleaners could be financially rewarding. Jay and I would go door-to-door, asking folks all over town if they had any coat hangers that we could have. Generally they were happy to oblige, for it relieved crowding in their closet space. When we had collected enough to fill our bicycle baskets, we would dead head to the dry cleaners with hundreds, for which we were paid a penny each (now with inflation, a penny then was worth precisely ten times as much today). We would come away with several dollars of easily-made money. We also occasionally would look for discarded *Coca-Cola* bottles, which also could be redeemed for a penny each, but the bottles were neither as plentiful nor as easy to handle as the coat hangers. At home, we would proudly hand over our gain to Mother, who would place it in her top bureau drawer in a cup until she needed to make another trip to the bank; and there she would deposit it to our savings account.

Saturday afternoon at the "picture show" was the norm in the late1940s. There was usually a double feature for the price of one. The Saturday features were always cowboys and Indians or Westerns, starring Roy Rogers and his wife, Dale Evans, or Gene Autry (both of whom were singing cowboys. Gene Autry later was the owner of the Los Angeles Angels Baseball team, and to this day, recordings of Gene Autry are heard on the radio throughout the Christmas season), Tex Ritter, Johnny Mack Brown, Hopalong Cassidy, and Lash Larue – the latter of whom was famous for his skill with a leather whip. The old westerns were essentially morally edifying. The good guys always wore white hats and the bad guys always wore black hats; and the good guys always prevailed. The matinees on Saturday would begin at 1:00 p.m.

When we wished to catch the later, 5:00 features, we first would walk to the Williams' Chuck Wagon, about 4:30 p.m., one city block away from Eupora Theater. The Williams' Chuck Wagon was a trailer with a side window. It was owned by Mr. and Mrs. Williams, and they lived in the trailer, too. There, for twenty-five cents one would buy a burger, and for ten cents an order of French fries, and for a nickel a Coca Cola, a complete meal for less than fifty cents. We would walk a little over a block to arrive well fed at the Eupora Theater, and the line would have already formed. The price for the movie was a dime. (At age twelve, the admission increased to fifteen cents. It was such a thrilling, prideful experience when, upon turning twelve years of age, you then got to pay the adult price of fifteen cents for the movie. A few years later, the admission went to twenty-five cents, which was regarded as outrageous). Popcorn was five cents, the price likewise for any one of the candies.

The featured "picture show," as it was called, almost always was preceded by a "serial," most often The Rocket Man, as well as a cartoon. And, always between the features the *MOVIE TONE NEWS*. Prior to television, the black and white *MOVIE TONE NEWS* was essentially the only mode by which one could see moving pictures, in black and white, of national and worldwide events. It was old news, two, maybe three weeks outdated, because once produced, it had to be distributed in a can to each movie theater. Yet, it served to keep one apprised of current events. Kids seldom read the newspaper, which our parents depended on for current information, along with the radio.

The movies during the week were generally directed to the adult audience, but many children went along with their parents. We did not find the movies during the week as easy to understand as the westerns, unless it was Tarzan, Lassie, or a science fiction, such as King Kong.

We boys always had a club of some sort. Often they were in name only, having to do with our play – Cowboys and Indians, Army, or Tarzan. We would dress for the occasion and as Tarzan, each of us would have two wash clothes pinned at the side, under which we wore our briefs. We built one tree house in a tree across the lane behind our house. We would gather there and talk, or whittle. We did a lot of whittling in our youth because we spent so much time in the trees. There is not much to do in a tree, other than talk, climb higher, or whittle. Many were the times that we carved our name or initials in the bark of a tree, while sitting fifteen or twenty feet above the ground. There, in the tree house, we formed a new club.

One day Jay climbed up into the tree house to join me, bringing his little kitten, which was only about six months old. Every kid knew that when a cat is dropped, it always quickly twists, rights itself, and lands on its feet. This truth was predicated on having been demonstrated many times. We decided to conduct an experiment with the kitty. Our tree house was about 18 or 20 feet from the ground. We wondered if the kitten would land on its feet. I took Jay's kitten, held it out arm's length, upside down, and released it. The kitten did indeed upright itself – three times, on the way down. However, it landed on its back. We had a rush of guilt when we observed that the kitty did not move. We believed that we had murdered the kitty. Quickly climbing down, we rushed to the side of the small animal. As Jay picked up his kitten he appeared lifeless. After a few seconds, the kitty began breathing, still stunned. The kitty had sustained the fall, without injury, merely knocking the breath out. Although relieved, we talked about how we could have killed him! We really had not thought of the harm, but only the experiment.

When the club was disbanded, the tree house fell into disrepair, and eventually fell apart, due to the expanding growth of the limbs of the tree on which the tree house had been constructed.

Our next plan for a club was a cave. We had never had a cave hideout before, and it seemed to be a perfectly good idea. But we needed a place where our club could meet secretly. This club would be unprecedented. We thought of the ideal location – behind Mrs. Wall's barn. Not only would no one see us excavating for the cave; it would be located clandestine, behind the barn. And underground. Taking shovels in hand, we began carefully removing the sod, with the weeds intact, setting the shovel loads aside. After several hours and much effort, we dug a big hole – about ten feet in diameter, and four feet deep. Adequate for our club members, namely Jay and me, Rob and Charles Sugg, Robert Miller, Buddy Reed, and Shorty Embry. We dug a tunnel of about three feet in width, beginning about six feet away under cover of a group of saplings. The tunnel opened into the side wall of the large area dug earlier. All of the dirt had been piled in a mound surrounding the wide hole. In Mrs. Wall's barn, we earlier had found several long boards two inches by six inches. These we hefted onto our shoulders, brought them out, and carefully laid them on the surrounding mound around the wide hole. Still as energetic as we had been when we started, we began shoveling a three to four-inch layer of the dirt on top of the boards. We transplanted the saplings and even the clumps of weeds that had been set aside. Next we brought in some more bushes. The result was a hideout with sufficient vertical space inside to stand almost upright. From a distance, it looked like a small hill. We had planned ahead for ventilation, having incorporated about four holes formed by large coffee cans, cut out at each end, and embedded end on end in the dirt surrounding the hole. Finally, we foraged around our homes and accumulated a stock of candles. A candle was placed inside the cave in front of each of the ventilation holes. Testing proved that the candles, when lit, provided sufficient light and the small amount of smoke made by the burning candle wicks was carried out through the coffee can ventilation holes.

A few months of meetings followed, during which time we handled important club business and planned various things. One day, after a meeting, we were outside playing. A fire started inside the clubhouse. Someone had been careless, leaving some paper near a candle. The burning paper led to the wood's catching on fire. We fled for safety, and watched as the smoke poured out of the ventilation holes. Realizing that the fire could worsen and possibly spread, and that the cave was but twenty feet from Mrs. Wall's barn, we all joined together and jumped up and down on the roof until it caved in. The fire was snuffed out. The clubhouse was destroyed, and the club was summarily dissolved. The hideout was soon forgotten.

Several months passed. The weeds had grown to the extent of obscuring the wide hole. Having heard some uncommon noise, septuagenarian Mrs. Wall decided to check on her property behind the barn. As the elderly lady walked into the deep weeds, she suddenly tumbled into the hole left by the collapsed hideout. There she lay helpless with a broken hip. For more than two hours she called out for help, and finally, a passerby in the lane heard her distressed outcry. Help immediately was called and she was transported to the Curry Clinic.

A whipping followed, first by Mother, and then by Daddy when he got home. After all, this was our landlady *and* T. F. Taylor's aunt!

After Mrs. Wall came home from the Curry Clinic with a cast, she was in bed for about six months. She hired a lady to look after her. The period in bed was followed by an equally long period confined to a wheel chair. (She always walked with a cane after that). She replied casually to anyone who questioned her affliction, "Those brothers, Jay and Si, are responsible for my broken hip. I fell into a hole that they dug behind my house."

Clearly we were not constantly being instructed at the knee of a Christian mother. We certainly did things that in hindsight could be viewed as overtly mischievous. This was regarded as a freak accident, yet in hindsight, it could have been avoided. We learned a life lesson. By and large, we were good kids and generally avoided even the appearance of prankish behavior.

In the summertime we could be entertained for hours playing under the spray of a garden hose or sprinkler. Occasionally a city employee would arrive in the neighborhood to test the fire hydrant, twisting it wide open. A strong stream of water shot out horizontally. Knowing that there was not time to run home and don a bathing suit, we played fully dressed in the powerful thrust of the gushing water until the man turned it off with his large wrench.

"Playing out" at night usually occupied our time in the summer months. We all would spend those warm, summer evenings playing *Red Rover...Kick the Can....Capture the Flag....May I...Red Light, Green Light... Slingshot*. The decision for who was "it" sometimes was made by rock, paper, or scissors: "rock" beat scissors, the "scissors" beat paper, and the "paper" beat rock. Once having determined who was "it," everyone else ran off into the dark of the night to hide, waiting for the warning to be declared: "Coming ready or not!" These games usually were conducted in front of the Embry house or the Sugg house, and we hid somewhere in the deep foliage surrounding the house.

Once, while hiding in the shrubbery, poised to rush out and "kick the can" at my first opportunity, I felt a bug crawl into my ear. It was horrible and terribly painful, but I had to suffer until I had the opportunity make a run to kick the can. I told my friends about it later. They looked in my ear, and although not seeing the insect, clearly *believed* my story. When I got home later, my parents were chatting with Lavinia and T. F. Taylors following dinner. They were still sitting around the Mahogany dining room table. Asking us how we had enjoyed "playing out," I told Mother of my torment. She looked into my ear, and seeing nothing, she told me that it was my imagination. I argued that such was the truth, and the grownups chuckled, thinking that I was just seeking attention.

About six or seven months later, Mother took us to Dr. Curry for an examination, in preparation to go off to summer church camp. In those days, it was customary for the doctor to remove the wax from a child's ears by simple irrigation of the auditory canal with the gentle injection of a warm saline rinse from a rubber bulb, which solution dissolved the wax. The spent liquid drained out into a kidney-shaped pan that was held gently against the neck. As this procedure was conducted, Dr. Curry exclaimed, "....expletive..., there was a bug in your ear." There it was in the pan, perfectly preserved in wax. Mother was both appalled and embarrassed with the finding. Immediately, she apologized to me for having not believed my story from the fall of the year before, and asked why I had not told her again. I replied that I had told her once, and by the next day, it no longer hurt nor bothered me at all. I simply could not hear out of that ear.

Jay and I went to summer church camp each year. The camp for boys was near Jackson. There were all of the trappings – nature trails, crafts, sports – but the emphasis was on Bible study and Scripture memorization. We had at least two hours devoted to study of the Bible each morning. I credit my life-time familiarity with many Scripture verses as based upon those verses that I memorized in those youthful years when one's mind is so uncluttered and memorization so easy.

I was a sleepwalker. I did not sleep walk often, but there were several times that I recall, and many more according to Mother. Occasionally I was found by one parent or the other in the dead of night, walking with my eyes closed and arms outstretched. I remember one extraordinary occasion when we had our Dollarhide cousins staying overnight. Adelaide Dollarhide was Daddy's younger sister. I was not yet eight years of age. Mother fixed pallets for the kids on the living room floor. We horsed around until we tired and bedded down for the night. Suddenly I was awakened by dogs barking at me and snipping at my ankles. I had been sleepwalking with my eyes open, in my briefs, halfway around our block. That block, as mentioned earlier, was huge, rhomboid in shape, with pasture land extending behind all of the houses. I was about two thousand feet from home, as the crow flies, but about a half mile from home on the paved road. I figured that it must have been about two or three a.m. I simply kicked at the dogs and yelled at them and continued to walk on home. I entered the front door and crawled back on the pallet and went back to sleep. The next day I told Mother about the experience. She smiled and obligingly acknowledged this story. I believe that she believed it. She knew first hand that I had often walked in my sleep within the house. And, she remembered my truthful story of the bug in my ear. But sleepwalking of this magnitude had never occurred before, nor did it ever happen again.

By and large, children abided by the instruction: "Children are to be seen, not heard." It simply was understood that we were not to disturb adults, either audibly or visibly. We were reared to honor our mother and father, as the Ten Commandments instruct, and the same principle applied to all adults, *especially* parents of our friends.

Discipline was widely permitted by another parent, without even a question from the parents of the child to whom it was administered. Almost always, discipline was administered in school. The most common disruptions or infractions of rules were the likes of talking, or throwing a spitball of paper or a stick of chalk. When one was derelict in class, the teacher took necessary measures – first, admonishment, which if not effective, was followed by the command, "Go stand in the hall." Being seen by other teachers or older students, standing in the hallway, brought instant and severe embarrassment to the punishee! Your own classmates, best friends, rolled their eyes, and anyone coming down the hallway looked at you with scorn. At the end of about an hour, the student was ordered back into the classroom with the expectation that no further disturbance would occur.

A more severe but not uncommon punishment was paddling by the teacher. With another offense by the same student, the accompanying, dreaded punishment with the paddle was immediately followed by the order: "Now, go to the principal's office." The principal first asked why, and then he verbally censured the student, and in the event that you were sent to his office *again* for another offense, the student often was paddled a second time. There was an unsubstantiated but terrifying rumor that the principal of our grammar school had an "electric paddle." No one had ever seen it, but the mental image of such a device, and of being spanked in that manner, was often sufficient to correct the attitude of all of our classmates. Furthermore, when one was spanked at school, he or she, but usually he, stood another almost certain spanking by his parent when he got home, because the notice of the malevolent behavior was sent home in a note from the teacher. One never dreamed of NOT delivering the teacher's note to one's parents. That would be dishonest and earn yet a second, separate whipping; for dishonesty.

A major pastime in the schoolyard during recess for boys was shooting marbles. Every boy had hundreds of marbles. One always went to school with several marbles in his pocket; the idea was to come home with more than you left home with. All you needed was a smooth, dirt surface. The circle – usually about four feet in diameter – was drawn with one's pocket knife, and the game began. One would use his aggie, or favorite marble, to shoot with. If you knocked one or more marbles out of the ring, you kept the "winnings" and you continued to shoot. Guys with big hands and long fingers could shoot the marble very hard. I had small hands and fingers! If they used a "steelie," they occasionally would shatter a glass marble. A steelie was actually a steel ball bearing from an automobile transmission. The ball bearings were available anywhere that cars were repaired, but we got ours from Lathem's Texaco. The game had no end unless someone won all of the marbles; and the game ended instantly when the bell rang signaling the end of recess or lunch hour. We also played marbles in front of our house, on the hard dirt under the big oak tree. It afforded about the best surface in the neighborhood, because no grass grew under that huge tree.

Every boy carried a pocket knife. A pocket knife was fundamental and absolutely essential. You never knew when you might have to whittle; but more, it was used in a variety of ways for prying, opening, trimming, and even sometimes cleaning under your fingernails.

The game Mumblety-peg had been popular since the 19th century. It was played with a pocket knife. The knife handle was held with your index finger, the point of the blade resting on your blue-jean covered knee, and the knife was flipped forcefully downward so that it would stick up in the ground. It was a game of skill. I don't recall anyone's ever sustaining an injury in the game, and certainly no one was ever threatened with a knife. Every Cub Scout knew knife safety: that when you whittled, it was always in an outward direction and away from the body.

Tops were conventional. We learned to spin tops in a variety of ways and were quite skilled. We could set a spinning top down on an area not much bigger than a silver dollar. Once it was spun on the ground, there was a way to encircle the metal tip of the spinning top with the three-foot string and cause the top to "walk" the string.

When we became bored of one of the above activities, we could always just chase one another around the playground. The energy of young children is almost unfathomed. One fun thing was for someone to lie down on the ground, stretch out, and stiffen spine, hips and legs. Then another boy would bend over and grasp under the neck and lift the stiff body to a standing position. Girls were not strong enough to do that. They always bent at the waist and simply were left sitting up. As the Bible states, women are the weaker vessel (a Scripture that is quite clearly explained by Paige Cothren in several of his Christian books).

Everyone in the neighborhood had a relatively new pair of roller skates – the kind that were tightened with a skate key at the sides of the sole of your shoe. We would skate for hours on end, principally in the smooth, paved driveway of the neighbor's driveway at the house at the top of the hill. Most of the sidewalks – and especially the pavement of the streets – had so many lines, filled with black tar, that it made for very rough, jarring, and unpleasant skating.

Boys and girls all had a bicycle. We often would ride alone, but usually in packs, all over town, sometimes the girls accompanying the boys. The bicycle was the chief means of transportation around Eupora for kids. The sidewalks were given over to us, and the streets also were safe, because automobiles were relatively few in number and drivers were exceedingly careful when they approached kids on bicycles. Jay and I each completely wore out a bicycle in about two years; scratches and scrapes gave over to rust, and fenders were dented and bent beyond reasonable repair.

One summer day, Jay and I were riding our bikes in the street in front of the school, and we came upon a pack of dogs barking and fighting viciously. The pack quickly moved toward us, blindly crashing into my bike and causing me to fall among the dogs. One of the dogs bit me deeply on the right calf and left me bleeding in the street from the several puncture wounds. I saw the dog that bit me and knew that I never had seen that dog before. We recognized most of the dogs and even knew the owners. However, rumor had it that there was a "mad dog" loose in town. We rode our bikes home, my thigh bleeding copiously. Mother had but to glance at it, grabbed her purse, rushed to the car, and again took me to Dr. Curry at the clinic. He saw me promptly, cleaned the wounds, and placed a bandage. From my precise description of the dog fight and the dog that bit me, Dr. Curry presumed that the dog may have been rabid, and the recommended rabies vaccination series was started immediately. Meanwhile, Sheriff Snyder was called and given the description of the dog, which he soon found and shot. The head of the animal was dispatched to Mississippi State College in Starkville for examination. Several days later, the report was received that the dog had been rabid. For 14 weeks this vaccination was followed up once per week alternating left to right descending down the spinal column. The follow-up shots were administered by a nurse. They hurt, I flinched, but I never cried (and from that time on, shots never bothered me again).

Behind the Sugg home was their two-story barn. There, in the loft, we had played in the hay often in our youth. By eight or nine years of age, Rob and Charles would hide out and smoke rolled cigarettes of rabbit tobacco, which grew voluntarily almost everywhere in the fields. Rabbit tobacco had a texture like tobacco, and it smoked as it burned. There the comparison ended. It was brown and white and it smelled horrible. They said it tasted even worse. To Jay and me, it appeared to be the same as smoking a real cigarette, which was absolutely forbidden by all of our parents. But after a while, Mr. and Mrs. Sugg allowed Rob and Charles this license – to smoke rabbit tobacco. Their rationale presumably was that such permission would deter the smoking of real cigarettes.

Mother had always encouraged Jay and me not to smoke behind her back, and we had honored her wish. She told me that if I ever was tempted to smoke a cigarette, to come to her and tell her, and we would sit down together and have a smoke. One day, after watching Rob and Charles smoke rabbit tobacco in their barn, I walked the short distance of two houses to our home. I entered through the back door, walked into the kitchen, and firmly and confidently as is possible for a ten year old, I informed Mother that I was ready to sit down with her and have a cigarette. She raised her index finger to her lips, hushing my brief diatribe, and motioned for me to have a seat at the table in the kitchen. She had already begun listening to Billy Graham on the radio. I knew Billy Graham and that he had recently begun his crusades. I listened intently, and when I less confidently broached the subject again (in my childish mind, this was the perfect time for a smoke, while listening to the radio), she gently raised her finger to her lips, and quietly asked me to listen to the rest of the sermon. It was providential. Billy Graham immediately moved to the subject of young people smoking, speaking with emphasis of the prevalence of the habit and the potential health hazard. Back then, children were told that smoking would stunt one's growth, that you would be short as an adult. Graham then exhorted the young listener to deny the temptation until the rational decision could be made in adulthood. Following the sermon, and the singing of a hymn, Mother turned the radio off. She stated: "Let's have a prayer." As she prayed, she thanked God for Graham's sermon – the text, but especially the timing. Following her prayer, she then offered praise for my honesty in coming to her as we had agreed. On closing, she asked, "Do you want to have a cigarette now?" I was ashamed. I had found it hard to believe that she would actually join me with a cigarette, but I knew she would not deny the request. But the Lord intervened on her behalf, so that she did not have to comply with her offer.

Along with Jay and me, Rob and Charles were taking piano lessons. Rob, who was older than Charles, would sit practicing at the piano in their living room with a smoking, rolled cigarette of rabbit tobacco in the ash tray. As we were already church choir members, these copiously practiced piano lessons to Jay and me seemed to be pushing things too far. I could sing well, but I never had the gift of playing any musical instrument. Finally realizing that Jay and I were far less than enthusiastic about piano, and possessing no evident gift to that end, Mother agreed to let us give up the piano lessons. Later I tried the coronet in the band, but that instrument soon was abandoned and my position in the band quickly was vacated. I must say, though, for the year that we took lessons, great dividends were realized. We had learned not only how to read music, but how to play the piano (That fundamental exercise profited us both, because we were in church choirs all through school and in the glee club in high school – even going to the state events in Jackson composed of glee clubs from all over the State of Mississippi. The life-long benefit, musically, of that one year of piano lessons was surpassed only by the life-long merit of a typing class that I had in the ninth grade in Hattiesburg. The typing course I regarded later as my most valuable school class. I type over 100 words a minute today).

During the summer months, it was our obligation to cut the grass at home. This was with a non-motorized push mower. We learned quickly that some neighbors, including Lady Mary Taylor, who had no boys, were willing to pay us to cut their lawns. We were paid about fifty or seventy-five cents for mowing the grass in the front, the side, and the back yards. It took over an hour for one large yard, but seventy-five cents was good pay, yet only equivalent to seventy-five coat hangers; but we could collect coat hangers only about twice a year.

The Eupora High School football games were watched by the parents and high school students from wooden bleachers, while the boys (and some tomboy girls) played on the red clay hill between the end zone and the score board. By the end of a game, generally we kids were dirtier than the football players. I remember the game's once being interrupted when a man apparently sustained a heart attack. After near silence, and patient delay, an ambulance reached the field. The man was carried away to the Curry Clinic. The game immediately resumed as though nothing had happened.

Already mentioned was my neighbor, Harriet Embry, the sister of Shorty. Harriet was my age; Shorty a year younger and, of course, short. Harriet and I never even walked to the picture show together, and I certainly never held her hand. It was just understood that she was my girlfriend.

My first true love was Nancy Johnson. My heart would race when I but laid eyes on her. She lived with her family on a home place about two miles outside town, and she and her older brother came to school on the bus. For my twelfth birthday, as a sixth grader, Mother granted my request to have a date with Nancy. About 2:00, Mother and I drove out to pick her up at her home place and we met Nancy's parents. We returned to the house for cake and ice cream, after which I opened some presents. Among the gifts were two silver dollars from my parents. Both coins had the same date. Mother suggested that Nancy take one to keep, as a memento of our first date. I walked with her the one block to downtown to see a picture show. The theater was at the end of the second block. When we returned home, Mother and I drove her back to her house. That was the only date that Nancy and I ever had, although we often sat with one another at the picture show, or at school during lunch or chapel. I believed, as I sat next to her, that I would literally melt down (today she would be the likes of a Meg Ryan).

Mother was consistently adamant in forbidding two things for her boys. First was playing football; second, owning a motor scooter. She had a life-long friend who had a crippling knee injury from high school football and had suffered his entire adult life from that impairment. I knew that. Yet Daddy was silent on the matter. Whereas Jay was not interested in the sport, I knew I was Daddy's rough and tumble boy. When I was in the seventh grade and eleven years old, football season was starting. I asked Daddy if I could go out for football practice. He readily approved and seemed proud of me.

I went to the gym the next day, and I was given the uniform and pads and dressed out the first day of football practice. The coach took notice of me. As a receiver, I ran down the field and caught a number of passes. What first startled me was when the opposing team member intentionally pulled the ball out of my hands. That didn't seem fair to me and it was an entirely new concept. We simply had never "stolen the ball" from an opponent in our neighborhood games. I was hit hard, again and again, but sustained the punishment. After practice, showering, and dressing, I headed home about dark. Soon we sat down for dinner. My hair still was damp from the shower and I had some visible abrasions and contusions. Mother asked: "What happened to your wrist and your elbow?" I replied gleefully: "I went out for football today!" Mother cut her eyes to Daddy and gave him a stern look, then began crying. Little else was said, but that was my first and only day as a football player. Mother's rule on the matter was sustained.

In a note that Mother made in her diary in December 1942, she stated: "Mac got some fresh pork from T. F.'s hog killing." In a 1943 letter from her mother, Grandmother Dobbs stated: "Haven't slaughtered the beef yet, tho Dad will try to get it over with this week....." That common event is described vividly by Paige Cothren in his 2005 2nd edition of *Home Sweet HOMOCHITTO, a backward glance at 150 years of one of the South's most unusual communities in Southwest Mississippi*, pp. 70ff:

HOG KILLING

Hog killing time was a special time at Brushy Creek for several reasons, the primary one being acquisition of a lot of necessary food. Subsisting at Homochitto in the earlier days would have been very difficult without pork.

Pork and the game we killed or fish we caught provided almost all of our meat...hogs were killed and eaten...

While "killing hogs" usually isn't that complicated, cleaning and cutting the swine up involved a little coordination. The first necessary job was to dig a large hole into the ground about three feet in diameter...deep enough to hold the bottom half of a fifty-five gallon oil drum. Then the black wash-pot was filled with water and a fire built under it. By the time the

first hog is killed, the water was boiling. The boiling water was
transferred into the drum…The pig then was thrust into the hot
water, first one end of him, and then the other. Following that,
the men placed the hog upon an outside table…There, he or she,
is scraped, with butcher knives, in order to remove all the hair
from the skin….

The explicit details above continue. Prior to the explanation above,
Paige had explained that the "killing" was accomplished with one carefully
aimed shot deployed from a 22 rifle to the head of the animal, precisely
between the eyes. Death was instant, the animal suffering no pain. Brother
Jay and I saw this procedure on a few occasions when we happened by the
home of a rural family. By the mid-1940s, the town of Eupora had taken a
giant step forward, a process quite advanced over the description provided
by Paige Cothren or practiced by my grandparents.

The Eupora Freezer Locker House was a facility located near the
ice house. It was a convenience for citizens who did not have the latest
luxury of a freezer in their home. The freezer locker facility was a large
building with a square center lobby in the front of the building. The lobby
was surrounded with freezer locker doors in the side and back walls, each
locker having a key lock. The freezer locker doors were about one third the
size of a home refrigerator. The window of the butcher shop was centered
on the back wall, through which window a large area extending back to
the slaughter house was visible. Here the slaughtered and dressed pigs and
steers were hanging on iron hooks from a rail attached overhead, and the
rail traced further to the back door. The skilled butcher would transfer
the pig or steer (cow) to a butcher table to be cut up. People purchased
their preferred cut of various meats from the butcher at the window of the
butcher shop, placed them in their personal, rented freezer locker, where
the meats were kept frozen until they owner chose to take the meat home
to cook. The freezer locker house was open every day except Sunday. Let
me explain how the slaughtered animals reached that stage of the process.

At the rear of the building, we quite often watched the slaughter of
both hogs and large pigs, as well as steers and cows. The butchers had the
procedure down to a precise routine. A cow would be led off of the bed of
a farmer's truck directly onto the concrete deck.

Alternatively, the pigs would be herded around through a series of metal fence-like barriers, then, one at a time, up a ramp to the deck. There the animals met their demise. The manner of slaughter differed.

With the large pig, a worker would quickly and deftly fasten a chain around the hind leg. Then, an electric motor overhead was activated with a handle connected with a pull chain and the hog was hoisted upward, front hoofs helplessly and desperately pawing at the concrete surface as the animal enunciated sounds of resistance. Once the pig stopped struggling and flailing about, the butcher stepped forward and with one quick wrist motion, he deftly slashed the throat with a razor-sharp butcher knife. Death came quickly. Next the pig was lowered onto a steel grate and lowered into a cauldron of scalding hot water for a precise and predetermined number of minutes. Then the pig's lifeless body, still resting on steel grate, was lifted out of the boiling water, and slowly rolled onto the deck. With the chain still cleaving the hind leg, the butcher slowly hoisted the pig back up into a vertical position and began to dress the pig, scraping the hair off. Finally the butcher would insert a hook, connected to a wheel on the rail, and push on pig and it would translate down the rail into the butcher shop. There it was prepared; more experienced butchers made the various cuts of meat for future public purchase and ultimate consumption. This was a modernized yet conventional form of "hog killing," as mentioned earlier.

The cow or steer was led forward with a rope passed through the steel nose ring. The rope was passed through a fixed metal ring imbedded in the concrete, and the cows head would be gently drawn down until the snout touched the floor. Then, with the appropriate small-ended but heavy sledge hammer, the beast was struck in the center of the skull between the eyes. The legs instantly gave way and the animal fell to the floor. Instant death occurred. It was so quick that it was virtually painless. Before the cow was sent into the butcher shop, it was skinned by hand with a razor-sharp butcher knife (and the skins were sold to a leather shop in Belfountain for retail sales – for leather whips and various other leather goods. Jay and I and many friends *always* had a six or seven foot whip. A strip of leather had been precut and we easily-plaited our whip from the properly cut piece of leather).

These slaughter tasks were regarded as "business as usual." The procedure was performed with skill. The animals essentially suffered no pain. It was almost as quick as shooting the animal in the head with a rifle, which is what the farmer did in his back yard. Again, the slaughter of a cow or pig was necessary to put food on the table, as it had been since the beginning of civilization. (My cousin, David Dollarhide, was veritably traumatized from seeing the procedure on one visit to Eupora, and he talked about it throughout his life).

Daddy bought a wire recorder. Although discovered in the 19th century, wire recording had its greatest popularity beginning about 1946 (and gave way to other forms by 1954). Wire recording was a form of audio storage resulting from recording on a thin steel wire as it was drawn across a magnetic head. Recording earlier had only been done on plastic records. Daddy had the recorder in Greenwood on a visit that we made to the Dollarhides' home, and the kids all cheerfully waited our turns to speak into the recorder, and then to hear the playback. We had the recording of that reunion for many years, cherishing it because it had Daddy's voice, as well as ours.

The first *new* car that I can remember our having was a 1946 Ford. Prior to that, new cars were not made, due to the war. Daddy frequently sold his new car for a profit and purchased another one in Jackson or Memphis. The owner of a new car had to break it in gradually, increasing the speed, little by little, over the months to come. After the prescribed mileage was reached on the odometer, and only then, could the car be driven at the posted speed limit on the highway. Mother said that when she asked Daddy why he traded so often and he remarked, "I'm working my way up to a Cadillac."

Mother told the story of their having traveled to Dallas, Texas, with the Taylors for a Saturday football game. On Friday, she and the other wives went shopping while the men played golf. Having had a passion for horseback riding since her youth, Mother bought a pair of fine riding boots at Neiman Marcus. They were on sale. When Daddy came back from the round of golf and saw her purchases, he gruffly asked her why she had bought the riding boots. Her reply was, "I'm working my way up to a horse."

Mother and Daddy had good taste, but they were practical and found joy in a good buy. In fact, Mother was consistently Scotch in her purchases. She had a silk scarf that she also had bought on sale at Nieman Marcus. Mother knew that Daddy needed a new bathrobe, and Mother decided to make one for him from red wool, lined in satin. She removed the label from the scarf and sewed it to the inside of the collar of the robe. When Daddy opened it on Christmas Day and saw the Nieman Marcus label, he was incensed. He immediately assumed that Mother had made an extravagant and unnecessary purchase. As soon as Mother explained to him that she had made the bathrobe, and explained the source of the label, he was thrilled.

Daddy got his first Cadillac in 1948. He continued to have it serviced at Latham's Texaco station, owned and operated by Mr. Jack Latham and his two sons. The station faced Highway 82 and was located between the Eupora Ice Company and Ross Ford Company. Both T. F. Taylor, Jr. and Daddy regularly had their Cadillacs cleaned and waxed at the Texaco station and were among the Lathams' best customers. In the late 1940s, service of the automobile was an integral part of the purchase of gasoline. Fluid levels were checked; the air pressure in the tires was inspected; all of the windows were washed, inside and out; and the car was thoroughly swept out with a whisk broom. All this was done enthusiastically and without waiting to be asked, and usually by two attendants. No thought ever was given to a tip for the service.

One egregious act occurred earlier at the Texaco station. Jay and I, at about age seven and eight years of age, were playing around the Texaco station. T. F.'s black Cadillac had been serviced and had just been cleaned inside, then washed, and waxed. For some reason – to this day I don't know why – Jay and I climbed on top of T. F.s car and were playing, with our dirty bare feet. Mr. Latham looked around and saw us; he was appalled, but more, terrified. He came running out of the building and swiftly and carefully lifted each of us off of the Cadillac. He was trembling with both fear and anger. When this loathsome matter was reported to T. F., he merely told Jack Latham to wax it again and buff the scratches out. However, later Daddy heard about it and was both embarrassed and angry. A whipping from Daddy followed for my older brother and for me. Daddy used a twelve-inch ruler for his measure of punishment.

We had always had the run of the Texaco station. We were a known entity, and our family business was appreciated. Following a puncture, we consistently had our bicycle tires repaired there by an attendant as we watched. There was never a charge. From the Texaco station we obtained discarded automobile inner tubes. They would repair the hole, again free. (Today you deposit three quarters in an air compressor for three minutes of air, which you must dispense yourself. What would our grandparents have thought? That air and bottled water one day would be sold for a high price). The tubes we took with us to Choctaw Lake or to the swimming pool. The men at the service station also had used ball bearing rings from repaired car transmissions. We would break them open with a small sledge hammer and take the ball bearings for playing marbles. As mentioned earlier, in shooting marbles, a ball bearing was called a "steelie." And here we got our used automobile tires for rolling down the street.

When Daddy had his first Cadillac in 1948, Mother drove a Ford. There was no Cadillac dealership in Eupora yet. Two or three times each year, Daddy would purchase a new Cadillac in Jackson or Memphis, drive it for a few months, and sell it for a small profit. He then would buy another new Cadillac.

Jay and I were forbidden by Mother to get our feet on the seats, a rule of Daddy's that we cautiously and meticulously followed in order to keep the car immaculate. Thereby, Daddy was successful in keeping his car clean, along with the diligent service at Latham's Texaco station. I cannot remember *ever* washing a car at home.

We always had made the trip to Ackerman by driving east from Eupora on Highway 82 to Mathiston and turning south on Highway 15. These were all paved, concrete roads, and Mother took the longer route to please Daddy, for he did not like to have his cars on gravel roads, due to the dust and potential damage from flying gravel.

Tuesday, November 2, 1948, President Truman and his family voted in Independence, Missouri. He retired early that evening, not knowing that history was about to be made in the form of a Chicago newspaper headline earlier printed for the morning edition. Indeed, the newspaper was circulated during the early morning with the headline: "DEWEY DEFEATS TRUMAN." By daybreak, it was determined that Truman had won.

Following a three-year study by the government, in January 1948, President Truman decided to end segregation in the armed forces and the civil service through executive order, rather than through legislation. After numerous committee meetings, on July 26, 1948, Truman signed Executive Order 9981, which stated, "It is hereby declared to be the policy of the President that there shall be equality of treatment and opportunity for all persons in the armed services without regard to race, color, religion, or national origin." The order also established the President's Committee on Equality of Treatment and opportunity in the Armed Services. On October 9, 1948, the Navy announced that it was extending the policy of integration that it had begun in the closing months of World War II. In December, the Army and Air Force acceded to the policy.

Also in 1948, the "Big Bang" Theory was formulated, regarding the formation of the universe. Proponents held that at one time, some one moment, all of space was contained at a single point, from which the entire universe had been expanding. Christians know full well that the book of Genesis gives the accurate description of creation.

More importantly, following Israel's War of Independence, the State of Israel was founded. That event had enormous eschatological significance, according to some conservative theologians. Your belief in "the end times" is not a saving doctrine. Therefore, it is a subject that should not divide believing Christians within their church.

Mother's cousin, Sara Margaret Moss, and husband Fenley had adopted a baby in 1947, naming him Spurgeon Adams Moss, after Sara's father. Although there was a seven-year age difference between Spurgeon and me, from 1950 to 1953, we had many adventures together on the expansive acreage behind their home which Fenley owned. The land was located on the edge of Ackerman, about a three minute drive from downtown.

Fenley's father, Richard Moss, had hired a young black boy to supervise his own two boys, Fenley and Richard, when they were growing up. So, Mr. Richard Moss decided that the same was needed for Spurgeon, his grandson. From that point, Tad was the constant companion for Spurgeon. Someone needed to watch Spurgeon because he always wanted to be outside, and there were hundreds of acres of land belonging to his family. Tad's given name was Floyd, and he was about our age, or six years older than Spurgeon. But to Spurgeon, Jay, and me, he was Tad. When we visited in Ackerman, the four of us would play together, roam in the woods, fish, or just wade in the creek.

Fenley was an avid hunter and had a nice gun collection. Some of the long guns belonged to Fenley's father. Fenley trained Spurgeon at an early age on gun safety and often took him hunting. When we visited, we would go rabbit and squirrel hunting with 22 rifles. One December, I wanted to surprise Mother with some mistletoe, but it existed only in the highest branches of the tall oak trees. Spurgeon went inside and got his 410 shotgun. One shot at the base of the stalk would bring down a bouquet of mistletoe, and we came home with an armful. There was an artesian well on their property that fed a small, man-made pond. We often played in the cold water at the artesian well and in the narrow creek originating there. And we fished in the pond.

Out in the neighboring counties, the smaller schools began classes in July and took about three weeks off when the cotton crop came in, in order that the school-age workers could earn money for their families. It was often the case that the owner of the farm employed his own children in this industry. Summer of 1949, the cotton crop came in early, before our school started. Jay and I decided that we could make some "easy money" picking cotton. The income would be in addition to that garnered from our paper route. We found a job at a farm out on Highway 9, no more than a half mile away. For a couple of weeks in late July and early August, Mother dropped us off there early in the morning, and we worked until it was time to deliver our papers. The cotton was picked by hand. The only equipment required was a ten-foot long cotton bag, which the owner supplied. Whereas an adult could straddle one row, and thereby pick three rows at a time, we managed just two at a time. The men would bend over, and their bag was pulled along fairly swiftly. It was amazing how quickly they could pick three rows clean. Jay and I soon would wind up sitting in the dirt, between two rows, and only occasionally would we tug our bag forward. This in the heat of the summer sun, and we were tired! It certainly was not the "easy money" we had envisioned. We would pick until the bag was full and then drag it to the weighing station. After being weighed and the weight documented, the cotton was dumped onto the bed of a truck by a worker, who then would return the bag to each of us and we would return to the field to continue picking cotton. Payment was deferred until the end of the day.

Cotton picking was a formidable experience. Many were farmhands, but others were farmers and their families. This was a big part of their livelihood. The men could pick as much as eight hundred pounds of cotton a day, and the women sometimes five hundred pounds. We picked about one hundred and twenty-five pounds. We were paid ten cents a pound at the end of the day. Earning twelve or thirteen dollars in one day for a twelve-year-old was good pay (equivalent to more than one hundred and twenty-five dollars today. The next year, as usual, the crop came in later, and we already had returned to school).

At an earlier age, we had found it fun to play at the Farmers' Cotton Gin. The gin was located on S. Dunn Street, between the Eupora Hotel and the Curry Clinic, literally a stone's throw from the train depot. Most farmers brought the cotton to the gin by truck, but there still were a few who came by mule-drawn wooden wagon. The process began when a cotton gin worker climbed onto a wagon load of just-picked cotton, and grasped the welded-on handles of a large, tin pipe that was about ten inches in diameter. The vacuum pipe was counter-weighted so that the operator needed only move the pipe laterally. The pipe had a spring-loaded extension, allowing vertical movement of the end. The cotton was drawn into the pipe by suction and carried through an elaborate pipe line up to and over the roof top of the two-story gin. The pipe then turned down, descending through a hole in the roof. Inside the gin, the cotton was spewed downward onto the second floor of the gin, where it collected in a pile on the wooden floor. We would get beneath the stream of cotton plummeting down from above and allow it to almost completely cover us before stepping out; it was not heavy. Sometimes a green boll would strike you on the head. (One was forbidden *ever* to pick a green boll because it added to the weight. Green boles were unacceptable if discovered while weighing in the field, and a penalty was extracted from the payment due to the picker).

From that second story floor, the cotton was sucked up later by another employee, to be sent through the ginning process. Jay or I or a friend would raise the suction pipe directly over our head. The suction was so strong, it would lift every hair on end – it was an amusing appearance to those looking on.

The cotton gin separated the seeds from the cotton. Eli Whitney, a Yale graduate, came South in the early 1790s as a tutor. While at Mulberry Grove, the plantation of retired General Nathanael Greene, Whitney invented the ginning process. Mulberry Grove is on the Savannah River, a few miles from Savannah, Georgia.

The end result of the ginning process, after the seeds were separated in some sort of combing process, was the baling of the cotton. Within the belly of the gin, the cotton was compressed by large, steel presses which first had been covered with a pre-cut piece of burlap material. Three steel bands were placed at equal intervals around the compressed bale by a worker. After positioning of the steel straps, and folding the burlap under the end straps, the worker slipped the loose ends of the bands through a steel fastener and clamped them with a large scissors-like tool. When the presses were released, the cotton expanded, and the straps tightened so tight one could not get a finger underneath the strap. The bales were then lifted by huge hooks cabled to a crane and transported over to the yard. There were scores of bales of cotton in the yard, waiting to be transported to the train depot and loaded onto the train.

We romped around inside the cotton gin as freely as if we were in our own home. The employees knew us and gave us the liberty to play. We actually were ignored, unless we got in their way, in which case a firm command was generated, such as: "watch out...don't do that...."

The greatest fun was found outside, running along the tops of the bales, and jumping long distances from one bale to another series of bales. I don't recall any of us ever being seriously injured at the Farmers' Cotton Gin, although one often sprained an ankle when he jumped short of a bale and fell to the ground, or if *almost* reaching the bale jammed stomach first into the blunt but soft bale, which would knock your breath out. It is only by the grace of God that we were not permanently maimed while playing rambunctiously at the cotton gin. For instance, consider a compound, comminuted fracture (and Mother was worried about my playing football? Not to mention all of the other dangerous adventures).

William Adams Dobbs, Sr., Mother's brother, had come home to Mississippi shortly after the end of the war. Soon thereafter, he joined Shell Oil Company in sales, moving first, in 1946, to Decatur, Georgia. The Dobbs family lived on Avery Street near Agnes Scott College when we visited them one summer at their home. Jay and I went with William to a summer day camp, which camp was situated in the forest adjacent to North Decatur Road (this same, vast area today is densely populated with single-family residences). One day, we waded along in a stream, in knee-deep water, searching for water moccasins, which we intended to catch with a loop of heavy string which was attached to a six-foot long stick. If one was successful in passing the loop over the snake's head, a quick, firm yank of the stick upward would clench the heavy string loop, securing the snake. Moccasins swim rapidly on top of the water. One had to be quick! Either to catch the snake in the loop, or run fast for safety, but more often the snake would swim in another direction.

Mother knew in advance that her brother, William, was to become ill.[39] In 1949, Frances, William's wife, called Mother from Decatur to tell her that Willie had been admitted to Emory University Hospital, and that his status was serious, with complications from a severe rash for which he had been hospitalized. Mother left for Decatur immediately. Arriving at Emory University Hospital, she met with Frances at Willie's bedside. She explained that his condition had worsened and had been downgraded to critical, having been complicated with respiratory problems. Then Dr. Strickler took the two of them into the hallway, and advised that Willie would not live through the night. Frances was terrified – almost hysterical. Mother embraced her and consoled her. First they went to the hospital chapel to pray. Then Mother took Frances home. They prayed and talked and prayed more. Mother told Frances that it appeared that Willie was going to die, and that she had to be willing to let him go and find peace in the Lord. Frances wailed, saying that she could not let him go. They cried together; they prayed more; and they waited. They did not sleep at all, but continued to pray through the night. Finally, Frances relinquished her will to God's will; she stopped crying, and appeared peaceful; she told Mother that she was ready to let God take Willie home, if that was His will.

Almost immediately, at 7:00 a.m., the telephone rang. It was Dr. Strickler. At his request, they hastened back to Emory University Hospital. Dr. Strickler was waiting and he told them that he didn't know what had happened, except that a "Higher Power had taken over," and that "Willie is better. He is sitting up and taking nourishment." Mother and Frances dashed to Willie's bedside. He was sitting up and eating. His condition improved by the hour, and the next day, his respiration was normal, the rash was completely gone, and he was released from the hospital.

Willie's recovery had begun to occur almost immediately after discontinuing the phenobarbital – a drug first made in 1904, but used only selectively. Medical doctors recently had begun using it for a variety of

---

[39]   In a 1977 letter, in discussing the supernatural, Mother recalled her experience in this way:

> Talking about "a word from the Lord," He told me of Brother's illness before I had had any word of it at all. When all was well, as far as I knew. So then, a couple of hours later, when Frances called me and said, "Mary, Willie is dying...." I KNEW the Lord was in it, and was able to go without panic and be of help. And, I know the Lord brought Brother back, because of prayer that was offered up.....

purposes, including the appeasing of a skin rash. Dr. Strickler explained to Frances and Mother that he had suspected that Willie was having a reaction to the drug, and late in the night, after Frances and Mother had left, he had arbitrarily stopped the phenobarbital infusion, thinking that it was doing no good.[40]

I am certain that Mother told us this story when she returned to Eupora. But over the years, I heard her tell of it on many other occasions. It was this kind of faith and "answered prayer" that was common to the instruction that Jay and I received at her knee.

Now knowledgeable Christians can easily argue that such supernatural acts simply do not occur today. I beg to differ. The first century church indeed had experienced "signs and wonders, with various miracles, and gifts of the Holy Spirit." But those days ended after the apostolic church age. (The church today may not have healers, but God still heals, responding to prayers of fellow Christians. Moreover, is not every Christian conversion a miracle? Conversion is a work of the Holy Spirit. Supernatural is defined as something that exists or occurs above and beyond the natural. Every believing Christian should know that God is in control of everything – little things, yes, but more, life and death, every day in every way. *Nothing* ever happens outside of the permissive will of God).

Daddy bought a new, 1949, red Cadillac convertible. Pete Fortner, Jr., son of the bank president, was a freshman at Mississippi State College, and he was at home one Saturday night when Mother and Daddy were having dinner with his parents. Pete Jr. told Daddy that he saw the Cadillac convertible outside, that he admired it, and he that he would love to drive over to Mississippi State College for Women (M.S.C.W) in the car on Sunday, just to see the reaction. Daddy tossed him the keys and told him to take it over on Sunday. Pete Jr. took care of that business and drove the some twenty miles back to Eupora late Sunday afternoon to return the car. He told Daddy that upon his arrival on the campus of M.S.C.W., he was surrounded by a crowd of at least a dozen girls. A couple or three months later, Daddy sold the convertible. Again, for a profit.

---

[40] About ten years later, Mother and Gene were talking with Dr. Strickler at a large medical meeting in New Orleans. He still was on the Emory University Hospital staff and when Mother asked, he clearly recalled Uncle Willie's case. He told them that he had reported the case, it was published, and it was the *first* recorded anaphylactic reaction to phenobarbital ever to be published. Nevertheless, in the opinion of Mother, this was the sovereignty of God.

In 1949, China became Communist; the first non-stop flight was made around the world; George Orwell published *Nineteen Eighty-Four*; NATO was established; and the Soviet Union had the Atomic Bomb.

Uncle Willie, except for five years while serving during the war, had been employed by Shell Oil Company since 1937 in various marketing positions, principally relating to industrial products and their application, rising to manager of their Industrial Sales Department, Atlanta Division, for three years (1946-1948). As noticed earlier, their home was in Decatur, near the campus of Agnes Scott College. In 1949, Shell Oil Company transferred Willie to Houston, Texas, where he was placed in charge of jobber sales for the Texas District of the Shell Oil.[41]

Mother began corresponding with C. S. Lewis in 1950.[42] Ostensibly she wrote him about April 1, 1950, and Lewis replied to her in a letter dated April 20, 1950, erroneously addressed to "Europa, Mississippi." The envelope was forwarded to "210 Taggart St., Houston, Texas," where we were visiting the William Dobbs family. In the letter, Mother apparently had offered praise to Lewis for his books:

> Magdalen College,
> Oxford
> 20th April 1950
> Dear Mrs. McCaslin,
>
> Many thanks for your most kind and encouraging letter of the 17th. It gives me great pleasure to know that my books have been of some service to you.
> With all best wishes for the success of your work,
>
> Yours sincerely,
> C. S. Lewis

Our family had planned on a visit with Uncle Willie's family in Houston, Texas, after school was out. Mother, Jay, and I flew to Houston, which was

---

[41] Although most of his civilian career was in the oil and heavy machinery business, during the last ten years, until his retirement, he served as a registered professional engineer in the U. S. Civil Service. He found time to enjoy one of his hobbies. A student of the visual arts, he visited most of the major art museums in the United States, Canada, and in some countries in Europe...."

[42] The thirteen letters that Mother received from Lewis are transcribed in *LETTERS TO AND FROM A CHRISTIAN MOTHER AND MORE.*

our first experience in a commercial propeller air plane, although we had been treated on many occasions to a flight in smaller airplanes in Eupora. I had never been above the clouds before, and for a nine-year-old, the event was exhilarating. Daddy drove to Texas in his car, because he had business to conduct on the way, as well as a married cousin he wished to visit with briefly in Corsicana. She and her husband lived in a second story garage apartment. As they talked, she complained about the dripping faucet in their small kitchen, saying that the owner had failed to have it fixed, even after their several polite requests. In their view, it was annoying and it wasted water. Daddy walked over to the wall-hung sink, stationed his feet firmly, placed his hands under the front lip of the sink, and lifted it up. The pipes burst and water spewed out, as the sink hung askew. Then Daddy went out to the owner's house and knocked on his door. When the man came to the door, Daddy told him that the sink needed repair, which repairs followed forthwith.

We have photographs of the visit in suburban Houston, with us all posing in their yard. William and his baby brother, Frank, had double bunk beds, and the windows were high and horizontal, in their contemporary home. We admired our Cousin William. He was three years older than I. William could grip a *Coca-Cola* bottle around the base section, while Jay and I could only lift the Coke by grasping the neck of the bottle. We were impressed with his maturity.

William had a stamp collection which Jay and I admired. Mother recognized our interest and when we asked, she agreed to let us start a collection. The next step was taken at the Houston stamp store, where we purchased a few inexpensive groups of stamps along with the stamp books and hinges for the stamps.

Daddy took me with him while he played nine holes of golf at a Houston country club. It must have been over one hundred and ten degrees that day. When we finished the course, we went into the club house for cold drinks. The ballroom was huge, with impressive pine-paneled walls and a high, vaulted ceiling. Jay and I went down to Galveston with Daddy for a swim in the Gulf. It was a cool, gray summer day. There was a high wind, and the waves were enormous; appearing to be fifteen feet high. Daddy instructed Jay and me to remain near the shore, and he swam out and over the high, braking waves. Our sight of him was temporarily obscured by the great swells and waves of the ocean, then we would see his head bobbing. I experienced sheer panic, an immense fear that Daddy was gone. (In hindsight, in 1954, I regarded this experience of terror as a premonition, a realization that my daddy was not invincible). After a few minutes, we saw his head and shoulders again, probably four hundred feet off shore. Soon, he began making his way back toward the shore, swimming the Australian crawl, yet as the waves broke, he would disappear completely, obscured by the high waves. Daddy was a fine swimmer, and I should have been confident that he was safe.

On another day, Daddy took us to the new Shamrock Hotel, a spectacular property, built far ahead of its time. In fact, it was said to be the largest indoor swimming pool in the world at that time. We had swimming privileges there for our entire visit.

That entitlement may have been through Daddy's association with National Old Line Insurance Company, because Daddy had made the arrangements in advance. The president of National Old Line, Bill Darby (T. F. Taylor, Jr. was the CEO), was a very close friend of Daddy's, with whom they visited on occasion in Little Rock and with whom they went to college football games. They vacationed twice in Havana with the Bill Darbys and the T. F. Taylors.

The swimming pool was shaped like a shamrock, at the deep end of which were one meter diving boards flanking at the far left and right; then three-meter diving boards; and in the center, a ten-meter platform, equivalent to over thirty feet. Daddy repeatedly dived from the platform. Finally I got the courage to climb the ladder to the platform and jump, which I then did many more times. Jay chose not to try. After the visit, we rode home to Mississippi with Daddy.

Among the first television sets in Eupora was at the Embrys' home, but of course T. F. and Lavinia were probably the first to own one. We often sat in the Embrys' living room in the early evening hours watching those shows. The "rabbit ears" antenna was awesome, spreading out beyond the width of the television console. Of course, the screen was black and white. The programing was good, but we often found that the commercials were even more exciting. I don't remember anyone else in our neighborhood's buying a television set, but I'm sure there were others. However, my parents did not acquire one at that time. I assume that the cost was a significant hindrance.

In June 1950, the Communist government of North Korea attacked South Korea. President Truman conferred immediately with his military advisers. In July, World War II General Douglas MacArthur was placed in command of U.S. troops in Korea.[43]

We continued to visit in Ackerman frequently. Sara Margaret Moss' grandparents lived in town in a fine old two-story home. We spent many hours there while Mother visited with Sara Margaret and her grandparents, the Scarbroughs. Sara's parents had been killed in the automobile accident several years earlier, and her grandparents then became like parents to her. Jay, Spurgeon, Tad, and I would play about the house and in the huge, red-painted barn behind the house.

Spurgeon was known all over the small town of Ackerman, and everyone adored him. Fenley continued with his rural mail route. Meanwhile, Fenley had purchased the movie theater in Ackerman. What a treat for a kid! To have relatives that owned the theater. Admission for us was free. Popcorn was free. To a young boy, it was the closest thing to Heaven![44]

The first modern credit card was introduced; the first organ transplant was accomplished; and the first *Peanuts* cartoon appeared, all in 1950.

Senator Joseph McCarthy led a campaign against Communist subversion in the early 1950s. His anti-communist charges often were not well documented, and the United States Senate voted to censure him for the tactics he used. President Truman ordered the construction of Hydrogen Bombs.

In 1951, T. F. and Lavinia Taylor traveled to Europe. At Daddy's request, while visiting in Geneva, Switzerland, T. F. purchased for Daddy an 18k rose gold, Rolex Oyster Perpetual, bubble-back wrist watch. T. F. already had a Rolex that Daddy had admired. The watch cost two hundred dollars and probably would have been five hundred dollars in the U.S. (In 2015, considering inflation, the 18k gold men's Rolex Oyster Perpetual costs over thirty thousand dollars). Later, while in the kitchen entertaining friends as they prepared dinner, Daddy often would remove the watch and gold band from his wrist, submerge it in a glass of ice water, and leave it for a while. Friends were amazed to see this first-hand demonstration of

---

[43] President Truman later wrote, "Complete, almost unspoken acceptance on the part of everyone that whatever had to be done to meet this aggression had to be done. There was no suggestion from anyone that either the United Nations or the United States could back away from it."

[44] Later, Fenley bought a drive-in theater in West Point – it was among the first drive-in theaters in north Mississippi. Drive-in theaters flourished but met their demise in the 1970's.

the waterproof capability of the Rolex. Daddy took great pride in owning the watch. The next year, upon another trip to Geneva by the Taylors, Daddy had him purchase a matching ladies' 18k rose gold Oyster Perpetual watch for Mother (In December of 2014, I gave my nephew, Alston Jones McCaslin VI, the Rolex that Daddy treasured. Jay was overwhelmed with appreciation, thinking that it could have gone to my son-in-law. But Suzanne, Jeff, Carey, and I agreed that it should stay in the McCaslin family. However, Mother's Rolex is for Carey).

As was noticed earlier in their married life, Daddy had been a faithful Presbyterian, but he had stopped going to church regularly. (In hindsight, I perceive that his master had become mammon [money] and material things in general, not the least of which were Rolex watches, Fleetwood Cadillacs, and the finest Wilson golf clubs and equipment). Mother had concluded (and she told Jay and me later) that Daddy was aware constantly of T. F. Taylor's opulent wealth, but also, Daddy was strongly lured by the kind of affluence which his family had experienced throughout his youth, prior to the Depression.

Our duplex on Adams Avenue was owned by Mrs. Wall, T. F. Taylor's aunt. (Ironically, Foy and Paige Cothren lived in the same duplex when Paige retired from professional football and they returned to Eupora; yet when Foy's parents moved to Ft. Lauderdale, she and Paige moved to the big house on Clarke Avenue). The duplex had two bedrooms. There was a huge living room with a bay window on the front. Family time customarily was spent in the kitchen, while Mother cooked dinner. Daddy's favorite chair was next to the doorway, and his crème-colored Zenith radio was at arm's reach on the counter. His chair was chrome, with a maroon leather upholstered back, arms rests, and seat. The latest, modern furnishing! After dinner, he would retreat to his armchair where he would sit and listen to the radio and read his magazines. The *Saturday Evening Post* was his favorite, but he had subscriptions to *Life*, *Look*, and *Readers Digest*. Daddy loved horse-radish. He would paste a generous amount of horseradish on a Saltine Cracker. Then, after biting off about half of the cracker, his eyes would water as he savored the sharp taste. He also loved fine cheese and purchased it at every opportunity, for it had been rationed all during the war.

Life in Mississippi as late as 1949 or 1950 was virtually without air conditioning. We had used a large three-speed window fan in the bedroom, which would circulate outside air throughout the house. During the summer months, it ran almost twenty-four hours a day; we slept with that fan running on high, drawing a stiff wind across the room. As noticed earlier, Daddy had two large, oscillating Westinghouse fans, one of which sat atop the Frigidaire refrigerator in the kitchen. The duplicate could be placed in the dining room or living room or bedroom as needed.

No one had central air conditioning in Eupora until T. F. Taylor, Jr., installed a system in his home. In fact, a Memphis, Tennessee newspaper ran an article stating that T. F. Taylor, Jr., had installed the first residential central air conditioning in the entire state of Mississippi (as authenticated to me by his son-in-law, Paige Cothren). With that amenity, T. F. gave Daddy one of the window air conditioner units that he had previously used in his home. The cream-colored unit was installed in our back bedroom window, replacing the window fan. Our friends would come over often, just to sit on the edge of the bed, in front of the air conditioner, to experience the cool stream of "air conditioned" air blowing into their faces. It was mesmerizing to us youngsters.

The advent of air conditioning changed the way of life in the South (and it has been said that corporate America literally was ushered into the South by the luxury of central air conditioning, beginning with the corporate offices that came to Atlanta).

Jiggs, our beloved dog, was pitiful as he aged. But, he was always loyal and ready to play with us. Jiggs died, in 1951. Later, Mother told us that, prior to our going out of town, on several occasions, she had asked our neighbor, Town Marshall Mac Coleman, to dispose of Jiggs, only to call him early in the trip requesting him not to do so. Jiggs had been limping most of his life from having been run over by a car.

On June 25, 1951, the Columbia Broadcasting System made the first commercial colorcast. Color television had been introduced. Lavinia and T. F. Taylor, Jr., had the first color television set in Eupora. We heard that it wasn't worth the money, for it did not look natural. The grownups were skeptical that color television would ever be as popular as black and white. (Almost three years later, on January 1, 1954, the first coast-to-coast color telecast would occur – The Rose Bowl parade and The Rose Bowl. The first television set retailed for over one thousand dollars, which was a huge expense for the mere sixty-eight hours of colorcasting that would be available on NBC during the whole of 1954. Significant sales of color receivers would not be significant for another ten years).

About 1951, at ten years of age, I was sitting in our kitchen at the corner of the kitchen table. Jay, Mother, and I were engaged in a conversation late in the day. I had my elbows on my knees and my head down low, almost between my knees. In response to a question directed to me, I raised my head rapidly, at the same time opening my mouth to reply, and the corner of the table caught my lower central incisor and peeled it right out. It lay on the table in front of me. Mother picked up the tooth and took me directly to Dr. Maddox' home, which was located further up Adams Avenue from our house. Dr. Maddox came to the door. Mother explained how the injury had just occurred, and she asked him what to do. He said there was nothing that could be done. I had a tooth-sized gap in my lower arch for quite some time, but it gradually closed. It was soon after this incident, before I was eleven years of age, that Mother began taking us to a dentist in West Point, some thirty-five miles away. Dr. Maddox' practice had evolved into mainly serving his older patients.

Having experienced this traumatic injury, combined with the awareness of having slightly crowded teeth, the nearest orthodontist being one hundred and ten miles away in Jackson (Harriett had braces and her mother had to take her to Jackson once a month for adjustments), and our having experienced our fair share of cavities in these days (before the advent of fluoride in the 1960s), I firmly believe that the Lord was leading me toward the selection of the profession of dentistry. (From dental school forward, when asked how I had chosen dentistry, my reply would be: "I knew a great deal about the practice of dentistry, from the patient's standpoint." Another severe dental injury sustained my freshman year in college galvanized my decision; I wanted to be a dentist. I wanted to go to dental school. Later, having worked with young children in my high school and college years, first as a life guard, then as a swimming instructor, it became apparent to me that specializing in children would be my choice in dentistry).

A near tragedy once occurred. Gordon and Evelyn Ebert, close friends of our parents, from Winona, had come over for dinner. Gordon was a veteran of the war. He owned and operated a large picture framing gallery in Winona. On that night, Gordon, a veteran, gave me a WW II military-issue cigarette lighter with a long wick that passed through the lighter and hung below. The wick was about the diameter of a pencil. There was a small ball, chain, and hook attached to the upper end of the wick. Gordon showed me how it worked. Pulling up on the ball and chain would lift the wick up next to the flint; striking the flint with the lighter wheel ignited the wick, but not in a flame. It gave off only a soft glow, which looked like a burning cigarette, and was adequate to light a cigarette. As one pulled downward on the wick that hung down beneath, the ball would cap the chamber and snuff out the smoldering wick. Gordon explained that in combat, one would never strike a match, or light a regular cigarette lighter, for fear of the enemy's seeing the flame and firing. I was honored that he had given me this souvenir of his from the European Theater of World War II. I had never seen one before, and we knew all about Army and Navy things from the Army and Navy Store.

I occupied myself in the bedroom striking the flint, lighting the wick, and snuffing it out. The trouble began when the flint was used up. I found a box of matches, skipped the first step, and continued to light the wick, tossing the spent matches in the trash can, an antique, wicker basket, under Mother's dresser. Finally becoming bored with it all, I went into the living room to study, which is what I should have been doing all along. In a few minutes, I was alarmed by yelling, and the sound of feet pounding the floor from the kitchen to the bedroom. One of the matches had not been extinguished and had ignited some paper in the wicker trash can. A fire started and quickly spread, burning up the wallpaper behind the dresser and burning the underside of the dresser. Gordon saw the flame from the kitchen, and as he ran into the bedroom, he tripped, fell against the bed and drove it into the flames. They grabbed the bedspread from the bed, and began beating out the flames. But for the grace of God, the house could have burned down!

Through all of this, I did not move one inch. I kept my eyes on the text of my book and my finger on the line, seemingly studying hard. However, I am certain that my face was red and that I certainly was NOT concentrating on my studies. The adults were baffled about how the fire got started, and, one after another, they began taking the blame for starting the fire. First, Mother said that she may have thrown a match in the basket; then, Gordon insisted that he remembered throwing a match aside. While Daddy was insisting that it was his fault, Mother glanced at me on the couch in the living room. She asked, "Si, do you know anything about how the fire started?" I replied, "Yes ma'am, I started it with a match, while I was playing with the cigarette lighter." They were all stunned by my quiet, polite admission, but it solved the mystery. Daddy and the Eberts rolled their eyes and shrugged shoulders and returned to the kitchen. But Mother came in and sat next to me. She asked how I could sit there, all that time, appearing to study, while they each were assuming the blame. But, she knew that I did not lie. Then, she firmly explained: "<u>Not</u> telling the truth, when all about you people are taking the blame falsely, is the <u>same</u> as lying." I was embarrassed and hurt by my action, and I told her that I would never do it again. This was a very early and clear lesson in the meaning of honesty, again, instructed at the knee of a Christian mother.

As a youngster, I often listened to the radio at bedtime until I fell asleep. One comedy program that I particularly enjoyed was *Fibber Magee and Molly*. I never missed an installment. Abbot and Costello were hilarious acts. I also developed a taste for hillbilly music, the precursor to country music, accompanied by the newly-invented electric guitar. The program was broadcast each night from Renfro Valley, Kentucky. Renfro Valley is located between Knoxville, Tennessee, and Lexington, Kentucky. Songs popular at the time were the likes of "Big Rock Candy Mountain," "He's In The Jailhouse Now," and "You Are My Sunshine."

Chapter Seven

VISITS IN GRENADA, GREENWOOD, AND GREENVILLE

From these days of the early 1950s are memories of family gatherings in Greenwood and Grenada. The Dollarhide cousins lived in Greenwood, where Uncle Roger was the band director at the high school. Adelaide had a musical gift (as did Roger), and she was the organist for their Presbyterian church in Jackson. At the same time, Roger bought the local music store downtown. At the doorway of the music store sat a life-size statue of a white and black dog, "Nipper," his head cocked to the side, listening to the phonograph. He had become the symbol of RCA. The Dollarhide home was within walking distance of everything of interest: the music store, the swimming pool, and the ball parks.

Our McCaslin family gatherings most often were in Grenada, at the home of Grandmother McCaslin. Christmas Day brought all of her children and grandchildren together. Although widowed in 1938, she had retained the large, two-story family home. My first memories were of the early to mid-1940s, when Granny still lived upstairs, occupying the entire second floor. When one entered at the front door, the mahogany staircase extended up the left wall to a landing, turned right, then after a few steps to a second landing, turned right again, with a few more steps toward the front. We enjoyed many happy hours of play on that elegant staircase.

From about 1950 Granny lived alone. She moved downstairs as all of the children had gone. She had the house divided, separating out three apartments. She used what formerly had been a dining room as her bedroom, next to the kitchen and breakfast room. The parlor remained her living room. She rented one apartment across the foyer and two tenants resided upstairs, where previously there had been several bedrooms and baths, previously occupied by her seven children. Everyone had access to the front door, which never was locked.

At the end of the driveway, there was a garage, with tongue-and-groove, pine-paneled walls. On the left wall there was a built-in, glass-front, pine gun cabinet in which Grandfather McCaslin once had kept his rifles and shotguns displayed but locked up, far away from the children. There never was any thought that the guns would be stolen simply by breaking the glass. In the rear of the garage there was a storage room. The back yard was huge, with large shade trees here and there. We were free to roam inside and outside of the garage. We thoroughly enjoyed our visits with Granny, particularly when we stayed overnight, and could sleep on a "pallet."

The McCaslin home was little more than a block from the City Square. We were allowed to walk to the Municipal Swimming Pool, about four blocks in the opposite direction of the square, still on Main Street. There we spent entire afternoons swimming and diving from the low and high diving boards. Filter systems were not present in the older pools, and the water was drained frequently. Jay and I arrived at the pool on several occasions when the pool was being refilled, and that process took several hours. We were allowed in the pool once the water rose deep enough at the deep end to play. Only after the water was at the optimal level were we allowed to dive from the diving boards.

While visiting one summer on the first weekend that the pool was to be open, I was concerned about not having a tan. Granny had a heat lamp. I concluded that I could get under the lamp and get a quick tan. Being impatient, I pulled the lamp down to about six inches from my thighs, and waited about ten minutes to tan. Very soon, huge blisters formed on both of my upper legs – water blisters! The painful blisters did not interfere with our plans to go to the swimming pool, but I had to roll up the legs of my bathing suit, because the material was painful when it rubbed against the blisters.

Daddy loved the game of golf, and he had been a member of the Grenada Country Club since the 1930s. Whereas he also held a membership at the Greenwood Country Club, the Grenada Country Club was where he most often played. He had many friends at both clubs. (Many years later, Louise told us that Daddy had paid for an entire sprinkler system to be installed throughout the eighteen-hole golf course. This enhancement he provided conditional upon its being anonymous. His generosity was disclosed to the membership shortly after his death).

Daddy often would take Jay and me to Grenada with him on Sunday, Mother staying in Eupora to attend church and sing in the choir. Arriving in Grenada about 9:00 a.m., Daddy would visit for a while with his mother, and then depart for the golf course about 9:30. We would walk the two blocks to Grenada Presbyterian Church to go to Sunday school and the morning church service. Afterwards, Jay and I would have lunch, change clothes, and wait for a ride. Daddy would send a driver in his car to get us and ferry us to the club. Once there, we played about the clubhouse with other kids our age. The kitchen was at one end of the ballroom in the clubhouse. The savory smell of the hamburgers permeated the entire facility, for the cook was preparing them throughout the day. Jay and I generally would have for lunch a hamburger or two, and a *Coca-Cola*, and our purchases were put on a tab that Daddy would pay later in the day. Once we got carried away. It had been a hot afternoon at the Club, and Daddy was paying the tab at service window of the kitchen. I had consumed twelve *Coca-Colas*, along with hamburgers and French fries. Jay had fewer. I was justly reprimanded by Daddy for this presumptive overindulgence and extravagance.

We had taken up the game of golf early. Never owning a child's set of clubs, we learned the game by choking up on an old set of Daddy's. Although we never had a formal lesson from the pro, we both developed perfect form and a good golf game, purely by imitation of the adults. (I played golf regularly until entering dental school in 1962. On weekends, I needed to study. But more, tee times were scarce and in high demand on the Atlanta golf courses).

Following eighteen holes of play, usually Daddy would eat a snack with his friends as they played hearts or gin rummy in the locker room. A small room extending off of the locker room was lined with rows of slot machines. They were illegal in those days. Once a friend of Daddy's, while sitting at the card table, handed me a quarter and told me to try my luck. I won two quarters. Then I won five. After a while, I had a handful of quarters, and I quit. They commended me on being smart enough to quit while ahead.

Once, on a tip from an authority that the Clubhouse would be raided to confiscate the slot machines, various members were asked to take one machine each home for a while. We had a nickel slot machine in our pantry for many months. The cash drawer on the back was removed, replaced by my baseball hat. Jay and I would play that slot machine for long lengths of time, replenishing our reserve of nickels from the baseball cap that served as a cash drawer. We learned quickly and painlessly that one cannot win at gambling.

About seven or eight o'clock, we would pile in the car for the hour-long drive back to Eupora. Often Daddy would let me drive. He had taught me, as well as Jay, to drive an automobile around Eupora, as well as on these frequent trips to Grenada. The training for me began when I was eight or nine years old. I would sit in Daddy's lap and steer, being too short to reach the brake and gas pedals. I would line up one of the screw heads, located in the trim of the front windshield, with the center line in the road ahead. I drove completely straight, never weaving. But, in my peripheral vision, when I saw an oncoming car, I would be terrified. Whereas I did not think that Daddy was aware of my terror, I realized later that Daddy had his thumb and index finger on the lower part of the steering wheel, and actually was in complete control.

We discovered how the golf ball was made by taking one apart. After cutting the white casing from a scarred golf ball, we uncovered the continuous rubber band inside. This continuous strand enveloped the internal rubber ball. We would unwind the tightly-wound elastic strand to expose the rubber ball in the center. The ball was filled with a slimy, off-white fluid, and we cut into only one. We found many uses for the long rubber bands and spent many hours stringing them around the yard. The rubber ball was fun to bounce off the ground or a wall.

Marlon Brando was not the recipient of the Academy Award in 1951 for his leading role in *A Streetcar Named Desire*. The Oscar went to Humphrey Bogart for *The African Queen*. Yet, it could be debated that no performance had more influence on modern film acting styles than Brando's work as Stanley Kowalski, Tennessee Williams' harsh, crude, and athletic hero.

Daddy bought a 1951 white four-door Cadillac Fleetwood for Mother and traded his Oldsmobile for another new one. Mother's Fleetwood was the first automobile that we had ever owned with power windows and a power "seek" bar on the radio, yet without air conditioning.

Before my eleventh birthday, on a Wednesday night, while Mother was at prayer meeting at the Baptist Church, I asked Daddy if he would take me out and let me drive his car. He rose from his chair in the kitchen, walked into the dining room, and reached for car keys on the top shelf of the corner cupboard. Handing me the keys, he said: "Take it around the block." I did, driving very, very slowly. I was gone for about five minutes. When I reached home, Mother's car was in the driveway. I entered the house, feeling very guilty, my heart pounding as though it would burst forth from my chest; for I knew full well that Mother was going to be angry with me. As I approached the kitchen, I overheard her fussing at Daddy for letting me go out alone in the car. There was no sustained argument, though, for times were different in the early 1950s. I suppose the law required one to be fifteen years of age and licensed, but law enforcement agents winked at country boys and girls driving at a young age; they made no issue of it at all. That simply was the way kids learned to drive.

By age eleven, I had been driving Daddy on forty to sixty-mile trips to Grenada or Sturgis. I had to sit up on the edge of the seat in order to reach the gas and brake pedals; and I could not see over the top of the steering wheel. My view was between the dashboard and the underside of the upper curve of the steering wheel. Daddy would sit entirely over on the passenger's side, perfectly relaxed and trusting, as he thumbed through "Life" or "The Saturday Evening Post." He had complete confidence in my driving ability, and I never damaged his car.

On September 8th, 1951, the San Francisco Peace Treaty officially ended World War II. It was a separate treaty signed between the 48 states and Japan, exclusive of other nations.

In August 1952, Uncle Willie resigned from Shell to purchase and operate a Cities Service Oil distributorship in Greenville, Mississippi. They returned from Houston, settling in Greenville. He had been determined to own his own business and had despised working for someone else. We visited with them there often. They had a large, single-level frame home, painted light green in color. William, by then fifteen years of age, was driving his parents' automobile, a light green, two-door Chevrolet with an AM radio. Here again, we were impressed with the maturity of our older cousin. He had begun smoking cigarettes, and he drove the car with one hand! He drove us all over Greenville, but I remember most vividly two sites. First, the Cities Service facility, and the hundreds of oil drums in the yard. Second, the levee along the Mississippi River; it must have been more than forty feet in height! Cars could drive up on the top of the levee and continue down the length of the levee for many miles in either direction. The levee afforded protection for the city in the event of rising water of the

Mississippi River. I spotted a red fox on the levee. It was the first fox I had ever seen in the wild, although Grandfather Dobbs used to go on fox hunts in Choctaw County when I was too young to accompany him. The song most popular that summer was *Jambalaya*. Each time we visited, Uncle Willie would mark our heights on the trim of the door to the pantry. We all were amazed at how fast we were growing up.

A very memorable occasion was the 1952 McCaslin reunion, when all of the family was gathered together at the Dollarhides' home in Greenwood on a Sunday. All of us twelve cousins, boys and girls, were romping all about the house and the yard; we were a host of rug rats. Just before an early dinner, the children were assembled with their parents standing behind them to pose in the backyard for a family picture. David Dollarhide had not put his shirt back on for the black and white photograph made of that family gathering. Every member of the family was present for the group picture, except Daddy. He was playing golf with friends.

Later, the Dollarhides moved to a large frame house on several acres of land a few miles from downtown Greenwood. There was a great expanse of farm land there to play. Our oldest cousin, Roger Dollarhide, Jr., was, two years Jay's senior and the oldest of the other eleven grandchildren. He would lead all of the cousins about in play, like a pied piper, while the parents remained in the house visiting. Often though, it was just the mothers, for all of my uncles were playing golf at the Greenwood Country Club. Daddy held a membership there, as well as at the Grenada Golf Club.

It was not infrequently that I went with Daddy to Sturgis, where he was the bookkeeper for the Sturgis Lumber Company. He was a partner in this business, owned by T. F. Taylor, Jr. Sturgis was on the highway that connected Ackerman and Starkville, and about a forty- minute drive from Eupora. There was little else in Sturgis other than the lumber mill. I don't recall that there was even a single red light. There was a general mercantile business and an ordinary, small café, where they served as good a hamburger as you could find anywhere. I always enjoyed eating a hamburger at that café with Daddy on my trips to Sturgis.

During the school year, I made this trip with Daddy to Sturgis on Saturday; in the summer, more frequently. While he occupied himself with his bookkeeping in the office, I was free to roam about the mill and the lumber yard. Cut lumber was brought to this mill to be planed, after which it was carried into the yard and stacked for curing. There, at about ten years of age, I enjoyed riding the work horse. The horse was used to pull a trailer, for moving the lumber from the mill to the yard. This old mare was the last of the work horses; they had been replaced by Ford tractors. My horseback riding was soon replaced by another activity. I began riding along with one of the lumbermen on a tractor.

Soon, I had permission from Daddy to drive a tractor, and therewith, given access to one of the tractors, if there was one not in use. Driving the tractor by myself was beyond any thrill imagined for a ten- year-old boy. I shiver now to think of the danger, as I careened down the dirt lanes, between tall stacks of lumber. With the hand throttle fully out, in order to stop you had to pull the hand throttle down, while depressing the clutch, and only then did you apply the brakes. If not coordinated, the engine would rev all the way up. I probably was going no more than thirty miles an hour (there was no speedometer) and would literally turn on two wheels as I jockeyed about the lumber yard. None of the lumbermen were concerned; I was the boss's son. On one occasion, I made a sharp turn, failed to depress the clutch and brakes in order to slow down, and ran straight-way into a stack of lumber. The lumber cushioned the impact, and I was able to hang onto the steering wheel. I eased off on the throttle for the roar of the engine to subside, as I first assessed the magnitude of the collision, then observed in sheer horror the outcome. I heard a low-level rumble. Then, I watched as the stack of lumber slowly shifted backward and fell over. I had knocked it off of the two railroad ties on which the lumber was stacked. This mess required the work of two men and a half day to dismantle the pile of lumber and re-stack it. When Daddy received word of the matter, he was not mad; he was amused with it all.

I went all over the area on the tractor – through the woods, across shallow creeks, and down dirt roads that bordered the lumber yard. Once, I got out on the open, gravel road that ran tangent to the mill grounds. While driving full-throttle, I saw a widening of the road near by and decided to turn off on the right shoulder and reverse my direction. On the left side of the road was a shack with a dirt yard and a large tree in the center of the yard. Without slowing or braking, I turned wide and began to make a U turn, circling into the yard and around the tree. My plan was to turn right and head back in the direction I had come. Something told me: "STOP." I believe it was the Lord. I certainly gave Him credit. I did stop, just as I had cut my front wheels to the right, directed back toward Sturgis Lumber Company. Not having heard or seen an automobile – or for that matter, not even thinking about it – the tractor skidded to a sudden stop, the front left wheel now being turned completely to the right and parallel to the road. My stopping had prevented me from lurching back into the road. A passing car came out of nowhere, speeding along at perhaps forty miles per hour, and clipped the baseball-sized hub cap off of the front wheel. One inch closer, and the car would have torn the front wheel off of the tractor. Three feet closer and surely I could have been seriously injured, or maybe killed, then and there! The driver did not slow down, nor did he return. Apparently he did not even realize that he had clipped the hub cap off of the front wheel. I never told Daddy of <u>that</u> experience. I suspected that he would not have been amused.

Cousin William, his brother and sister, Frank and Cathy, along with their parents, occasionally visited with us in Eupora. I recall a few of the visits occurring during the summer, and the many memories of those youthful, carefree days. We depended on our bicycles both for simply riding, but also to get about town. Riding our bicycles down the steep hill and around Dead Man's Curve was defying injury. Laying our bikes aside, we would go romping about in the woods on the edge of town; Jay and I even shared Poker Man's Palace with William.

Rolling automobile tires along the streets in the rolling hills of our block was an activity that William particularly enjoyed. These automobile tires we got for free behind Latham's Texaco station. Mr. Latham had no objection for otherwise they would have been hauled away. You would run alongside the tire, whipping it with your hand to speed up or pressing on the tire to slow down. It was great fun. We would go completely around the huge rhomboid-shaped block, often several times. That amounted to about one mile each round. Traversing counter-clockwise, after rounding Deadman's Curve, we would race upward to a short plateau, and then the hill would begin a steep descent, adjacent to Judge Eudy's house and long front yard (the judge's house and property occupied at least two, perhaps three city lots). Given a good start, a tire would accelerate down that hill reaching a speed of about thirty miles per hour. The street dead-ended at S. Dunn Street at the base of the steep hill. A large, white house was situated there, with the sidewalk leading directly up to the high, wooden steps of the house. The tire would meet the curb at such a high velocity that it would bounce about 15 feet high, and when it hit the ground, still spinning, it would race up to the house, climb the steps, and slam into the lady's front door. There, the energy fully spent, it would wobble around and come to rest. Before the lady could come to her doorway, we already had retrieved the tire and were out of her sight. I don't remember her name, but I am certain she knew who we were. Only occasionally did we do harm. Once my tire got away from me going down another long hill and slammed into the back bumper of a parked car. No harm occurred to the car because the bumpers, then, were attached directly to the car frame.

This same steep hill in front of Judge Eudy's house was a half-block long, and his front yard was the best hill on that side of town for sledding, when we had a three to four-inch-deep snow. (Everette Eudy served two terms as Mayor, then City Attorney, then Judge, and then State Senate 1944-1952). The Town was named for his Aunt Eupora Eudy. His wife, Mrs. Olive Eudy, wrote a weekly column in the Webster Progress for ten years.

Chapter Eight

DILIGENT WORK ETHIC

During our early years, we mowed the grass at home, as expected, but we also mowed the lawns for some of our neighbors. Earlier discussion was given to our diligence in occasionally collecting coat hangers from door to door to redeem at the laundry. The same was achieved by collecting discarded *Coca-Cola* bottles. Those tasks were the genesis of our Protestant work ethic, which ethic was instilled in us by our parents, as it was by the parents of most of our friends. The objective? The fundamental desire to work was to achieve a financial goal, and that end being to muster up a savings.

At the appropriate age, Jay and I had voluntarily accepted the responsibility of a *The Jackson Daily News* paper route in Eupora. We purchased deep baskets from Mr. Miller at Western Auto, from whom we also acquired our bicycles. The basket was attached to the front axle and handle bars. Our routes covered the entire town, Jay one side and me the other. The bundled newspapers were dropped at the Doolittle Pontiac dealership, directly across highway 82 from the Eupora Ice Company. This building also served as the station for *Trailways* and *Greyhound* buses, and the ticket counter was along the back wall inside the Doolittle Pontiac showroom. Upon their arrival, and we often were there at the time of delivery, we rolled the newspapers. After loading them into our bicycle baskets, we were off on our individual routes.

To begin with, we had in excess of fifty customers each, and it took about an hour to run our routes. After completing the afternoon route, we would meet again at the Doolittle Pontiac place. The two remaining stacks of papers we did NOT roll; they were transported down the road to the

Wells Lamont Glove Manufacturing Plant at 5:00 p.m. to sell to the workers as they came out of the plant. These folks mostly lived in the surrounding rural areas. Boy that was easy money! No rolling of the papers; no pedaling on the bicycle required, half the time of which was uphill. The Sunday paper we delivered in the morning before Sunday school and church. We developed skill in tossing the rolled paper precisely to the spot that each customer preferred. The goal was to have the tossed rolled paper barely clear the edge of the porch and slide up near the door. Our paper route customers were very pleased with our services. We were diligent and dependable. Actually, our customers adored us and told Mother at every opportunity. Again, the Protestant work ethic was established early in our character.

Once a year *The Jackson Daily News* ran a special drive for delivery boys to acquire new subscribers. As an incentive, they offered a prize for each group of five new subscribers. We buckled down, going to folks who did not subscribe; they were folks that we did not know by name, yet we were able to sell them on the idea of home delivery. The first drive offered the premium of a genuine leather football. We were awarded six footballs! We kept them all, proudly using one at our neighborhood games. Another time, the prize was a steel throwing dagger, the handle wrapped in leather. We received six of the daggers, but gave the extras to our friends. During the two or three years that we had the route, we had to buy a new Western Auto bicycle almost every year, because the paper route was so rough on the bikes. A new bicycle cost about twenty-eight dollars. It was awesome getting a new bike almost every year!

We went to Morristown, Tennessee, during the summer of 1952, to visit Mother's college roommate. Lois Harrell Shaver and Mother had been roommates and very close friends for over three years at Blue Mountain College. Lois had married Jay Shaver, and they had one son, Max, who was almost my age. His parents had divorced! This concept was not new for Jay and me. We simply had never known *anyone else* who was divorced! I don't recall the basis for the divorce. Let us call it irreconcilable differences. In fact, in the 1940 South, the divorce rate was 2.3 per one thousand inhabitants, and in the 1950 South, 3.2 per one thousand. Applying that statistic to Eupora, I suppose Mother knew two couples – the ones that they whispered about. Yet, I have no memory of who they were.

On May 26, 1952, Mother wrote to Daddy, describing events of the vacation:

Friday night
Dear Mac,

We had the most perfect trip up here. That Oldsmobile just purred like a kitten. It is a lot better to drive on the highway then it is around town, for some reason.

Jay and Si and I wanted to see Rock City on Lookout Mountain, so we stopped there about 4:30 Wednesday - 5:30 Eastern time. We all loved the sights we saw. We then ate supper, went to prayer meeting at the beautiful hundred-year-old First Baptist Church, went to a drive-in theater, then spent the night in a motor court.

Next morning, I mentioned going through the Smokies, and we all wanted to. We stopped and inquired about the route. A man told us it would be about 100 miles farther, but one fellow said the drive was worth $500! So, we went that way. The children were simply overwhelmed. And it <u>was</u> worth far more than those extra miles cost, to me as well as Jay and Si. I will never forget that day and I know they won't. We stopped at the Cherokee Indian Reservation, then on across the highest mountains – 5000 feet. It was better than an airplane ride to them. I wish you could have heard their precious conversation and cute remarks. Oh, they were so happy.

As we came down out of the mountains, Si prayed aloud. He thanked the Lord for taking such good care of us, and for all the lovely things we had done and seen, and for giving us a Daddy who would let us have such a good "vacation."

Max is nine, and the three of them are so excited. They are having real fun together and we all will have a grand time, I know. Lois has already seen in one day how much finer our boys are than Max – will have to tell you this. Max squirted Coke on the wall and later lied about it, saying that none of them did it. Si looked so pained that I asked him if he knew about it. He said, "Yes Ma'am." I said, "Well, tell the truth." So he did. Lois said, "Do they <u>always</u> tell the truth? Max lies to me all the time." I called to Si and said, "Si, would you tell a lie?" He said, "No Ma'am." I said, "Why is it wrong?" And standing so straight he said simply, "Because the Lord doesn't permit it."

Oh Mac, I know they will tell lies sometime. They might even <u>now</u>, if tried too sorely. They are only human, as we <u>all</u> are. But the <u>point</u> is, their <u>consciences</u> are developed properly, their characters are being molded in the <u>right</u> way, and they have a deep sense of <u>security</u> in Jesus, and <u>love</u> for Him as their <u>Lord</u>, and desire to be <u>good</u> for <u>His</u> sake! And I believe they will <u>never</u> lose this, if we do our part for as long as they will listen to us. I believe they will <u>always</u> hold to the good, and <u>if</u> <u>they</u> <u>fail</u> to do so, I think their consciences will pull them back every time, before it is too late, because their faith is the Lord is REAL and powerful. I praise Him every day for putting <u>me</u> back into recognizing Him, in time for me to <u>teach</u> my children! Your mother told me with emphasis, years ago, "Teach your children, Mary Margaret, teach your children. No one else can do it but you."

....Will write again soon.

Love
M. M.

Let us hear from you. We love you and miss you.

M. M.

Lois and her son, Max, lived alone in a small house. We all enjoyed the vacation in Morristown, and planned to go back again the next summer. However, Max was spoiled. His mother had to work full time, and Max was virtually undisciplined. I vaguely remember how Mother explained to us that Max's behavior was a byproduct of divorce. We felt sorry for him.

On our return home, Jay and I were anxious to show our friends the genuine Indian bow and arrows that we had purchased at the Cherokee Reservation, Cherokee, North Carolina. We were on the vacant lot where we played ball. Jay and a couple of friends were one hundred and fifty feet away, and I was with two buddies. Jay would shoot an arrow with a steep trajectory into the sky. It would loft, arch, begin to level, and then come down, plunging deep into the ground. I would run over to pull the arrow out of the ground and then return it to Jay's crowd the same way. It was great fun. Finally, after Jay's shot arched and started down, I lost track of it. Looking up for the descending arrow, it would have been no wider than a quarter of an inch. As I was crouched on one knee, with my right hand resting in front of me in the grass, the arrow slammed into the ground with a distinct sound, plunging about three inches into the grass between my index and middle fingers of my right hand. I think my heart stopped. Then when I felt my heartbeat return, it occurred to me that it could have imbedded itself into my skull. That activity never was performed again. Yet another close call! (Two years later when we lived in Hattiesburg, Lois and her son, Max, came for a visit in June. We packed up to visit for a few days on the Gulf Coast, taking two cars and staying at the Alamo Plaza Motel. On the second day, we three kids had found a fishing boat moored in the shallow water of the Gulf Coast. We released the rope and were about to paddle off when the owner yelled at us. By the time we got the boat back, the police had arrived. Realizing that we were NOT stealing it, that we were but young teenagers, the owner brought no charges against us, but the policeman did transport us back to the motel in his cruiser. Mother and Lois pulled up in their car at the same time, and we were delivered to our parents, tormented by the dread of the presumed punishment. Max was very upset and embarrassed, having been handed off to them by the policeman. As we got in their car, Max began cursing his mother. We had discovered during the two summer trips to Morristown that Max was spoiled and disobedient, and we were not surprised at this behavior. Mother turned around in the front seat and said sternly, "Max, do not curse your mother!" Lois was furious with Mother's admonition. She said something like, "You have no right to talk to my son like that." Lois went directly and quickly to her room, packed, and she and Max left! Mother later explained to Jay and me that Max probably was the way he was because his parents were divorced, and Lois was struggling so hard to raise him on her own). Divorce results in serious collateral damage to family relationships.

Ben Hogan was already known as America's best golfer in 1952. He was the tour's leading money winner in 1940, 1941 and 1942 before going into the military. He won the Professional Golfers' Association title in 1946. In 1948, he won both the U. S. Open and the PGA Tournaments, and was the leading money-winner on the tour. But, he lost almost all of the 1949 season after the car he was driving was involved in a head-on collision with a bus near Van Horn, Texas. He sustained a broken collar bone and fractured rib, but worse, a double fracture of the pelvic bone and a fractured ankle. It was believed at the time that he would never play golf again. He recovered from the trauma, winning the 1950 U. S. Open Championship sixteen months following the near-fatal accident. He won his first Masters in 1951 and then won the U. S. Open, all while moviegoers were watching an inspiring Hollywood version of the dramatic comeback story in the movie, *Follow the Sun*. We watched the movie in the local theater.

In 1952, Hogan's ability appeared to wane. He failed to repeat his championships at the Masters and the U. S. Open. He had his fortieth birthday in August 1952, and that generated speculation that Hogan's comeback was finished. In 1952 Ben Hogan visited Grenada Country Club. Daddy was privileged to play a practice round with him. Louise had first-hand knowledge of this event.[45] Ben Hogan and Daddy were contemporaries, Daddy being four years older.

Mary Foy Taylor was two years older than Jay. She was the only child of Lavinia and T. F. Taylor, Jr., each of whom had a Cadillac parked in their carport. The garage was located totally out of sight, around to the left side and in the basement level of their three-story home. When Mary Foy (Foy, as Paige called her) was a sophomore in high school in 1952, she got her driver's license. Her parents bought her a new yellow Cadillac convertible for her 15th birthday. It was pictured in the school year book parked in front of the high school building with the top down. Mary Foy and her fellow cheerleaders were perched around the rear seat and on doors of the car during a football rally. When Mary Foy graduated from high school, her parents gave her a large diamond ring of just over two carats. What more could a girl who has everything need? I don't recall anyone's being envious. It just seemed natural for her to have all of these things. Like Kim Curry, the son of my parents good friend, Dr. Hugh Curry.

In November 1952, General Dwight D. Eisenhower was elected as the thirty-fourth president, with Richard M. Nixon as his vice president. It was a sweeping victory. Jay and I were not the least bit interested in politics at that age. I was almost twelve years of age.

Truman decided not to run again for president, but to retire. Following the inauguration, Harry and Bess Truman drove their own car home to Independence, Missouri.[46] They moved in with Bess' parents, for lack of money to have their own home. He had no secret service and no retirement

---

[45] In a conversation that I had with the Editor of *THE GRENADA SENTINEL* in the 1990s, I told him this story and I asked if the paper had back issues. Once affirmed, I asked if they were on microfiche. They were not, but the Editor advised that he would be happy to escort me to the stacks of archived papers for me to look. I never had the chance to go to Grenada and search for an article.

[46] Truman died at 88, December 26, 1972, after a stubborn fight for life.

income, other than a small Army pension. Former presidents simply did not have such in those days.

Daddy bought a new 1953 green and white Oldsmobile 88. My parents decided to take the family to New Orleans for the Sugar Bowl. On December 30, we drove to Grenada and got Grandmother McCaslin. We stayed the first night at the Alamo Plaza Motel in Biloxi – a motel was a contraction of motor hotel the invention of which was recent. Driving on to New Orleans on the 31st, we arrived late in the afternoon. Jay and I noticed a hamburger place called "A Meal-a-Minute." That's where we wanted to eat. Contrary to the claim in their name, the service was slack, and Daddy squared them away on that matter.

In downtown New Orleans, we checked into the Monteleon Hotel in the French Quarter. Early that evening, we met with T. F. and Lavinia. The Taylors and Mother and Daddy wanted us to see the two piano players at Pat O'Brien's in the French Quarter. We rounded the corner off Bourbon Street, and the line waiting to get in extended the entire length of the block. We got in line at the end. Grandmother was not with us. In a minute, T. F. went to the head of the line and soon returned. The doorman came around moments later and called for the party of T. F. Taylor, leading us back through the front door of Pat O'Brien's and seating us in the big room with the huge mirrors hanging at a forty-five degree angle from the ceiling. Sitting at a table, one could view the piano players and the heralded black waiter behind the bar. The waiter had huge, long fingernails with which he would thump the metal tray in his other hand and the tips, the coins, would bounce three inches high. It was thrilling to see and hear, albeit briefly. We had no sooner gotten our drinks (*Coca-Colas* for Jay and me) when the manager came over, objected to mine and Jay's ages, and we were told that we had to leave. We were there less than ten minutes. When Mother inquired how T. F. had gotten all of us in so quickly, it was disclosed that T. F. had tipped the doorman fifty dollars. Although that was a lot of money (in today's dollars, over eight-hundred dollars) it did not appear in any way to bother T. F. He always was a big tipper; he had millions. And, he found pleasure in our having seen the show at Pat O'Brien's.

Mother told us on more than one occasion, that T. F. had a custom that he followed when they dined out at fine restaurants. She advised that a fine steak dinner, French fried potatoes, and a salad would cost about three dollars. She said: "When the waitress would first come to the table and was ready to take our order, she would notice a stack of ten silver dollars

163

on the corner of the table next to T. F. He then would point to the stack and say, 'Young lady, this will be your tip IF you give my guests your finest service.' We got excellent service. However, if *anyone* needed anything and the waiter was not there, when she returned, T. F. would get her attention and take one silver dollar off the stack. That usually would do the trick. No one in the dinner party suffered any want for the rest of the evening." (That ten dollar tip in 1938 would be equal to over one hundred and sixty-five dollars in 2015).

January 1, 1953, we were up early, preparing to go to the Sugar Bowl. Georgia Tech was playing Ole Miss. This was the first college football game that Grandmother McCaslin had ever attended, and the first bowl game for Jay and me.

The game was exciting. Of course, we all were pulling for Ole Miss. Coach Bobby Dodd was at the beginning of his heyday. Tech had beaten its opponents by a combined score of 325 to 59 and had allowed only one team, Florida, to score in double figures. Legendary Georgia Tech football coach Bobby Dodd once said that his 1952 co-national champions was the best team he had ever coached. They had recorded a perfect twelve to zero season by beating Ole Miss in the 1953 Sugar Bowl. The team was voted No.1 by the International News Service, while Michigan State was voted tops in the AP and UPI polls, therefore attaining a co-national championship.

I'll never forget one thing. A man, sitting with friends about four rows in front of us, became so excited during the game that he sustained a fatal heart attack. The ambulance crew came in and whisked his body away. Only those spectators in the immediate vicinity were even aware of the death, and the game never stopped. Georgia Tech, with quarterback Pepper Rogers, had mastered this win over Ole Miss. (Many years later, after Bobby Dodd, Pepper Rogers coached Tech).

In 1952, the polio vaccine was created by Dr. Joseph Salk. Princess Elizabeth became Queen of England at age twenty-five.

Ben Hogan rebounded in 1953 by winning five of the six tournaments he entered. His greatest victories were a sweep, as follows: he started his 1953 season at the Masters in Georgia, where he set a tournament record in a five-shot victory; he missed the PGA Tournament, because it was scheduled at the same time as the British Open, which he won; and he won the U. S. Open in Pennsylvania, beating longtime rival Sam Snead by six shots. No golfer had ever won three majors in one season. Hogan was the first since Bobby Jones to capture four U. S. Open titles, and he was four-time PGA Player of the Year.

The 1953 Eupora Telephone Book had on the mailing label our name, 2102 telephone number, and our address, Adams Avenue.

Jay and I watched the inauguration of President Eisenhower on television on the ground floor den of T. F. Taylor, Jr.'s home while our parents viewed the ceremony upstairs in the library. The inauguration made the front page of all of the newspapers, text and pictures. Eisenhower brought to the Presidency his prestige as Commanding General of the victorious forces in Europe during World War II.[47]

In April 1953, Mother and Daddy were in Little Rock with the Taylors and Fortners for the "ONE HUNDRED MILLION" celebration of National Old Line Insurance Company. That mark had been reached with insurance coverage by the company, and the President of National Old Line, Bill Darby, threw a party in a Little Rock hotel. T. F. Taylor was Chairman of National Old Line. The Darbys were close friends of Daddy and Mother.

I continued to go frequently to Sturgis with Daddy right up until the end of June, at which time I was twelve and one-half years of age. And, by then, it was often just Daddy and me who traveled to Grenada on Sundays. We were very close. Although we did not talk much, I sensed that we had a mutual love and respect for one another. Clearly he simply enjoyed having one of his sons with him. I consider it a distinct privilege to have had this close relationship with my father, one that boys often do not experience in the busy suburban family today. I had finished the seventh grade, and Jay the eighth.

Julius and Ethel Rosenberg were executed for espionage shortly after 8 p.m. in Sing-Sing Prison on June 19, 1953. This event closed the book on one of the most sensational cases in history.

We vacationed in Morristown again in summer of 1953. This year, Mother drove her Cadillac. Looking again at a diary that Mother kept, entries were made for July 1, 1953, in this way:

> Wednesday, July 1, 1953. We (Jay, Si, and I) left at 6:30
> on our trip to Morristown. Mac got up sleepily to tell us good

---

[47] Ike was successful in obtaining a truce in Korea and strived ceaselessly during his eight years in the White House to ease the tensions of the Cold War. He followed the moderate policies of "Modern Republicanism," and left office saying, "America is today the strongest, most influential, and most productive nation in the world."

bye. We went in the Cadillac, taking water and sandwiches in Mac's nice ice bag.

We were so happy–had our prayer and went gaily on our way. I wore the green cotton seersucker sun dress.

We did not stop for lunch, as I remember. We ate sandwiches and pushed on, reaching Chattanooga about 2:30 (3:30 EST). Went up the mountain and took in Ruby Falls. The guides were so cute...

Checked in at Read House. Ate supper there and went to prayer meeting at First Baptist. Visiting speaker spoke on "Complete in Christ." Jay and Si went to picture show and I got ready for bed and wrote some cards.

Thursday, July 2. Up about 7:00. Breakfast at Read House, then off. Debated about driving through Smokies, but decided to do so, for fear we would not be able to come back that way. Beautiful, lovely drive. So much fun with my boys.

Lunch at roadside restaurant. Then on to Bryson City to stop a moment to shop. Jay bought Cecile a mustard seed necklace and mailed it there. Then on to Cherokee. Shopped all over town, but bought little, for it was all "old stuff" to us this year. Then entered the park and drove up the mountain. Some rain, but not bad. Down the mountain to Gatlinburg, where I found a straw bag for myself and Lois. Took Max a little plastic dog.

Arrived about 6:30 in Morristown – saw a mule overcome with sunstroke! Lois was so cute. Told me about her engraved invitation she sent, which I did not get before I left (but Mac got it). We unpacked, made beds, and talked. Jay came home and we ate supper. To sleep, happily. (Later Mother added in her hand-writing: Mac ate supper with Ovid and Gladys Senate on this night).

Friday, July 3. Lois went to work at court house. I slept late. Then washed the clothes and started lunch. Lois came home at 11:30 and we ate and planned our visit. She left at 12:30. I cleaned the kitchen and took a nap. Then dressed and rode around–down the highway by the place where the kids and I ate last year. Then around and back. Started to go to town to get my hair cut, but was so hot I came home. Lois came home at 4:00 and we bought groceries and planned a picnic for Saturday...

Saturday, July 4. Cleaned up, packed for our picnic and took off. Went to Carson Springs, and kids swam...Then home to Morristown...Mac played golf on this day at Grenada and spent the night with Evelyn and Gordon Ebert in Winona, leaving there early Sunday Morning for home to bathe and change.

Sunday, July 5. Pressed my new black organdy skirt and white blouse, and dressed for Sunday school. Went to Mrs. Hale's class with lesson on Romans. I put in one word, "*Have* been saved, *are being* saved, and *will be* saved." Church. Man with big diamond. Jay said that he bet he owned a jewelry store. Don't remember sermon. Home....

July 5 was the final entry. Mother kept a bound, daily ledger of expenses most of her entire life. In this one from 1953, she recorded expenses to the penny, for items such as church, Sunday dinner, milk, coffee, meat, snap shots, W.M.U., telephone bill, water bill, ice bill, gas, stamps and papers, shoe shop, football game, haircut, etc.., including particular articles of clothing and household purchases. She records deposits "to boys' bank account," which were earnings from our paper routes. Her contribution to church is noted each week. She made marginal notes of important things. For the first week of July, her manuscript header reads "Morristown." For July 8, she has circled Wednesday, and her note reads: "Mac died – Waverly, Tenn."

Mother sent a picture postcard to Daddy, depicting "Lake at Camp Ridgecrest for Boys, Ridgecrest, N.C." The card is postmarked Asheville, July 7, 1953, 8:30 p.m. (This is unsettling. This was the day Daddy left Eupora and the day before his death). The card reads as follows:

Mr. A. J. McCaslin
Eupora, Miss.

We are staying at the Morristown cabin here, swimming and eating here at Montreat. We are really having a marvelous time. This place & Montreat are just as beautiful as everyone says they are. We haven't decided what to do this afternoon. There are so many choices. We will be home Monday.

Love,
M.M.

The only other extant picture postcard was postmarked Asheville, July 7, 1953, 8:30 p.m., and conveys similar information to the Taylors – their best friends:

> Mr. and Mrs. T. F. Taylor
> Eupora, Miss.
>
> We are staying here at Lois' church cabin – eating and swimming here and at Montreat. It is just wonderful up here! Just right.
> Don't know exactly when we will be home.
>
> Love,
M.M.

The *Webster Progress* later reported, along with the foregoing information, that reliable reports from Tennessee authorities acknowledge that Daddy had been murdered, and that an investigation was being conducted.

Apparently, Daddy was planning to surprise us by joining us in Morristown for the duration of our two-week visit there. Judging from the statement made by T. F. Taylor, Jr., in the newspaper article that follows, Daddy left Eupora on Monday, July 6. According to the local authorities, he died Wednesday, July 8, 1953, in Waverly, Humphrey County, Tennessee. T. F. Taylor, Jr. and Marshall Mac Coleman, both very close friends, had driven to Waverly to make an identification.

Mother was reached by telephone at Lois' home in Morristown early in the morning and explicitly informed of the matter. She immediately told us of the tragedy; then we quickly packed our things and left, driving two hundred and ninety miles straight through to Waverly, which was located west of Nashville. Upon arrival, we took a motel room. There Jay and I remained while Mother met T. F. Taylor, Jr., Marshal Mac Coleman, and the authorities. Mother made a positive identification. Soon she returned to the motel.

Mother's first telephone call from the motel had been to Daddy's mother. She had not wished to call until identification was made. When she answered, Mother said, "Mother Mac, I have some bad news." Grandmother McCaslin replied, "I know." Mother said, "You know? You know what?" She calmly stated, "I know that Mac is dead. I read a brief article in the newspaper, in which it was stated that an Oldsmobile with Mississippi license plates had been found on the bank of the lake where the unidentified body was found. The Lord told me that it was Alston." Granny had already dealt emotionally with the loss of her oldest son; Mother's telephone call merely confirmed the fact. Mother often said that this revelation was the intervention of the Holy Spirit. (It is amazing to me. In Mother's own words later, she said that she knew three months in advance that Daddy was going to die. She regarded the premonition as an act of the Holy Spirit. Having only in recent years lost both her mother and her father, she was forewarned. I, too, while at the coast in Galveston in 1952, believe I had somewhat of a premonition of Daddy dying).

We left for home the next morning and I remember absolutely nothing of the drive home to Eupora, Mississippi, a distance exceeding two hundred and fifty miles. We all must have been in a state of shock; of unspeakable loss. Our strong, male role model was gone.

Mother saved several obituaries as well as twenty-two newspaper articles pertaining to Daddy's untimely death. Three are provided as representative:

BODY BEING EXHUMED BELIEVED EUPORA MAN
Wife, Partner "Almost Certain" Of Identification.

Waverly, Tenn., (Friday) July 10. A body tentatively identified as that of a Eupora, Miss., lumber dealer was being exhumed Friday night after the businessman's wife and his partner told Humphrey County Sheriff J. Lawrence Bradley they were "pretty certain" the body is the missing Mississippian.

Sheriff Bradley said he tentatively identified the dead man as A. J. McCaslin, 45, partner in Sturgis Lumber Co. of Eupora. He said he notified McCaslin's family after a car registered in Mr. McCaslin's name was found abandoned near the point where the body was found in nearby Kentucky Lake Wednesday...

Mrs. Mary Margaret McCaslin arrived here Friday from Morristown, Tenn., where she was visiting relatives, and T. F. Taylor, Jr., the business partner, came from Eupora.

Mr. Taylor said earlier Friday, before leaving Eupora for Waverly, that he last saw Mr. McCaslin Monday, shortly before Mr. McCaslin left town without saying where he was going...

The coroner's office said Mr. McCaslin apparently died of drowning. Sheriff Bradley said he is checking reports that two men were seen riding in Mr. McCaslin's car in this area earlier this week....

Another article added more information:

> Sheriff Bradley said ignition keys were still in Mr. McCaslin's car, as well as freshly-pressed clothing, golf balls, and a set of golf clubs. Mr. McCaslin was a golfing and swimming enthusiast...

Still, another article had this information:

> A Humphreys County coroner's jury held that Mr. McCaslin died from drowning. There was no indication of foul play, the report said, but Mrs. McCaslin said her husband usually carried several hundred dollars with him. His wallet and clothes are missing....

One article stated that among the articles found in Daddy's car were letters addressed to T. F. Taylor, Jr. It is presumed that with Marshal Mac Coleman's consent, T. F. took those letters – they were his. Mother neither knew the contents of the letters, nor did T. F. mention them to her. T. F. had lost his best friend. The once-intense companionship of two couples who enjoyed each other's company had ended. The friendship of two men who worked together and traveled together, enjoyed football games and fine eating in notable restaurants, would no longer to be. Those days were gone. Mother now, suddenly, was a widow with the responsibility of her two boys. (Later, Mother said that the Taylors seldom corresponded after the tragedy, except for cards and notes at Christmas. And as will be seen later, we moved to Hattiesburg the next year).

There was a gathering of the entire family at the Garner Funeral Home in Grenada and a large crowd of Grenada people. I can recall having a feeling of such great importance. This was my daddy for whom everyone had assembled. Jay and I were the center of attention among our cousins. Daddy's funeral followed, at Grenada Presbyterian Church, in which he had been reared. Grandfather McCaslin had been an esteemed elder in the Grenada Presbyterian Church. Daddy was buried in the family plot at Odd Fellows Cemetery, Grenada. (The remaining grave sites were quit claimed to me from Aunt Louise and Uncle Henry in the early 1990s. Our already having burial plots in Savannah, in 2012, Jay's wife, Pam and I gifted eight cemetery grave sites in the McCaslin family plot to First Presbyterian Church of Grenada, to be used for any church family member who made the need known).

It was later disclosed by family members that Grenada Country Club had closed the day of Daddy's funeral in honor of him – a precedent in the history of the club. Daddy had been a loyal member.

There were further reports from the authorities that Daddy had been followed presumably by someone that he knew; and it was disclosed that he was accompanied by another man just prior to his death. Furthermore, there was evidence that Daddy's body had been in the trunk of his car. The clothing that he had been wearing, as well as his money clip and money, were not found. Mother was not satisfied that the Tennessee authorities had done all that they could, even though the F.B.I. had been called in on the case. The circumstances remained a mystery and eventually, with Mother's consent, the case was closed by the F.B.I.

(For more than a year, I had a recurring dream. Perhaps it was the Lord's way of comforting me in the loss of Daddy. The dream varied slightly, but it was always the same situation, that of Daddy's returning home from an extended trip. The setting always was at the intersection on Highway 82, where the Doolittle Pontiac dealership was located, which was the drop-off point for our newspapers each day. In the dreams, Daddy would drive up in his Oldsmobile and get out of the car and walk up, as though nothing had happened. Jay and I were all so happy to see him again that there was no concern about where he had been for all those months. In the dream, Daddy provided the perfectly plausible explanation – but my dream never revealed the explanation).

On July 27, 1953, the UN, North Korea, and China signed an armistice agreement – South Korea refused to sign – and the fighting ended. The armistice established a demilitarized zone 2½ miles wide across the middle of Korea at the 28th parallel, from which troops and weapons were to be withdrawn. This demilitarized zone, or DMZ, was in fact heavily fortified.[48]

---

[48] Suzanne and I would visit the DMZ in 1969, while I was stationed in Korea, at which time the U. S. had 25,000 troops in Korea. With no peace treaty signed, North and South Korea remained technically still at war. The armistice and the DMZ served to maintain a delicate peace.

Six weeks later, in the fall of 1953, Mother was offered a teaching position in speech and English at Eupora High School by the Superintendent of the schools, John Sanders. Whereas she did some work with the schools and worked with private students, she did not accept the teaching position. She was determined to resume and earn her college degree and then obtain a graduate degree in speech therapy.

We had Daddy's car, a 1953 Oldsmobile, and Mother's car, a 1951 Cadillac Fleetwood. Mother was advised by Uncle Henry McCaslin in a letter that the Cadillac would be more reliable, even though two years older. She sold the Oldsmobile.

In August1953, I entered the eighth grade, and Jay the ninth. I was honored to be elected eighth grade class president. Jay continued to surpass me with his grades. In fact, I believe that I studied harder than he, but he made all A's. There was a procedure that the principal followed. If one reached the end of the semester with an "A" average, he or she was not required to take the final exam – which covered the entire semester. All of the students were gathered in the assembly hall. The principal would take the microphone in hand to name those who were "exam-exempt," and once recognized, each of those students would proceed up front to receive their report cards, and then they were dismissed. Free to go home. They left gleefully. Before the announcement, I would find myself praying that my name, too, would be announced "exam-exempt," and then realizing full well that it was simply not going to be. For me, that was a very early and clear object lesson in wrongfully-employed prayer. Jay, like Mother, was very bright. I was simply smart.

There was an elderly widowed lady, an octogenarian, with whom her two old-maid daughters lived in a duplex on Adams Avenue, a half of a block toward town. They were poor. The three women made monkey dolls out of socks, as well as many other gifts by hand. Everyone in town felt sorry for the three women, particularly the old woman, and they visited their home to purchase things just to help them out. It was rumored that the two daughters, both of whom were in their sixties, never married. Rather, they stayed with their mother to help her. At Christmas each year, many people in the community would take them gifts and boxes of food – home canned goods as well as store-bought things. I know that Mother did, for I was with her on one occasion.[49]

Mother's booklet, first printed Dec. 1951, was the Guest Editorial in *THE WEBSTER PROGRESS*, December 24, 1953. She wrote as follows in the booklet:

Concerning Gifts

A little boy was heard to pray, "Lord, help us to remember that this is YOUR birthday, not ours!" What is Christmas, anyway? But quite another thing is what we have made of it. To many it is an orgy, and ordeal, instead of a gracious, grateful time of praising Him for the gifts He came to bring. SALVATION, PEACE, and LOVE, and JOY unspeakable! There are those who still reject His marvelous gifts. Incomprehensible it must be, this unbelief, to the angels around the throne of God.

Just imagine for a moment that you were transported to another realm, transformed perhaps to a veritable angel of God, being now permitted to have your first glimpse of this earth and the vaunted human race. An angel, knowing well the incomparable Love of God, the matchless Grace, poured out for centuries...but having just now your initial view of the proposed recipients of that Grace–those creatures known as men. Imagine then the consternation of this angel as he speaks:

"So those are men! But what is all the darkness they have made between? Doubt and fear and unbelief! Why can't they see the Light of Heaven, the glorious Light of our God has beamed to them, through Bethlehem and Calvary?

"What are they doing at this Christmas time, in such a mad and scurrying unconscious rush? How miserable they are and worried, most of them. There should be reverent silence on the earth or joyous songs of praise–but so much blatant noise there is instead. Strife and hatred, graft and greed, and senseless revelry. What is it all about? Oh, God, don't people know what Christmas is?

"Where is the PEACE You offered them? I cannot see it... oh, yes–I catch a glimmering, a single heart just here and there

---

[49] Shortly after we left Eupora, Mother heard from a friend that the old lady had died. In the duplex, the daughters had found money stashed here and there, estimated to be over one-hundred thousand dollars. We heard that each daughter bought a new convertible automobile and left Eupora, in opposite directions.

which has in faith accepted Your measureless gift of peace. But oh–so rare! Do they not want it? They don't believe it's true.

"And where is LOVE? Is there no love–no love at all to meet and share in our God's love–or care? Oh, God–show me some love on this Your earth. Oh, yes–I see a scattering–in the hearts of little children, trusting, sweet, too young to hate. And in an older heart–one here–one yonder–another over there; those hearts that have been crushed, and learned of love by turning first to Thee, in faith believing. Of course, there is no other way. For human love is selfish, circumscribed, until it has been purified by Thee. Oh, God–why can't they see, and hear, and feel the love You have for them–and rise above those other lesser things, the tinsel trinkets with which they think they are satisfied?

"Oh, men! Men of earth" cries the anguished angle from above. "Look up and see! It is bound to be dark if you shut your eyes. But look–just look, and see 'light of the knowledge of the glory of God in the face of Jesus Christ.' And your hearts will fill with love to overflowing.

"And JOY. Peace, love and joy–the gifts Salvation brings. Where is the joy that Christ was sent to give? Nineteen hundred years it's been more–and yet, the world is farther now from joy than it has ever been. Oh, yes, they call it joy–this harried, feverish hurry they are in–this frantic rush to buy and wrap and send a lot of things that perish with the using. 'Tis well, of course, to share one's good with others who have less–but oh, how rare a gift of lasting value, and free, but priceless!' These gifts of God in Christ.

PEACE – LOVE – JOY

"Oh, God–God," cries our angel in despair. "You went down once into the world, and, dying for their sin you offered all these things. Go down again!"

And God might well reply, "I'm there–beside each fainting heart. I only wait for them to ask of me. My gifts are free–to anyone who will believe and see."

And myriad angle voices sing, "Amen."

Mother received an invitation sent in error, the envelope addressed to "Mr. Bull McCaslin, Eupora, Miss.," postmarked Feb. 25, 1954, Greenwood. Enclosed was an engraved invitation:

> The Greenwood Country Club cordially invites you to play
> in the Seventh Annual Invitational Golf Tournament to be held
> May 13th, 14th, 15th, and 16th, 1954 at the Greenwood Country
> Club Greenwood, Mississippi

Many of Daddy's friends called him "Bull." Taurus the Bull is the sign of the zodiac for period including May twentieth, Daddy's date of birth. His golfing friends gave him this nickname. Inadvertently, he had been left on the invitation list.

In a step of faith, Mother determined to complete her college education, which had been disrupted in 1932, during the Great Depression. She corresponded with the President of Blue Mountain College in February 1954, seeking advice on her desire to pursue her college course work. In her first letter to the President of Blue Mountain College, Mother spoke of the unusual difficulties that she had endured over the prior six months since Daddy's death. She shielded Jay and me from the adversities that she was facing.[50] She mentioned the challenges facing her in the future with her two teenage sons; that John Sanders, the Superintendent of Eupora High School, had offered her a full-time teaching position in speech; but that she preferred to pursue a degree in speech therapy, for both qualification and credibility. She said that she had considered taking courses at Mississippi State College, in Starkville, located about twenty-five miles from Eupora. We have copies of her letters to the admission offices and the replies from Blue Mountain College and Mississippi State College.

By March, she had decided to make application to Mississippi Southern College in Hattiesburg. The Speech Department at Mississippi Southern had the most exalted reputation in speech therapy in the State of Mississippi. Speech pathology and speech therapy was essentially a new field and Mother's chosen field of study, her having had courses in elocution while

---

[50]   All that we knew about the ordeal was what little that Mother told us over the years. She really talked little of the tragedy, and we had to prod her for the details she did offer.

at Blue Mountain College in the early 1930s. We have several carbon copies of letters that she wrote to the President of Mississippi Southern.[51]

We have a letter received from George Hughes, of whom we spoke earlier. George was a close friend and a classmate of Uncle Willie's at the Naval Academy. Mother had been invited to the senior prom at Annapolis, and her escort was Cadet George Hughes. He had fallen in love with Mother, but the feeling was not mutual. Nonetheless, Mother had stayed in touch with Hughes over the years. He married later and had a son, Joe, who followed his father into the Navy. George rose to Admiral in the Navy and retired to California. Mother boldly and consistently witnessed her Christian faith to him each time they exchanged letters, apparently not persuading him.

On May 17, 1954, Brown vs. Board of Education was handed down by the Supreme Court, in which the Court declared that schools would be integrated, that "separate educational facilities are inherently unequal." (The ruling was gradually followed by integration of the public schools. Several states in the deep South responded with actions to prevent integration, beginning in 1957 in Arkansas. The first phase of the Civil Rights Movement began in 1896 and continued through to the second phase in the late 1940s, which stretched to 1968. I was a sophomore in dental school at Emory University when Atlanta had "sit-ins." Much more unrest unfolded during and after the life and efforts of Martin Luther King).

In May 1954 I came to a stark realization. Daddy truly was gone. It had finally impacted me. The recurring dream of his return home ceased. I had a very difficult time dealing with this sudden realization of his loss, even though he had died almost a year earlier. My obstacle, as Mother perceived it and explained, perhaps stemmed from the closed-casket funeral service – that I, as a twelve-year-old, had not actually seen Daddy's body, and that I was in a state of denial of his death. The anguish of this final reality lasted for several weeks. It was a hard thing for a thirteen-year-old! Yet God had His plan for us.

Also, by May in 1954, Mother had narrowed her search for her continued education, ruling out Mississippi State College, which was only about thirty miles from Eupora. Speech therapy was a relatively new field and Mississippi Southern College in Hattiesburg was reputed to have the

---

[51]   In later years Mother explained how imposing was the thought to her of moving so far from home, but that the decision was made, based upon faith in God, which faith had continued to grow, particularly since the death of her father.

best graduate program in the state. She was not only accepted at Mississippi Southern, but also was awarded a stipend. A marginal note in her weekly register in May reads, "Bought house May 5." Mother received letters in April and May of 1954 from the President of Mississippi Southern College, in which he confirmed her acceptance, along with a paid staff position. We were bound for Hattiesburg, Mississippi.

We drove to Hattiesburg May 16, 1954, following the moving van, and moved directly into our house at 101 South 21st Street. Located two houses off of Hardy Street, the gate to Mississippi Southern was less than ten blocks up the hill, close enough that we could get there easily by bicycle. Mother resumed her college studies, now matriculating at Mississippi Southern College, beginning summer quarter 1954. As she had taken a correspondence course on short story writing from the University of Chicago, as well having taken a course at Mississippi State College, these hours transferred, along with her credits from Blue Mountain College.

On July 5, 1954, Elvis Presley, from Tupelo, Mississippi, recorded "That's All Right," at Memphis Recording Service. Memphis, already the Home of the Blues, became the birthplace of Rock 'n Roll. As a matter of fact, Sam Phillips, the studio owner, overheard the young boy playing the song on his guitar during a coffee break, and it required a few takes to make the recording, using studio musicians. (In 2008, I completed the genealogy of our good friends, Heber and Sister Simmons of Jackson, Mississippi. I had met Heber, a colleague, in 1971 at a meeting in Williamsburg, Virginia. Heber, six years my senior, was from Tupelo. He was a couple of years ahead of Elvis in school and in the early 1950s he and his classmates had said: "That boy can sing." Heber is a storyteller. He said: "During my graduate training in Memphis at the University of Tennessee Dental School, a classmate and I were walking up the street to go to lunch. From over his shoulder I heard my name called loudly. Now when your name is Heber and someone calls out your name, you turn to see who it is. The fellow had a black leather jacket on and his hair was greasy and combed back in a duck tail. As he approached, I recognized him. Elvis came up and grabbed my hand to say hello. A few minutes later, Elvis had left. My classmates were impressed).

I attended ninth grade at Hawkins Junior High School, and Jay entered Hattiesburg High School. Mother benefited financially from the paid staff position during the time that she attended Southern – a stipend. The staff appointment must have been based upon her scholastic acumen, as well as her need. She earned enough from her work to meet all the expenses, never encroaching upon the corpus of twenty thousand in savings, proceeds from a National Old Life Insurance policy from Daddy's death.[52]

Among the most essential things that we did upon arriving in Hattiesburg was to join the First Baptist Church, which congregation had only recently moved into a huge new brick complex. The church was located downtown. Here again, we never missed Sunday school or morning or evening church service, and we returned for Wednesday night Prayer Meeting. Along with our other church friends, we were active in the "Royal Ambassadors." The program was well organized, and an emphasis was given to Bible verse memorization. It was through this organization that we met many of our friends. And we participated in a summer camp sponsored by the church.

Three letters were received from C. S. Lewis. Mother must have written Lewis on the occasion of the first anniversary of Daddy's death. Apparently, she was looking for consolation and "guidances" from Lewis. The first letter pertained to the "terrible calamity" that had occurred in Mother's life, and the loneliness from which she was suffering:

Magdalen College,

Oxford
Aug. 2nd 54
Dear Mrs. McCaslin,

Than you for your letter of the July 25th. I will certainly put you in my prayers. I can well believe that you were divinely supported at the time of your terrible calamity. People often are. It is afterwards, when the new and bleaker life is beginning to be a routine, that one often feels one has been left rather unaided. I am sure one is not really so. God's presence is not the same as the feeling of God's presence and He may be doing most for us when we think He is doing least. Loneliness, I am pretty sure, is one of the ways by which we can grow spiritually. Until we are lonely we may easily think we have got farther than we really have in Christian Love: our (natural and innocent, but merely

---

[52]   Jay and I did not know that Mother had used only the interest from the insurance money. After her death in 1980, the twenty-thousand had been equally divided and willed to me, Jay, our step-sister, and step-brother.

rational, not heavenly) pleasure in <u>being loved</u> – in being, as you say, an object of interest to someone – can be mistaken for progress in love itself, the outgoing, active love which is concerned with giving, not receiving. It is this latter which is the beginning of sanctity. But of course you know all this: alas, so much easier to know in theory than to submit to day by day in practice! Be very regular in your prayer and communion; and don't value special "guidances" any more than what comes thro' ordinary Christian teaching, conscience, and prudence.

I am shocked to hear that your friends think of following <u>me</u>. I wanted them to follow Christ. But they'll get over this confusion soon, I think.

Please accept my deepest sympathy,

Yours sincerely,
C.S. Lewis

Six weeks later, Lewis replied to a doctrinal question posed by Mother.[53]

The two sons of a widow obtained work. Jay worked at the counter in a dry cleaners near our high school. I found a job as a waiter in a restaurant directly across from Mississippi Southern College. These jobs we did with diligence, responsibly depositing the financial proceeds in our respective savings accounts. Then, Jay and I began again what we knew well; delivering newspapers. This time it was the New Orleans *Times Picayune*. We always carried our papers by bicycle, equipped with the one-foot-deep basket attached to the handle bars. Each of us had a lengthy paper route. We arose at about 5:00 a.m., returning home about 7:00 a.m., and following breakfast, the two of us and our mother were off to classes.

Jay and I both took up golf and tennis. As children of a student, we had access to both. We had already acquired skill in golf, having grown up on the Grenada Country Club property. But tennis was entirely new to us. The tennis court was virtually in the shadow of the football stadium. We met the Voss brothers, the younger of whom was Didi. They had played the game for many years, and we benefitted in learning the swings and the overall style by playing doubles with them. Jay and I never had a lesson.

---

[53] As noted earlier, all thirteen of these letters from Lewis were published by Walter Hooper in his continued, seminal work, published in 2006, entitled *C.S. LEWIS – LETTERS AND CORRESPONDENCE*, Vol. III, and are all transcribed in *LETTERS TO AND FROM A CHRISTIAN MOTHER AND MORE*, published 2011.

(Our second year in Hattiesburg, Didi Voss and I played Jay and the older Voss brother in the city championship. Didi and I won the match, for which we each received a trophy. In singles, it came down to Didi vs. me, and he beat the socks off of me).

Mother had a washing machine, equipped with a wringer. Following the washing cycle, the wet clothes were fed through the wringer, and the excess water ran into a drain and into the sink. The clothes had to be hung to dry on a line behind the house. This was our job. Jay and I wore blue jeans all of the time. Mother provided metal stretchers. They were, with difficulty, inserted into the legs of the wet jeans, and then stretched to the limit, for the purpose of removing the wrinkles from the wet jeans, which were then hung on the line in the back yard to dry, thereby eliminating the job of ironing the jeans. This was our job, and it was a pain!

Earlier, it was mentioned that Mother refused to let us play football, out of fear of the possibility of permanent, debilitating injury. He had had a good friend who ruined his knees for life with football-related injuries. The second thing that Mother denied us in our youth was a motorbike. She deemed them as unsafe. I believe that most all of the paper carriers had either a motor bike or a "Cushman Motor Scooter." But not Jay and Si! I thought often of owning one, but it never was going to come to pass, just like my intention of playing football. Both playing football and having a Cushman had a common flaw. Mother's determination precluded the possibility of both activities.

The paper routes engendered within us a growing sense of responsibility, which feeling was compounded with the discipline that we had learned with the similar occupation in Eupora.

My best friend was Wayne McWhorter. He and I were fourteen years old and we went all over our part of town together, usually by bicycle. His parents were very fond of me, the widow McCaslin's boy. Wayne's grandfather lived with the family. I would whistle frequently as I delivered their paper, before dawn. And, I was punctual. Wayne's grandfather once gave me ten dollars extra as reward for my whistling as I came by his bedroom window. He had grown to depend on my regularity, rather than on an alarm clock. The rewards continued, but not that much. (In 1995, Wayne called me as he was headed home to Winston-Salem, North Carolina, where he practiced neurosurgery. He had been in Savannah for a conference and had seen our office sign as he drove to the Neurological Institute. Forty years had passed since we last talked! Small world).

One cold winter morning, the alarm clock went off, we sat up in bed, saw that it was raining and very cold, and decided to stay at home. It was about an hour later that Mother appeared at the door. The telephone was ringing off the hook. She was infuriated that we had shirked our duty. We dressed in less than a minute, and Mother took us in her car, first to pick up the newspapers, and then to deliver them. Throughout the duration of running the two paper routes, she said nothing. She just cried. We never did anything like that again.

While juggling college courses and rearing two teenagers, Mother continued with her Christian admonition, exhortation, and instruction. (*LETTERS TO AND FROM A CHRISTIAN MOTHER AND MORE* has many details of these two years). As briefly mentioned in the INTRODUCTION, Mother completed her degree requirements at Mississippi Southern in one year, graduating with a degree in psychology, cum laude. Straight A grades, except for a hostile B given by the head of the psychology department, whose name need not be disclosed. When she confronted him, explaining and insisting that she had an A, he told Mother that he had purposely given her the B to prevent her from having an A in every subject. There was nothing that she could do about it. He was the head of the speech department.

On July 11, 1955, Mary Foy Taylor, the daughter of Lavinia and T. F. Taylor, Jr., married Jennings Paige Cothren. Mother told us of the wedding at the time and we were very pleased for them.

Parenthetic: Paige Cothren made All Big 8, All State, All South, and All American as a high school fullback in Natchez, Mississippi. He was No. 40 at Ole Miss, where he made All SEC, All South, and All American as a fullback, and set national collegiate records as a kicker. Ole Miss won the SEC championship two years while Paige played. He led the SEC and the nation in field goals kicked and in kick scoring in both 1955 and 1956.

He played in the Sugar Bowl, the Cotton Bowl, the College All-Star game, the North-South All-Star game, and the Hula Bowl. The *SATURDAY EVENING POST* carried an article in 1956 by Tom Siler, including two photographs. The piece is entitled "HE MADE OLE MISS A MENACE," and tells of how Coach Vaught turned the Ole Miss Rebels, once the underdog of the other powerful teams in the Southeastern Conference, into a big-time football opponent. The top photo in the feature article is of Vaught and team members. The lower image pictures Ole Miss fullback Paige Cothren carrying the ball as he ran a twenty-one yard play against Texas Christian at the Cotton Bowl on New Years day.

Cothren was drafted by the Los Angeles Rams for whom he played in the 1957 and 1958 seasons, there again setting kicking records, but he sustained a serious knee injury. He played for the Philadelphia Eagles in 1959 and retired from professional football in 1960. Paige returned to Foy's home town of Eupora to run a small chain of grocery stores that he acquired.

In 1966, the inaugural team of the Atlanta Falcons tried to lure him out of retirement as their kicker, but he opted for the New Orleans Saints, who offered to pay him $5,000 more. He signed on February 4, 1967, as the "first signee" with the Saints, but was beat out at spring practice by another kicker, Charlie Durkee, who had a steel toe in his kicking shoe. Although not as accurate as Paige, he could out-distance him. The NFL outlawed steel-toed shoes the next year. Page, never played for the Saints

Following his Christian conversion, he and Foy moved to Memphis, Tennessee, where they both attended seminary. He first pastored a church at French Camp, Mississippi. Then Paige earned the Masters degree from Dallas Theological Seminary. In Memphis, he ran a Christian counseling service for twenty-five years, and was a full-time Christian counselor with an average of over fifteen-hundred counselees every year. He authored twenty-nine books in three decades, principally on Christian subjects, but including a series of six novels and two books on football at Ole Miss.[54]

Mother completed the two-year Masters program in five quarters, magna cum laude. She then searched for work in speech therapy. Her cousin from Texas, Helen Wright, the daughter of Aunt Arlin, who visited

---

[54] On November 24, 2014, I reached Paige by telephone. We reminisced of early 1950s Eupora. I asked to purchase four copies of his book on football, *Walk Carefully Among the Dead*, inscribed to Jay, Byron, Jeff, and me. He kindly agreed. When I asked if Lavinia and T.F. had attended all of his professional games, he paused, then replied: "Well, not *all* of them." He offered to send me copies of several of his Christian books as gifts. I reciprocated, sending copies of *LETTERS TO AND FROM A CHRISTIAN MOTHER AND MORE* to Paige and his two children.

Ackerman often in the early years, had married and lived in Gainesville, Georgia. When she received word from Mother of her job search, the timing was perfect. Helen was a part of a committee of the Junior League in Gainesville, and their project was to fund the salary for a new speech therapist for Gainesville public schools. Mother was invited for an interview, hired on the spot, and shopped for a house to live in. On her return to Hattiesburg, we gathered together to discuss the prospect of moving; we prayed over the decision of leaving Mississippi; and we unanimously agreed to do so. More valued than the friendships that we had made in Hattiesburg during the two years there was Mother's happiness and sense of fulfillment. Mother flew back to Georgia, bought a new home on Lake Lanier in Gainesville, and returned to Hattiesburg. We moved immediately.

Having joined First Baptist Church of Gainesville, Jay and I quickly became involved there, just as we had been in Hattiesburg. We attended Sunday school, the morning and evening services, and the Wednesday night Prayer Meeting, just as we had in Hattiesburg and Eupora before. In fact, we also joined the Royal Ambassadors, again.

Both Jay and I sang in the choir. Dr. Warner Fussell was the distinguished pastor of the church. His sermons were very formal, almost rhetoric.

Chapter Nine

A GLIMPSE AT THE YEARS
THAT FOLLOWED

Jay lived in Gainesville only for his senior year at Gainesville High School, graduating in 1957. He had excellent grades and was accepted at Georgia Tech in their Co-Op Program, whereby he alternated, attending college classes one quarter, then working for Dupont in Camden, South Carolina the next quarter (which program ended as he began his sophomore year, having been awarded a place in the Naval Scholarship Program).

I worked as the head life guard at Green Street Swimming Pool during the summers. Not only did I keep a nice tan, but our city pool was a magnet for kids. It was where all of the pretty girls were around all day. All this, and I was paid a salary, too! It was like Heaven for a sixteen-year-old! The City of Gainesville hosted Saturday night dances on the deck at the Green Street Pool all summer. The Tricks[55] played and sang. We danced almost non-stop from about 7:00 to 11:00 p.m., every Saturday night.

I had become a close friend of Eugene Ward, Jr., who was a year behind me. Gene's sister, Barbara, had been a classmate of Jay's. In fact, at one point, when Barbara had broken up with her boyfriend, Jay had one or two dates with her. In September, Jay left for Georgia Tech, Barbara attended Stephens College in Columbia, Missouri, and I began my senior year at Gainesville High School.

---

[55]   The Tricks were a band composed of contemporaries of ours. These guys were gifted. They stayed together for many years. Prior to Nashville fame, Ronnie Milsaps was the pianist and the lead vocalist.

On December 26, 1957, Mildred Ward died at home. She was forty-five years of age. Gene and Barbara's dad, Dr. Gene Ward, suddenly was living alone in his five-bedroom, two-story house, except for his son, a junior in high school (many other details are supplied in *LETTERS TO AND FROM A CHRISTIAN MOTHER AND MORE*).

It was customary at the loss of a spouse that the partner spend a year in mourning. This custom Gene intended to honor. However, he was president of Kiwanis, and as president, he served as host to and sat next to the weekly guest speaker. For this particular early 1958 meeting, the program chairman, having known of Mother's work as the new speech therapist for the public schools, some weeks earlier had arranged for her to be the invited speaker. She was seated next to Gene. Most folks would regard this as a chance meeting. (Mother and Gene always regarded it as the sovereign will of God). They visited in clear view of many prominent Gainesville Kiwanis members.

Upon encouragement from his closest friends, Gene secretly invited Mother to go to Atlanta for dinner. Their romance began, and on future dates, they usually would drive the fifty miles to Atlanta for a play, a movie, or just dinner. I graduated from Gainesville High School in June 1958 and worked through the summer as the life guard and teaching swimming to young children.

I began college at North Georgia College, Dahlonega. I knew not what my future would hold. As noticed earlier, I wanted to be a dentist, but a widowed mother could ill afford the cost of an additional four years of tuition. I considered a major in physics, then chemistry, then physical education, or finally, at least a business degree. But God had already made other plans for me.

One year after Mildred's death, at the end of December 1958, Mother and Gene went public with their courtship. Of course the four children, along with a few close friends, had known of their interest in each other. Now, the news spread quickly.

Mother was looking for closure regarding the mystery of Daddy's tragic death that had occurred in July of 1953. We have an exceptional two-page letter to Mother from her former pastor, Richard A. Bolling,[56] minister of First Presbyterian Church, Cleveland, Mississippi. Written on

---

[56] Reverend Bolling had been their pastor in 1934, and, as earlier noted, he signed Jay's cradle roll certificate in 1940. By 1959, he had been Pastor at First Presbyterian for thirty-three years.

letterhead church stationery and dated January 21, 1959, the letter offered consolation and advice:

Dear Mary Margaret,

My connection with the McCaslin family goes back to 1916 when I was driving a T-Model Ford raising money for Belhaven College and enjoying the friendship of Rev. John Young, then pastor at Itta Bena, Miss. John later officiated at my marriage and I attended his funeral at Grenada last year. I looked again at the McCaslin monu-ment in the cemetery and remembered how Mr. McCaslin in 1916 was a millionaire Ford dealer and an honored elder in the Presbyterian Church there. The 1929 panic or recession broke him and many other automobile men.

In 1926, I came to Cleveland and found Henry McCaslin of Grenada in the Bank at Beulah nearby. I have been with Henry and his wife in some of their troubles and count them among my warm friends. Henry is an elder in the Rosedale Church where I have preached often.

Then Alston McCaslin came here with the bank and you and he were among the very charming attractive young couples of the church and very dear to Mrs. Bolling and myself. We loved you dearly and regretted greatly to lose you.

Then came little brother Byron McCaslin working with Cleveland Lumber Co. And he married Juliet Watson in our church with Uncle Paul Watson officiating. Mrs. Bolling and I drove Byron and Juliet to Leland to take the train to Vicksburg on their honeymoon. We continue to see Byron and Juliet and their son Bill often as they visit her sisters Nona and Adelaide and Virginia here. They live in Tunica now where Byron is with an architectural firm.

And we met Mother Mac from time to time at church meetings, etc. She is a great soul; a real, real Christian.

Of course Byron's wife told her sisters all she knew of Alston's death and they confided in us. I read all the papers said and made inquiry also as I was able and I reached this firm conclusion – NOBODY KNEW JUST WHAT HAPPENED. Nor do I believe anybody knows NOW.

My purpose in writing this is to remind you that your boys have a goodly inheritance from their McCaslin grandparents in Christian faith and character. Their own father, Alston, was an earnest Christian when I knew him. You and they were left under a cloud of uncertainty as to whether violence was connected with his death from unknown parties never discovered.

Since the veil was drawn over this by the investigating authorities, I cannot lift that veil nor can you. Nor can we see behind that veil. I do know, "Whosoever believeth that Jesus is the Christ shall be saved," and Alston so believed.

Now, Mary Margaret, I want to say this to YOU. If God leads to you a man you can love and respect and whom you wish to marry, you are surely entitled to marry and be happy the rest of your days. You have been a fine mother to your sons and they must indeed appreciate it.

AND when and if you find this man and marry him, I do not think he would press you for details about Alston which concern nobody now. That chapter in your life is closed. Why open it again?

The miserable fact is that past events DO haunt us and the gnawing fear of such events being recalled does breed an unhealthy fear in us. But God said "As far as the East is from the West, so far have I removed your transgressions from you." If a merciful, forgiving God so far removes our own sins from us—why should we be haunted by the sin or mistake of others? And what do we KNOW about this which you are brooding on? Nothing!

My conclusion is then that Mrs. Bolling and I still love you very much. God loves you and your boys infinitely and wants your welfare promoted in every way.

Any man who falls in love with YOU will not think he is entitled to know things you do not know and cannot know. He will be marrying YOU and loving YOU. Jesus meant more than we know when he said, "Let the dead bury the dead....Follow thou Me."

So my dear lady – trust God, follow Him, forget as much as you can of the sad yesterdays and live in the sunshine of God's love and your family love NOW.

With the earnest hope this letter may bring you some comfort or help and reminding you again we still love you and ALL the McCaslins, I am,

Devotedly yours,
R. A. Bolling

That singular letter served to confirm in my mind and heart that I will see Daddy in Heaven. I am as convinced as any human can be that Daddy was an humble, believing Christian.

In the providence of God, Gene proposed to Mother in the winter of 1959 and they married on May 2, 1959. During the summer that followed, my stepfather assured me that he would provide the financial means for me to go to Emory University School of Dentistry. I had only to make the grades. I returned to North Georgia College for my sophomore year. (I am a debtor today first to the generosity and encouragement of my late stepfather, Gene Ward and second, to my mentor and friend, the late Dr. Robert M. Jennings, for his kind enthusiasm, his advice, and his two letters of recommendation, first to Emory University, and then to Emory University School of Dentistry. By the time of Robert's retirement, he was the honored recipient of a unique award from the Georgia Dental Association for having brought ten men into the profession).

My junior and senior years were completed at Emory University. Four years of dental school followed, and I entered the two-year Masters in Dentistry program at Emory, graduating in 1968.

Meanwhile Jay had graduated in 1961 from Georgia Institute of Technology with a degree in industrial management and moved to Chapel Hill, to manage the flagship location of a men's clothing store, which had two locations in Atlanta, as well as stores in Charlotte and Dallas. Jay had worked at the West Peachtree store in Atlanta while a student at Georgia Tech. Jay's girlfriend, Pam Stanley, whom he had met his freshman year while in the Georgia Tech co-op program working for Dupont in Camden, South Carolina, enrolled at Agnes Scott College, Decatur, Georgia, in order for them to be closer. However, upon Jay's move to Chapel Hill, she transferred to the University of North Carolina. They were engaged, and then they married June 23, 1962. In 1966 they had fraternal twins, a boy and a girl of whom more will be said later. Jay was two years behind me, graduating third in his dental school class at UNC in 1968. Pam was Phi Beta Kappa and took the Masters Degree at UNC in special education. Although accepted at UNC, as I had been, Jay chose to do his residency in pediatric dentistry at Emory, during which two years I served in the Dental Corps of the U.S. Army.

With me at Ft. Hood, Texas, and Jay at Emory University, we carefully planned and developed a partnership practice with an established colleague in Savannah. My second year in the U.S. Army took Suzanne and me to

Korea where I served as Chief of Dental Services, Seoul Military Hospital. In June 1970, Jay completed his second and final year in pediatric dentistry at Emory. I completed my two-year tour of duty in July, returned from Korea, and we launched our private practice the first week of August.

We struggled with our practice and were forced to travel to distant public health facilities just to stay busy. For three years we often were despondent. All the while, Mother encouraged us from home. Interestingly our dental practice slowly began to improve and outpace the earlier months. God began working His will in our lives.

Beginning in the spring of 1974, three marvelous things happened to me. These happenings perfectly coincided with my decision to follow the Lord Jesus Christ. First, the notable improvement of our practice perfectly coincided with my decision (on the insistence of Mother) to personally establish and support the local radio broadcast of Changed Lives, the radio and television of the ministry of Ben Haden, Senior Pastor of First Presbyterian Church, Chattanooga, Tennessee. Second, once I committed to that work and the radio ministry gained traction, I was called by the congregation to serve as a deacon at the Independent Presbyterian Church. Third, a month later, on September 16, God provided a baby girl for us to adopt, utilizing my attorney and best friend, Morton (Salty) G. Forbes. In tandem with our life changes, Brother Jay and his wife, Pam, became very active in their church. God was broadening His plan for all of us.

Each successive year, our practice continued to thrive. My daughter, Carey, was joined by her adoptive sister, Nancy, in June 1977. Again, Salty Forbes was the catalyst used through the grace of God. My brother served dentistry, beginning at committee level (and eventually rising to the presidency of both state and national dental associations and academies), while I preferred and was content to remain in Savannah practicing. We opened a satellite office across town. Our faith in Christ grew, and we continued in our pursuit of the knowledge and the love of God.

Mother had articulated to Jay and me on several occasions that her mother had died at age fifty-eight and her father at sixty-two, and that she did not believe that she would experience longevity. Indeed, she died at sixty-six years of age on August 1, 1980, three days after sustaining a massive heart attack.

God continued to shower His great blessings on both Jay and me and our families, exceeding abundantly. Our practice grew steadily, year after year (the extraordinary manner in which the Lord brought Jay's son into dentistry is described in graphic detail in *LETTERS TO AND FROM A CHRISTIAN MOTHER AND MORE*), and in 1998, Jay's son, Alston Jones McCaslin VI, joined our practice. Three years later, H. Byron Colley III came in, both as full partners. Byron married the oldest daughter of my best friend and attorney, Morton G. Forbes. Therefore, Byron was almost family to us all.

The Lord continued to manifest His gracious will for us. Jay's son-in-law was hired as our practice administrator in 2004. Bryan Lobel was married to twin Jennifer Dobbs McCaslin. I have always said that good professional partnership is like a good marriage. That we had, by the grace of God. Our practice was centered around Christ. And the Lord continued to bless our families and our practice.

In July 2006, Brother Jay had assembled the largest privately held collection of C.S. Lewis first editions. While Jay was still adding to this collection, a dealer provided him with the email address in Oxford, England of Walter Hooper, who was the personal secretary to C.S. Lewis the last year of his life. Jay, having been informed by that book dealer of the book in progress, immediately wrote Hooper, telling him of our thirteen letters received by Mother from Lewis. Upon Walter Hooper's request, copies and transcriptions of all thirteen of the letters were quickly emailed to him just in time to be included in his latest and final work entitled: *C.S. LEWIS, COLLECTED LETTERS,* Vol. III, pub. November 2006. My brother and I produced *THE ANCESTRY OF C.S. LEWIS* during the first of his three months of terminal illness. The genealogy was posted immediately on the web, public domain (where it remains today).

www.silasdobbsmccaslin.com

Copies of *C.S. LEWIS, COLLECTED LETTERS,* Vol. III, were graciously and personally inscribed by Hooper to Jay, to my daughters Carey and Nancy, to our pastors, Terry Johnson and Ron Parrish, and to me. The books were immediately shipped by air mail to us from Oxford, England. Jay was quite gratified to see the work and hold it in his hands merely days before his death.

My brother and I practiced together side by side for thirty-six years. Jay did not fear death – he but mourned the separation from loved ones. The Lord took Jay home at age sixty-seven, November 24, 2006. Death came from that dreaded disease, metastatic lung cancer, after his having been in remission from colon cancer for nineteen years

Our younger daughter, Nancy, while pursuing a course of study in Atlanta, died accidentally on April 30, at age twenty-nine. Her death followed a tumultuous few years resulting from severe ankle injury in an automobile crash in 2001. In all of this tragedy we clearly saw the loving hand of God.

By the grace of God, Bryan Lobel was converted to Christianity in the summer of 2006, which is surely the most astounding miracle in our family. He observed the family during Jay's illness from September 2006 until his death in November. Then, he witnessed how our family dealt with the loss of Nancy in early 2007. Without equivocation, Bryan credited his conversion to "the way my father-in-law lived his life and faced his illness and death."

These closing reflections are glimpses of our later life. Begging indulgence once again at this final juncture, there is much more autobiographical information provided in the work entitled, *LETTERS TO AND FROM A CHRISTIAN MOTHER AND MORE*, where a unique statement is provided, to wit:

Most of Mother's genealogical correspondence to distant cousins had at least some reference to Christianity, and in many of her letters the emphasis on the subject was intense. We have copies of hundreds of her letters to friends and relatives in our genealogy files, because she always kept a carbon copy. Often a distant cousin would reply with the family information Mother had requested, probably asking in closing: "How is your family?" Mother's reply to them often was as follows:

> You asked about our family. Everyone is doing just fine,
> while most of the rest of the world is fast going to Hell.
> (This writer's note: Hell is used in the Biblical sense).

As the whole world speedily spins out of control, we grieve for our morally-degraded nation, from the top down to the grass roots. The singular, most important decision that one can make in one's life is couched in the passage below.

> *But if our gospel be hid, it is hid to them that are lost: In*
> *whom the god of this world hath blinded the minds of them*

*which believe not, lest the light of the glorious gospel of Christ,
who is the image of God, should shine unto them. For we preach
not ourselves, but Christ Jesus the Lord; and ourselves your
servants for Jesus' sake.*

(II Cor. 4:3-5)

Let us praise God continually for being among His elect, as contrasted with those whom we have spoken of above who have been "judicially blinded."

EPILOGUE

Permit me to emphasize a verse of Scripture:

> *Train up a child in the way he should go: and when he is*
> *old, he will not depart from it.* (Proverbs 20:6).

That Proverb is known both to believers and unbelievers. In the phrase, "and when he is old," God clearly ratifies the patience that He has with His wayward children.

> *If the root be holy, so are the branches.* (Rom. 11:16b)

Another old proverb states:

> *As the twig grows, so grow the branches.*

Hanging framed on the wall of my bedroom in my youth was an oil painting that Mother had created. The tree was dwarfed, scraggly, gnarled, and growing out of the rocks on the side of a cliff. Yet its leaves were bright green, lush, and the tree clearly was vital, with a beautiful blue sky as the backdrop.

Although raised at the knee of an outspoken Christian mother, I was not convicted of my sinful life until eight years of age at a revival, as mentioned earlier. I was faithful in church attendance and prayed continually. But I was not a consistent, committed Christian.

I had reached age thirty-three before I made it my purpose to lead a Christian life. However, I was thirty-nine years old when Mother died, at which time I made a vow to God that, in the future, I would read my Bible daily, continue with my involvement in our church, and strive faithfully and meticulously to apply Christian principles in my everyday life. Now, at seventy-four years of age, I perceive that I have not departed from the training given me by my mother and that garnered from other Christian teachers.

My dear wife and I endeavor every day, in every way, to provide the Christian counsel, exhortation, and admonition that we received to our family members – our daughter, her husband, and their two young daughters. Specifically, we encourage their attendance of Sunday school and church, and we know of their daily devotionals and their prayer time.

The Westminster Confession of Faith, Shorter Catechism, Question One, asks: "What is the chief end of man?" The answer: "Man's chief end is to glorify God and enjoy Him forever." We find our chief enjoyment now is in our daily witness to Christ. Yes, we have planted; others will water; but only God will give the increase.

May these reminiscences redound to the praise and honor and glory of God and to the furtherance of His kingdom.

FURTHER READING

SEABISCUIT, by Laura Hillenbrand (published in 2001) and her book, *UNBROKEN* (published in 2010), both were best sellers and both became important movies. They are veritable masterpieces. Although *SEABISCUIT* was fictionalized, *UNBROKEN* was true, recounting facts in real time about real people and real events. Both stories are morally uplifting, edifying, and explicitly detailed. The genius and literary talent of Laura Hillenbrand were exercised, resulting in gratifying stories of human interest in this literary genre. *SEABISCUIT* was nominated for seven Academy Awards.

TO KILL A MOCKINGBIRD, by Harper Lee, published in 1960, received the Pulitzer Prize in 1961. The story is set in 1936 Monroeville, Alabama and is partially based on incidents experienced by Harper Lee of her own family and neighborhood when she was ten years of age. The novel is renowned because of the writer's skill in portraying serious subjects. The character of the fictional father, Atticus Finch, played by Gregory Peck, touched a wide audience, as it illustrated the quiet integrity of a small-town lawyer. The plot is complex from a moral view. The movie was nominated for eight Academy Awards and won three.

REMINISCENCES OF A CHRISTIAN FAMILY IN THE MID-20TH CENTURY SOUTH tells true and factual stories, affirmed by both first-hand family tradition and authentic family correspondence. Some of the stories are unique. Others are quite typical for children, especially boys, who grew up in small, towns in the deep South. The stories cascade down, year after year, interwoven with biographical information. See how this author attracts the interest of Christians seeking wholesome literature.

ABOUT THE AUTHOR

Silas Dobbs McCaslin was born in 1940 in Louisville, Mississippi. He was eight years of age when. upon hearing the message of an evangelist at a revival, he came to the clear realization that he was a sinner, that Christ had died for his sins, and he walked the aisle to confess Christ as the Son of God and his Savior. His mother, widowed at thirty-nine years of age in 1953, returned to college first to complete the one remaining year for her BA degree and then for a Master's degree, both with honors. She then moved with her two teenage sons to Gainesville, Georgia, where she practiced speech therapy in the public schools.

Dr. McCaslin holds three degrees (BA, DDS, and MSD) from Emory University, Atlanta, Georgia. At thirty-three years of age, he recommitted his life to Christ and six years later, reaffirmed his vows to study the Word daily, to "pray without ceasing," and to serve the Lord continuously. He has practiced pediatric dentistry for 49 years, the last 45 years of which have been in private practice in Savannah, Georgia.